MW01001341

Making a Case

Making a Case

The Practical Roots of Biblical Law

SARA J. MILSTEIN

UNIVERSITY PRESS

Oxford University Press is a department of the University of Oxford. It furthers the University's objective of excellence in research, scholarship, and education by publishing worldwide. Oxford is a registered trade mark of Oxford University Press in the UK and certain other countries.

Published in the United States of America by Oxford University Press
198 Madison Avenue, New York, NY 10016, United States of America.

Library of Congress Control Number: 2021942376

ISBN 978–0–19–091180–5

DOI: 10.1093/oso/9780190911805.001.0001

9 8 7 6 5 4 3 2

Printed by Integrated Books International, United States of America

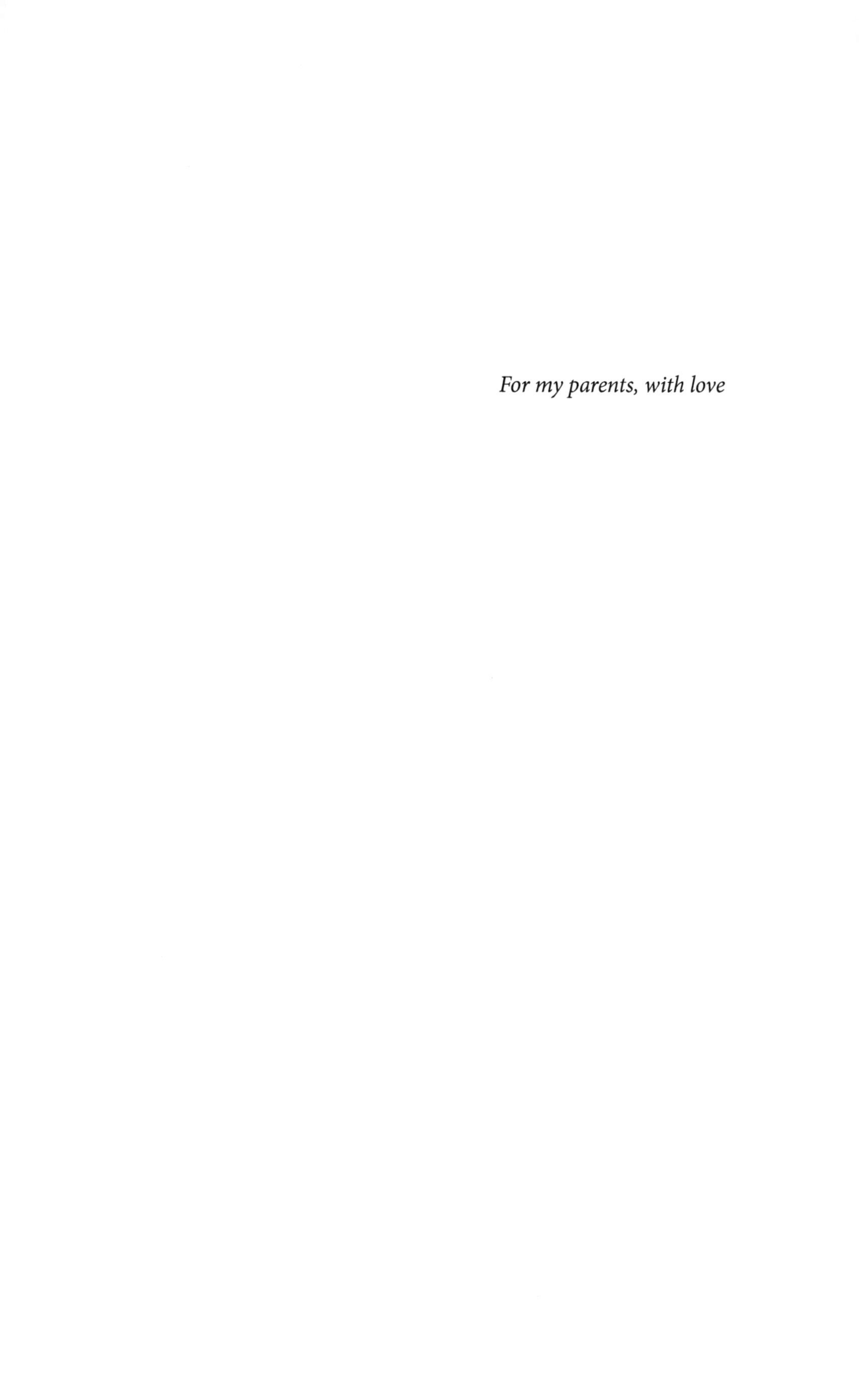

For my parents, with love

CONTENTS

LIST OF ILLUSTRATIONS

ACKNOWLEDGMENTS

IF TIME IS the most precious commodity that scholars have, it is all the more remarkable when they give so generously of it. I am deeply grateful to those who took the time to provide invaluable feedback on different chapters: Lisa Cooper, Daniel Fleming, Martha Roth, Bruce Wells, Paul Delnero, Gabriella Spada, K. Lawson Younger, Reinhard Müller, Andrew Gross, and Juha Pakkala. I am especially grateful to Martha Roth and Gabriella Spada: even though I had never met either of them, they were both quick to offer feedback and warm encouragement. Gratifying exchanges like these are what make me feel part of a community. Special thanks also go to Paul Delnero and Daniel Fleming for reading the entire book and for pushing me to sharpen my arguments in crucial ways. Paul, your sharp eye always illuminates a new angle that I had overlooked. Dan, your provision of space and time for thought to deepen allows me to think through new ideas fearlessly. I also benefited much from conversations with Bruce Wells and Reinhard Kratz. Bruce's nuanced studies on biblical and Near Eastern law are partly what inspired me to delve into this area in the first place, and he has been nothing but welcoming, encouraging, and helpful. Reinhard helped me tighten the argumentation in Chapter 2 and generously hosted me in Göttingen, where the ideas in this book first took shape. Christoph Levin was an enthusiastic guide to me in Munich and helped me access the ample resources there. I also appreciate Bernie Levinson and Ted Lewis for their incredible generosity and ongoing support of my career. I am grateful to Reinhard Müller and Juha Pakkala for the countless stimulating and inspiring exchanges over the last decade. Finally, many thanks to Martin Sauvage for generously providing the excellent map that accompanies the book; and to Susanne Paulus at the Oriental Institute of the University of Chicago and Agnete Lassen at the Yale Babylonian Collection at Yale University for kindly providing several of the images for the book.

Presenting this work at different stages has been vital. I am grateful to the attendees at the workshop, "The Scribe in the Biblical World," hosted by Michael Langlois and Esti Eshel at the University of Strasbourg, for their input on some of the content in Chapter 1. The attendees of the doctoral seminar at the University of Göttingen (hosted by Reinhard Kratz) and the attendees of the workshop "Supplementation and the Study of the Hebrew Bible" at Brown University (hosted by Saul Olyan and Jacob Wright) provided crucial feedback on the arguments in Chapter 2. My colleagues in the Baltimore Biblical Colloquium also provided useful feedback on the arguments in Chapter 4.

I am grateful to Cynthia Read, Preetham Raj, and the staff at Oxford University Press for expertly bringing another project to fruition. This project has also benefited from funding from the Killam Foundation and the Social Sciences and Humanities Research Council of Canada. This funding allowed me to hire my fantastic research assistant for this project, Nicole Tombazzi, who is now a budding legal scholar in her own right. I am also grateful to the staff and the 2018–2019 scholars-in-residence at the Peter Wall Institute of Advanced Studies for challenging me to make my scholarship accessible and meaningful to a wider audience. Their openness to the strange wonders of Near Eastern law fueled my excitement about the project. Our year together was a gift. To my colleagues in the Department of Classical, Near Eastern, and Religious Studies at the University of British Columbia, I feel lucky to bask in your generosity, sense of humor, and passion for all things ancient. Special thanks to Tony Keddie, Leanne Bablitz, and Kat Huemoeller for their enthusiasm and support of this project.

An earlier version of some of the arguments in Chapter 3 was published as "Will and (Old) Testament: Reconsidering the Roots of Deuteronomy 25, 5–10," in *Writing, Rewriting, and Overwriting in the Books of Deuteronomy and the Former Prophets: Essays in Honour of Cynthia Edenburg*, ed. Thomas

Römer, Ido Koch, and Omer Sergi, BETL 304 (Leuven: Peeters, 2019), 49–63. Earlier phases of some of the arguments in Chapter 2 were also published in "Making a Case: The Repurposing of 'Israelite Legal Fictions' as Deuteronomic Law," in *Supplementation and the Study of the Hebrew Bible*, ed. Saul Olyan and Jacob Wright, BJS 361 (Providence: Brown Judaic Studies, 2017), 161–81 and will appear in "The Origins of Deuteronomic 'Law,'" Congress Volume Aberdeen 2019, International Organization for the Study of the Old Testament, ed. Joachim Schaper, VTSup (Leiden: Brill, forthcoming). I am grateful to these presses for granting me permission to reprint some of this material.

During the pandemic, I have been most grateful for my family: without your love I would be nowhere at all. To my partner in life, Aaron, your supportiveness allowed this project to flourish and enabled me miraculously to keep my head above water. I could never thank you enough. Aviva, Asher, and Ezra: I am grateful to you for all of the love and hugs at a time when hugs were few and far between. Han and Mark, Josh and Annie, Sally and Ron, Marni and Craig, and Tara and David: our bonds are an anchor. Ell and Bill: you are my home away from home. I dedicate this book to my parents, Alan and Audrey Milstein. Ma, your unwavering attentiveness, insight, and ability to be present buoy me. Dad, your boundless curiosity, devotion, and zest for life are inspiring. Our distance is in miles (or kilometers) only.

ABBREVIATIONS

AAAS	*Les Annales Archéologiques Arabes Syriennes*
AASOR	Annual of the American Schools of Oriental Research
ABS	Archaeology and Biblical Studies
AfOB	Archiv für Orientforschung: Beiheft
AHw	Wolfram von Soden, *Akkadisches Handwörterbuch*. 3 vols. Wiesbaden: Harrassowitz, 1965–1981.
Ai	*ana ittišu*
AIL	Ancient Israel and Its Literature
AION	*Annali dell'Università degli Studi di Napoli "L'Orientale"*
AJSR	*Association for Jewish Studies Review*
AMD	Ancient Magic and Divination
AOAT	Alter Orient und Altes Testament
AoF	*Altorientalische Forschungen*
AOS	American Oriental Series
ATD	Das Alte Testament Deutsch
AuOr	*Aula Orientalis*
BBB	Bonner biblische Beiträge
BDB	F. Brown, S. Driver, and C. Briggs, *The Brown-Driver-Briggs Hebrew and English Lexicon, Coded with Strong's Concordance Numbers*. Peabody, MA: Hendrickson, 1906. Repr., 2003
BETL	Bibliotheca Ephemeridum Theologicarum Lovaniensium
Bib	*Biblica*

BibMes	Bibliotheca Mesopotamica
BiOr	*Bibliotheca Orientalis*
BJS	Brown Judaic Studies
BN	*Biblische Notizen*
BZAW	Beihefte zur Zeitschrift für die alttestamentliche Wissenschaft
CAD	*The Assyrian Dictionary of the Oriental Institute of the University of Chicago*. Edited by Martha Roth, et al. 26 vols. Chicago: The Oriental Institute of the University of Chicago, 1956–2006
CANE	*Civilizations of the Ancient Near East*. Edited by Jack Sasson. 4 vols. New York, 1995. Repr. in 2 vols. Peabody, MA: Hendrickson, 2006
CBQ	*Catholic Biblical Quarterly*
CC	Covenant Code
CDLJ	*Cuneiform Digital Library Journal*
CHANE	Culture and History of the Ancient Near East
CM	Cuneiform Monographs
CNIP	Carsten Niebuhr Institute Publications
CT	Cuneiform Texts from Babylonian Tablets in the British Museum
CUSAS	Cornell University Studies in Assyriology and Sumerology
DJD	Discoveries in the Judaean Desert
DMOA	Documenta et Monumenta Orientis Antiqui
Emar	Daniel Arnaud, *Recherches au pays d'Aštata, Emar VI/3: Textes sumériens et accadiens*. OBO 20. Paris: Éditions Recherche sur les Civilisations, 1986
FAT	Forschungen zum Alten Testament
FRLANT	Forschungen zur Religion und Literatur des Alten und Neuen Testaments
GMTR	Guides to the Mesopotamian Textual Record
GSCC	Groningen Studies in Cultural Change
HANE/M	History of the Ancient Near East/Monographs

HANEL *A History of Ancient Near Eastern Law*. Edited by Raymond Westbrook. 2 vols. HdO. Section 1 The Near and Middle East 72. Leiden: Brill, 2003

HCOT Historical Commentary on the Old Testament

HdO Handbuch der Orientalistik / Handbook of Oriental Studies

HeBAI *Hebrew Bible and Ancient Israel*

Hen *Henoch*

Ḫḫ ḪAR-ra = *ḫubullu*

HL Hittite Laws

HLFs Hebrew Legal Fictions

HSS Harvard Semitic Studies

HThKAT Herders Theologischer Kommentar zum Alten Testament

HUCA *Hebrew Union College Annual*

IEJ *Israel Exploration Journal*

ILR *Israel Law Review*

JAOS *Journal of the American Oriental Society*

JBL *Journal of Biblical Literature*

JCS *Journal of Cuneiform Studies*

JCSSS Journal of Cuneiform Studies Supplemental Series

JEN Joint Expedition with the Iraq Museum at Nuzi

JEOL *Jaarbericht van het Vooraziatisch-Egyptisch Gezelschap (Genootschap) Ex oriente lux*

JESHO *Journal of the Economic and Social History of the Orient*

JNES *Journal of Near Eastern Studies*

JSJ *Journal for the Study of Judaism in the Persian, Hellenistic, and Roman Periods*

JSOT *Journal for the Study of the Old Testament*

JSOTSup Journal for the Study of the Old Testament Supplement Series

LE Laws of Eshnunna

LH Laws of Hammurabi

LL Laws of Lipit-Ishtar

LOx Laws about Rented Oxen

LSTS The Library of Second Temple Studies

LTT	*Law from the Tigris to the Tiber: The Writings of Raymond Westbrook*. Edited by Bruce Wells and F. Rachel Magdalene. 2 vols. Winona Lake, IN: Eisenbrauns, 2009
LU	Laws of Ur-Namma
MAL	Middle Assyrian Laws
MC	Mesopotamian Civilizations
MSL	Materialen zum sumerischen Lexikon / Materials for the Sumerian Lexicon. 17 vols. Rome: Pontifical Biblical Institute, 1937–2004
NEB	New English Bible
NHT	Nippur Homicide Trial
OB	Old Babylonian
OBC	Orientalia Biblica et Christiana
OBO	Orbis Biblicus et Orientalis
ÖBS	Österreichische biblische Studien
OBML	Raymond Westbrook, *Old Babylonian Marriage Law*. AfOB 23. Horn, Austria: Verlag Ferdinand Berger & Söhne, 1988
OECT	Oxford Editions of Cuneiform Texts
OTS	Old Testament Studies
RA	*Revue d'assyriologie et d'archéologie orientale*
RE	Gary Beckman, *Texts from the Vicinity of Emar in the Collection of Jonathan Rosen*. HANE/M II. Padova: Sargon srl, 1996
RSO	*Rivista degli studi orientali*
SAAS	State Archives of Assyria Studies
SCCNH	Studies on the Civilization and Culture of Nuzi and the Hurrians
SLEx	Sumerian Laws Exercise Tablet
SLHF	Sumerian Laws Handbook of Forms
SP	Samaritan Pentateuch
TAPS	Transactions of the American Philosophical Society
TBR	Daniel Arnaud, with Hatice Gonnet, *Textes syriens de l'âge du Bronze Récent*. Aula Orientalis Supplementa 1. Barcelona: Ausa, 1991
VT	*Vetus Testamentum*

VTSup Supplements to Vetus Testamentum
WAW Writings from the Ancient World
WMANT Wissenschaftliche Monographien zum Alten und Neuen Testament
WVDOG Wissenschaftliche Verfföffentlichungen der deutschen Orient-Gesellschaft
YBC Tablets in the Babylonian collection, Yale University Library
YOS Yale Oriental Series, Texts
ZA *Zeitschrift für Assyriologie*
ZAR *Zeitschrift für altorientalische und biblische Rechtgeschichte*
ZAH *Zeitschrift für Althebräistik*

Introduction

IT HAS LONG been taken for granted that the Bible preserves several "native" expressions of the Near Eastern law collection genre: Exodus 20–23, Deuteronomy 12–26, and the so-called corpus of Priestly law, especially Leviticus 17–26.[1] The genre has its roots, of course, in southern Mesopotamia, with the Laws of Ur-Namma, a work that dates to the late third millennium BCE.[2] Over the next five hundred years, law collections

1. More precisely, what scholars call the "Covenant Code" (after the phrase in Exod 24:7) is commonly demarcated as Exod 20:22–23:19. The category of Priestly law includes what scholars call the "Holiness Collection" or "H" (Leviticus 17–26).

2. All of the dates in this book use the Middle Chronology, and the dates for the law collections correspond to those in Martha T. Roth, *Law Collections from Mesopotamia and Asia Minor*, 2nd ed., WAW 6 (Atlanta: SBL Press, 1997). There is much debate regarding an absolute chronology for Mesopotamia prior to the fourteenth century BCE, with competing proposals ("Ultra-High," "High," "Middle," "Low," "New," and "Ultra-Low") that vary by more than 150 years. The "Ultra-Low Chronology," for example, situates the fall of the First Dynasty of Babylon in 1499 BCE, nearly a century later than the corresponding date for this event (1595 BCE) in the Middle Chronology (Glenn M. Schwartz, "Problems of Chronology: Mesopotamia, Anatolia, and the Syro-Levantine Region," in *Beyond Babylon: Art, Trade, and Diplomacy in the Second Millennium B.C.*, ed. Joan Aruz, Kim Benzel, and Jean M. Evans [New York: Metropolitan Museum of Art / New Haven, CT: Yale University Press, 2008], 450–52). According to Sturt Manning et al., the latest dendrochronological measurements at Kültepe and Acemhöyük in Turkey support the Middle Chronology ("Integrated Tree-Ring-Radiocarbon High-Resolution Timeframe to Resolve Earlier Second Millennium BCE Mesopotamian Chronology," *PLoS ONE* 11.7 [2016]: e0157144 [doi:10.1371/journal.pone.0157144]). For alternatives, see also Amanda Podany, "Hana and the Low Chronology," *JNES* 73.1 (2014): 49–71; and Steven W. Cole, "Chronology Revisited," in *Mesopotamian Pottery: A Guide to the Babylonian Tradition in the Second Millennium B.C.*, ed. James A. Armstrong and Hermann Gasche, Mesopotamian History

Making a Case. Sara J. Milstein, Oxford University Press. © Oxford University Press 2021.
DOI: 10.1093/oso/9780190911805.003.0001

of a similar type—the Laws of Lipit-Ishtar, the Laws of Eshnunna, and the Laws of Hammurabi—were produced in Sumerian and Akkadian. In the second millennium BCE, the genre was also put to use by two groups outside of southern Mesopotamia: the Hittites in Anatolia (modern-day Turkey) and the Assyrians in northern Mesopotamia. In the cases of the Laws of Ur-Namma and the Laws of Hammurabi, the production of a law collection was tied to the king's expansion of territory and his consolidation of power. Other collections, such as the Laws of Eshnunna, the Middle Assyrian Laws, and the Hittite Laws, were similarly generated by powerful kingdoms in the ancient Near East. Leaving the Bible aside, it is possible to state that all of the Near Eastern law collections were produced in the third to second millennia BCE, in cuneiform on clay tablets, and in major capital cities in Mesopotamia and in the Hittite Empire: Ur, Isin, Eshnunna, Babylon, Hattusha, and Assur (see map I.1).[3]

The notion that more than five hundred years later, the kingdoms of Israel and/or Judah likewise produced their own Hebrew law collections is thus highly unexpected, to say the least. None of the five major sites in Syria to have yielded troves of cuneiform tablets (i.e., Ebla, Mari, Ugarit, Emar, and Alalakh) has borne even a fragment of a law collection, despite the fact that these sites have yielded ample legal documentation of other types. Excavations at the northeastern Mesopotamian site of Nuzi likewise have turned up numerous practical legal documents, but again, no evidence of a law collection. Even Egypt has not yielded a collection of laws, though some speculate that such collections did exist.[4] As such, the

and Environment, Series II, Memoirs VI (Ghent: University of Ghent / Chicago: Oriental Institute of the University of Chicago, 2014), 3–6.

3. It is not evident that the work that scholars call the "Neo-Babylonian Laws" constitutes a law collection in the Near Eastern tradition. The text dates to the seventh century BCE and is attested only in the form of a single tablet that originally contained fifteen to eighteen laws (Roth, *Law Collections from Mesopotamia*, 144).

4. Given the elaborate nature of royal edicts, trial records, and other private legal documents in texts from the Old Kingdom, some have surmised that a law collection probably did exist (Richard Jasnow, "Egypt: Old Kingdom and First Intermediate Period," in *HANEL* 1:93 n. 3). References in some texts from the Middle Kingdom to thematic sets of laws imply the existence of limited groups of laws, if not an extensive collection (Richard Jasnow, "Egypt: Middle

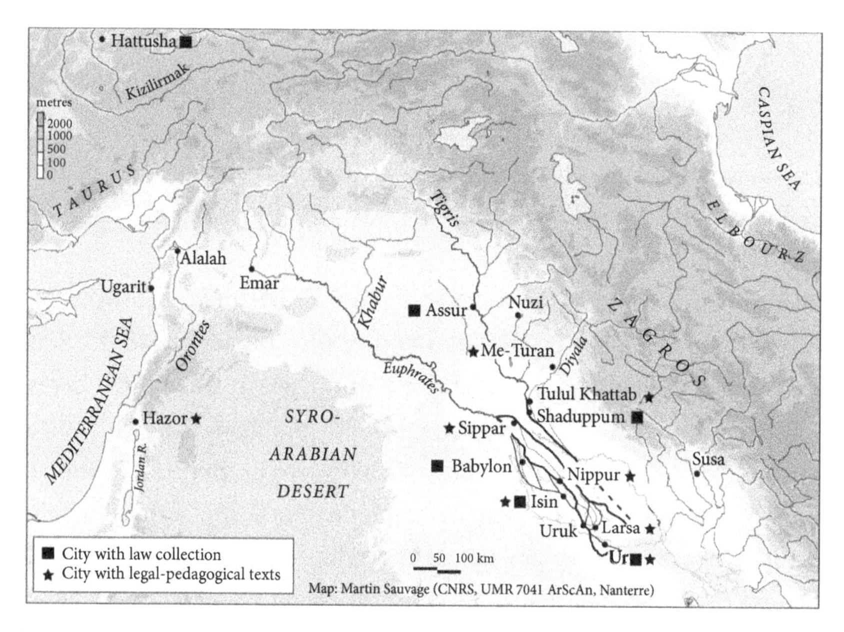

Map I.1 Map of the ancient Near East, with denotation of sites that yielded law collections and/or legal-pedagogical texts. Image designed by Martin Sauvage.

biblical texts that scholars identify as legal corpora would represent the only "western," non-cuneiform expressions of the genre in the ancient Near East, produced by societies that were not known for their political clout, and separated in time from the aforementioned collections by centuries.[5]

Kingdom and Second Intermediate Period," *HANEL* 1:256). Finally, some references to "laws" in texts from the New Kingdom may suggest the presence of such a collection (Richard Jasnow, "Egypt: New Kingdom," *HANEL* 1:289).

5. Outside of the ancient Near East, it is also important to mention the early sixth-century BCE laws of Solon, attributed to the Athenian *archon* Solon (available only in the form of later quotations and reformulations in a range of later texts); the Gortyn laws, a late seventh-century BCE collection of laws from Gortyn, Crete, that covers a number of civil and criminal topics (inheritance, adultery, divorce, adoption, etc.) in casuistic format; and the mid-fifth-century BCE Twelve Tables from Rome (available not as a complete text, but rather in the form of hundreds of quotations and paraphrases of its laws). For a translation and commentary on the Gortyn laws, see Ronald Willetts, *The Law Code of Gortyn*, Kadmos/Supplemente 1 (Berlin: De Gruyter, 1967). For an overview of the Gortyn laws and their parallels to "biblical law," see Anselm C. Hagedorn, "Gortyn—Utilising an Archaic Greek Law Code for Biblical Research," *ZAR* 7 (2001): 217–42; and for a discussion of the legal sections of the Pentateuch in the context of these three collections, see Gary N. Knoppers and Paul B. Harvey, Jr., "The Pentateuch in Ancient Mediterranean Context: The Publication of Local Lawcodes," in *The Pentateuch as*

In addition, the biblical corpora contain much material that would have no place in the Near Eastern collections: cultic regulations, ethical precepts, stipulations regarding judicial protocol, and harsh punishments for failing to worship Yahweh alone. Notwithstanding these differences, scholars have nonetheless retained the classification of these biblical texts—or parts of them—as "law collections."

With this monograph, I propose that the scribes of ancient Israel and Judah neither made use of "old" law collections nor set out to produce a law collection in the Near Eastern sense of the genre. They did, however, put the conventions that are associated with the genre toward radically new ends. These compositional processes involved repurposing and supplementing different types of legal-pedagogical texts, the outlines of which are still evident in Exodus 21–22 and sporadically in Deuteronomy 19–25. When we view this material in the context of legal-pedagogical texts from Mesopotamia, the practical roots of biblical law begin to emerge.

THE NEAR EASTERN GENRE OF THE LAW COLLECTION

The earliest expression of the law collection genre—the Sumerian Laws of Ur-Namma of Ur (LU)—dates to around 2100 BCE, more than a millennium after the emergence of writing in southern Mesopotamia.[6] Although

Torah: New Models for Understanding Its Promulgation and Acceptance, ed. Gary N. Knoppers and Bernard M. Levinson (Winona Lake, IN: Eisenbrauns, 2007), 105–41. For examples of specific links between the Mesopotamian law collections and Roman law, see Raymond Westbrook, "The Nature and Origins of the Twelve Tables," *LTT* 1:21–71.

6. The most up-to-date edition of LU (omitting the prologue) is Miguel Civil, "The Law Collection of Ur-Namma," in *Cuneiform Royal Inscriptions and Related Texts in the Schøyen Collection*, ed. Andrew R. George, CUSAS 17 (Bethesda, MD: CDL Press, 2011), 221–86. Prior to this publication, all of the extant copies dated to the Old Babylonian period. Civil's edition focuses especially on the contents of a cylinder (MS 2064) that appears to date to the period during or shortly after King Ur-Namma's reign. The cylinder originally featured ten columns; parts of eight of these are preserved (221). Scholars previously attributed the laws either to Ur-Namma or to his son and heir, Shulgi. As Civil notes (221), however, the connection to Ur-Namma is confirmed in the new cylinder in §E3b: "In the reign of Ur-Namma, the king of the *níg-diri*-tax, after he had been enthroned by Nanna over the people, if the one [who sold] the slave, [either] the slave's owner or his(?) . . . , if he does not bring a *ginabtum*-officer, this man is (declared) a thief" (251–52).

earlier Sumerian kings had propagated reforms that promised the eradication of social inequities, LU represented a new genre, one that would be replicated in both Sumerian and Akkadian in southern Mesopotamia for centuries.[7] It is only fitting that King Ur-Namma would have been the first sponsor of the genre. He founded the Third Dynasty of Ur and united the city-states of southern and northern Mesopotamia for the second time in history.[8] The production of a law collection, with its promises to protect the vulnerable, would have signaled the king's commitment to justice throughout the entire area under his jurisdiction.

Although LU is rudimentary in comparison with its legal-literary heirs, it already featured the main building blocks of the genre: a prologue lauding the king's relationship to the gods, his military prowess, and his commitment to justice; a set of casuistic laws, grouped by topic and pertaining to specific legal quandaries; and an epilogue promising curses on anyone who dared to efface the inscription. This template was mirrored shortly afterward in the Sumerian Laws of Lipit-Ishtar (LL), a work that dates to about 1930 BCE and is attributed to King Lipit-Ishtar of Isin. Once again, a set of casuistic laws was framed by a prologue and epilogue that linked the king to the gods, emphasized his role as the enforcer of justice "in Sumer and Akkad," and promised curses on anyone who destroyed the work or replaced Lipit-Ishtar's name with his own. Like LU, the force of LL was also communicated by its physical representation: in both cases, the original monument was apparently inscribed on a stone stela.[9] Next followed the first Akkadian collection, the Laws of Eshnunna (LE). The work is

7. Two rulers of Lagash, Enmetana and Urukagina (read alternatively as Irkagina or Uruinimgina) were known to have established edicts against social inequity and the abuse of power (Claus Wilcke, "Mesopotamia: Early Dynastic and Sargonic Periods," *HANEL* 1:141). Though the genre of LU is unique, its prologue does draw on the Reforms of Urukagina (J. J. Finkelstein, "Ammiṣaduka's Edict and the Babylonian 'Law Codes,'" *JCS* 15.3 [1961]: 104).

8. Roth, *Law Collections from Mesopotamia*, 13. My nomenclature throughout relies on Roth's designations.

9. Civil concludes that LU was evidently written on a stela because there is a list of offerings in the prologue; such offerings are associated with these types of monuments ("Law Collection of Ur-Namma," 226). Regarding LL, Roth notes the existence of two fragments of a stone stela that may have belonged to the original monument (*Law Collections from Mesopotamia*, 35 n. 1). The king indeed states in the epilogue to LL that he "erected this stela" and makes reference to a pedestal for it.

known primarily from two tablets that were discovered at Tell Harmal (ancient Shaduppum) and dates to about 1770 BCE.[10] LE lacks a prologue and epilogue, but its date formula compels scholars to associate it with King Dadusha, a ruler of Eshnunna, a powerful kingdom in the early second millennium BCE. Although LE does not follow the template, its casuistic laws echo the style and content of those in LU and LL. LE also exhibits a heightened preference for *clusters* of law: that is, a basic legal scenario followed by additional laws that modify certain factors, such as the status of the person or the severity of the injury, so as to yield different outcomes.[11] This "cluster format" would reach its apex with the Laws of Hammurabi, a work that would come to define the genre.

The Laws of Hammurabi (LH) is of course associated with Hammurabi, the great king of Babylon who reigned 1792–1750 BCE. When Hammurabi inherited the kingdom of Babylonia from his father, Sin-muballiṭ, it was relatively modest. In defeating and annexing a series of rival kingdoms, including Larsa, Mari, Eshnunna, and Elam, Hammurabi managed to build an expansive political empire. As with LU, the production of a law collection seems to follow logically from the expansion and consolidation

10. Another fragment was found at Tell Haddad (ancient Meturan) (Dominique Charpin, *Writing, Law, and Kingship in Old Babylonian Mesopotamia*, trans. Jane Marie Todd [Chicago: University of Chicago Press, 2010], 72).

11. On the structure of LE, see Barry Eichler, "Literary Structure in the Laws of Eshnunna," in *Language, Literature, and History: Philological and Historical Studies Presented to Erica Reiner*, ed. Francesca Rochberg-Halton, AOS 67 (New Haven, CT: American Oriental Society, 1987), 71–84. Eichler emphasizes the inclusion of "polar cases" with the maximum amount of variation in LE, as compared with LH and the Middle Assyrian Laws, both of which provide more elaboration and/or additional laws (71–81). He concludes that LE is best understood as a "legal textbook," designed for teaching Mesopotamian legal thought and for "appreciating the complexities of legal situations." In this reconstruction, students would have had the opportunity to debate the gray areas in between the polarized cases. The elaboration present in LH would then reflect expansions that grew out of scholastic discussions regarding LE (81–84). Eichler's proposal is intriguing, but there is no way to determine with certainty that LE is either a legal textbook in origin or in secondary use. Roth notes that there are only three attestations of LE: two large tablets that preserve nearly complete copies of the collection and one student exercise with extracts (*Law Collections from Mesopotamia*, 58). She observes further that the date formula that begins the text preserved on "Source A" is comparable to the beginning of royal edicts and debt-cancellation edicts known as *mīšaru*-edicts; and the initial provisions of LE concern the standardization of measurements, a topic that appears in the prologue to LU (57).

of territory, though in this case on a much larger scale. It is widely recognized that LH was composed toward the end of the king's long reign, and indeed, the epilogue looks ahead to (warn) the kings who will follow in Hammurabi's stead.[12]

The most famous exemplar of LH is an imposing 2.5-meter diorite stela that is inscribed in archaic script and presented in horizontal bands (Fig. I.1).[13] Excavated at the site of Susa (in modern southwestern Iran) in three separate pieces by the French Archaeological Mission in 1901–1902, the stela now stands in the Louvre Museum in Paris. Prior to this act of repossession, the stela was confiscated as booty and brought to the Elamite capital of Susa either by the king Shutruk-Nahhunte I or his son, Kutir-Nahhunte, in the twelfth century BCE, a testament to the power that the monument still held after six centuries.[14] Fragments of at least two other stelae, most likely structures that once stood in the temples of other Babylonian cities, were also found at the same site. LH was not represented only in the form of imposing monuments, however. Hammurabi's collection—or parts of it—was copied for centuries in schools and scribal centers throughout Mesopotamia, with over fifty attestations to date.[15] The latest copy dates to the fifth century BCE and was found at a library in Sippar, postdating the original masterpiece by over a millennium.[16]

12. Scholars draw this conclusion about the date of LH because the prologue refers to a number of cities under his domain that Hammurabi was known to have captured late in his rule. Most of Hammurabi's military action was conducted in an intense four-year period prior to his thirty-third year of rule (Marc Van De Mieroop, *King Hammurabi of Babylon: A Biography*, Blackwell Ancient Lives [Malden, MA/Oxford: Blackwell, 2005], 79).

13. On the effect of this visual display, see the excellent discussion in Martha T. Roth, "Mesopotamian Legal Traditions and the Laws of Hammurabi," *Chicago-Kent Law Review* 71.1 (1995): 21–24.

14. Ibid. It is generally accepted that the stela was erected in Sippar, though Tallay Ornan contends that it was originally erected in Babylon ("Unfinished Business: The Relief on the Hammurabi Louvre Stele Revisited," *JCS* 71 [2019]: 87).

15. Roth, *Law Collections from Mesopotamia*, 74; see also Roth, "Mesopotamian Legal Traditions," 19–20.

16. Charpin, *Writing, Law, and Kingship*, 81.

Figure I.1 The famous diorite stela with the Laws of Hammurabi, dating to the early second millennium BCE. Now housed in Musée du Louvre, Paris, France. Photo credit © RMN-Grand Palais / Art Resource, NY.

The top third of the "Louvre stela" displays an image of Shamash, the god of justice, seated on his throne before the standing Hammurabi. As Tallay Ornan emphasizes, the visual component—with its depiction of Hammurabi and Shamash at eye level, Shamash's furnishing of Hammurabi with the symbols of power, and the physical parallels between the two figures—imbues Hammurabi with godlike status.[17] The extensive prologue then complements the visual by detailing Hammurabi's devotion to the many patron deities and temples within the city-states under his rule. The nearly three hundred laws that follow cover a range of topics, including obligations for soldiers, the rental and cultivation of land, debts and interest-bearing loans, safekeeping of property, family law, torts, ox rentals, hiring fees, slavery, and more, and in this context, serve to highlight the king's facilitation of justice. The epilogue is finally dedicated to Hammurabi's role as just king and protector of the people. It also identifies the preceding provisions as the *dināt mīšarim* ("verdicts of justice") of the king. This claim prompted Fritz Kraus to regard LH as a set of Urteilssprüche or Rechtssprüche (judgments) from cases that Hammurabi had actually adjudicated; that is, they were descriptive, not prescriptive. In turn, he characterized LH not as a code of laws but rather as "ein Werk der babylonischen wissenschaftlichen Literatur" (a work of Babylonian scientific literature), similar to the omen collections.[18] Kraus's "reclassification" of LH was enormously influential, as exemplified in essays by Jean Bottéro and Raymond Westbrook that compared the style and presumed development of "other" scientific collections (respectively, the medical treatises and omen collections) to the style and development of LH.[19] Yet while some, including Bottéro, upheld Kraus's conclusion that the provisions of

17. Ornan, "Unfinished Business," 89–92.

18. Fritz R. Kraus, "Ein zentrales Problem des altmesopotamischen Rechtes: Was ist der Codex Hammu-rabi?," *Genava* 8 (1960): 283–96. With this classification, Kraus pays homage to Benno Landsberger, who in an earlier essay ("Die Babylonischen Termini für Gesetz und Recht," in *Symbolae ad iura Orientis antiqui pertinentes Paulo Koschaker dedicatae*, ed. Johannes Friedrich, et al., Studia et Documenta ad Iura Orientis Antiqui Pertinentia 2 [Leiden: Brill, 1939], 219–34) had observed that the Babylonians had no word for "law," and in a pair of speeches delivered in 1950 and 1951 had more or less reached the same conclusion (Kraus, "Ein zentrales Problem," 284). The classification of LH as a "code" dates back to the first edition of the work by Father Vincent Scheil (*Textes élamites-sémitiques, deuxieme Serie*, Mémoires de la Délégation en Perse, Tome IV [Paris: Leroux, 1902], 11–12).

19. Jean Bottéro, "The 'Code' of Ḫammurabi," in *Mesopotamia: Writing, Reasoning, and the Gods*, trans. Zainab Bahrani and Marc Van De Mieroop (Chicago/London: University of Chicago Press, 1992), 156–84, esp. 169–79; Raymond Westbrook, "Biblical and Cuneiform Law Codes," in *LTT* 1:1–10, esp. 7–9.

LH were not normative, others, including Westbrook, contended that LH nonetheless served some sort of judicial function.[20]

If we leave aside the question of applicability, there is some evidence, albeit limited, that certain provisions in LH are rooted in actual disputes. There are over two hundred letters sent by Hammurabi, and many of them deal with problems arising in the management of the royal domain that required a decision from the king.[21] Although they are rare in the collection, a couple of these letters do appear to parallel specific laws in LH and potentially served as sources.[22] Nonetheless, it is important not to take Hammurabi's "own" statement at face value, given its contextualization in a work that is designed to glorify him at every turn. Not only must a number of the laws in the clusters reflect scribal inventions, but it is also clear that LH draws liberally on the contents of other collections.[23] By

20. Bottéro also emphasized the fact that there were major lacunae in LH, casting doubt on its role as normative in society ("'Code' of Ḫammurabi," 161–64). He concluded that LH was not a code but rather "a treatise, with examples, on the exercise of judicial power" (167). Westbrook instead surmised that LH was a reference work that judges would have consulted for difficult cases ("Biblical and Cuneiform Law Codes," 10). For Godfrey R. Driver and John C. Miles, LH reflects "a series of amendments to the common law of Babylonia" (*The Babylonian Laws*, vol. 1, *Legal Commentary* [Oxford: Clarendon Press, 1952], 41). Sophie Démare-Lafont takes a different tack, emphasizing the statement in the epilogue to LH that the "wronged man" facing a lawsuit should consult the stela for his verdict and thus be granted reassurance. To her mind, this statement indicates that a person who was living abroad and felt wronged by his local judicial system would have had the right to demand the application of LH and to appeal his case before a Babylonian court ("Law Collections and Legal Documents," in *Handbook of Ancient Mesopotamia*, ed. Gonzalo Rubio [Berlin: De Gruyter, forthcoming]). Yet cf. Martha T. Roth, who concludes that the statement indicates that the "wronged man" should bring his lawsuit not before Hammurabi but before his stela, where he can offer prayer and blessings to the king and thus be granted solace ("Hammurabi's Wronged Man," *JAOS* 122.1 [2002]: 45). In another publication, see also Roth's humble "confession" that she does not ever expect to know what the law collections meant for their ancient scribes, judicial authorities, and for the mostly illiterate population at large ("Mesopotamian Legal Traditions," 13).

21. Charpin, *Writing, Law, and Kingship*, 19; see also Dominique Charpin, *Hammurabi of Babylon* (London: I.B. Tauris, 2012), 146.

22. For examples, see Bottéro, "'Code' of Ḫammurabi," 165–66; and Charpin, *Hammurabi of Babylon*, 155.

23. On this latter point, see, e.g., Roth, *Law Collections from Mesopotamia*, 71; Martha T. Roth, "The Law Collection of King Hammurabi: Toward an Understanding of Codification and Text," in *La codification des lois dans l'Antiquité: Actes du Colloque de Strasbourg, 27–29 novembre 1997*, ed. Edmond Lévy, Travaux du Centre de Recherche sur le Proche-Orient et la Grèce Antiques 16 (Paris: De Boccard, 2000), 16–17; Charpin, *Writing, Law, and Kingship*, 71–73; Barry

my count, more than seventy laws in LH overlap with content in LU, LL, and LE.[24] These laws were not reproduced verbatim, however. Typically, Hammurabi's scribes appear to have revised older precepts and supplemented them with additional provisions, some of which reflect recurring interests.[25] In general, the clusters in LH are far more elaborate than those in the preceding collections, and its provisions are typically more verbose. In sum, LH is squarely rooted in its antecedents but simultaneously stands as the most sophisticated and elaborate expression of the genre in history.

As alluded to above, although the law collection is most closely associated with kingdoms in southern Mesopotamia, two other major powers in the ancient Near East—the Assyrians and the Hittites—produced their own takes on the genre. Scribes at the Assyrian capital of Assur generated what is known as the Middle Assyrian Laws (MAL), a set of fourteen tablets with about 120 preserved laws. Although copies of MAL date

Eichler, "Examples of Restatement in the Laws of Hammurabi," in *Mishneh Todah: Studies in Deuteronomy and Its Cultural Environment in Honor of Jeffrey H. Tigay*, ed. Nili Sacher Fox, David A. Glatt-Gilad, and Michael J. Williams (Winona Lake, IN: Eisenbrauns, 2009), 365–400; and Van De Mieroop, *King Hammurabi of Babylon*, 109. It is worth adding that the prologue and epilogue to LH likewise demonstrate awareness of the frameworks for older collections, given the overt overlap in themes and terminology. Interestingly, although Driver and Miles observed that all but one-quarter of the laws in LE were reproduced in LH, they were disinclined to conclude definitively that Hammurabi made use of older collections (*Babylonian Laws* 1:8–9).

24. The following demonstrate close parallels in form and content: LE §40 // LH §7 (man purchases something without evidence); LL §12 // LE §50 // LH §19 (man detains a runaway slave); LE §§12–13 // LH §§21–24 (theft and robbery); LU §31 // LH §§53–55 (man floods his neighbor's field); LL §10 // LH §59 (man cuts down another man's tree); LU §32 // LL §8 // LH §§60–63 (gardener does not plant the land); LL §11 // LH §e (man fails to cultivate his land, leaving his neighbor's property vulnerable); LE §§36–37 // LH §§122–26 (man gives goods for safekeeping and they are stolen); LU §14 // LE §§26–28 // LH §§127–32 (marriage, adultery, and assault); LE §§29–30 // LH §§133a–36 (woman's husband is captured or deserts his city); LU §9 // LH §§137–43 (dissolution of marriage); LE §25 // LH §§159–61 (refusal to complete a marriage); LL §31 // LH §165 (division of the paternal estate); LE §§42–47a // LU §§18–23 // LH §§196–208 (penalties for injuries); LL §§d–f // LH §§209–14 (man strikes a pregnant woman); LE §5 // LH §§236–38 (boatman allows boat to sink); LL §§34–37 // LH §§247–49 (mishaps involving a rented ox); LE §§53–55 // LH §§250–52 (goring ox); LE §3 // LH §§271–72 (cost of renting cattle and a wagon); and LX §§j–k // LE §§7–11 + 14 // LH §274 (costs for hiring various workers). This is not to say that LH is primarily based on recycled law, however. A number of precepts deal with groups or roles that are wholly unique to LH, including merchants, soldiers, different classes of priestesses, doctors, apprentices, veterinarians, builders, and others.

25. We thus see a notable emphasis in LH on oath-taking (see, e.g., LH §§9, 20, 126, 131, 266), contracts (e.g., LH §§47, 52, 122, 123, 128, 151, 264), and proof for accusations (LH §§1, 2, and 127).

to the eleventh century BCE, it is assumed to be based on fourteenth-century BCE originals.[26] Scribes at the Hittite capital of Hattusha produced the Hittite Laws (HL), a collection of about two hundred laws that originated in the early Old Kingdom (1650–1500 BCE). The tablets were found in the archives at Hattusha at the site of the Hittites' "supreme court."[27] One copy of HL from the mid-second millennium ("the Late Parallel Version") then revises the laws, suggesting that the provisions were indeed normative.[28] Unlike LH, however, MAL and HL do not make ample use of the precepts of the earlier collections, and neither one appears to have included a prologue or epilogue. Rather, MAL and HL exhibit strongly local interests and individual styles. Tablet A of MAL is particularly unique in its focus on women, with nearly sixty highly detailed precepts that feature women as either perpetrators or victims. Although fragmentary, the other tablets are also apparently devoted to individual themes, including inheritance, agriculture, pledges and deposits, theft, false accusation, and the like. HL includes a plethora of unique laws on damages to animals, plants, and implements; "TUKUL"-obligations; and prohibited sexual pairings.[29] In both cases, the uniqueness of the provisions, together with the findspot, suggests that MAL and HL served some sort of judicial function. In short, both the Assyrians and the Hittites adopted the casuistic style and cluster format of the genre, though neither group produced a collection in precisely the same form as the southern Mesopotamian tradition.

26. Sophie Démare-Lafont, "Mesopotamia: Middle Assyrian Period," *HANEL* 1:521.

27. Richard Haase, "Anatolia and the Levant: The Hittite Kingdom" (henceforth, "Hittite Kingdom"), *HANEL* 1:620.

28. As Harry Hoffner, Jr. points out, the Old Hittite copies already point to a process of revising, given the inclusion of the phrase "Formerly they did X, but now he shall do Y" in some provisions. Curiously, other late copies revise only the wording but not the content ("Hittite Laws," in Roth, *Law Collections from Mesopotamia*, 214). See also Haase, "Hittite Kingdom," 620.

29. The Sumerogram TUKUL can mean both "weapon" and "tool" (Haase, "Hittite Kingdom," 633). The term refers to an obligation of holders of land to the state (Hoffner, "Hittite Laws," 245). While LH does proscribe incest in several laws, the scope of prohibited sexual unions in HL is far wider.

In this company, it is thus especially curious that the only other Near Eastern society to appear to yield anything close to the Mesopotamian genre of the law collection would be ancient Israel/Judah.[30] Exodus 21–22 and Deuteronomy 19–25 in particular feature topics similar to those in the Near Eastern collections, such as physical damages, property damages, divorce, and inheritance disputes.[31] A number of the laws in Exodus 21–22 even parallel specific Mesopotamian provisions. Laws dealing with an ox that gores either a person or another ox are represented in Exodus 21, LH, and LE. The "famous" problem of an injured pregnant woman is attested in Exodus 21 and in LH, MAL, HL, and LL. Exodus 21 also features a talionic refrain ("Eye for an eye, tooth for a tooth, hand for a hand, foot for a foot") that loosely echoes the personal injury laws in LH §§196–205. Beyond these and other points of overlap, Exodus 21–22 and Deuteronomy 19–25 display features that are characteristic of the Near Eastern collections: the use of third-person casuistic format (i.e., a "protasis" outlining a particular situation, followed by an "apodosis" stating the penalty or prescription); clusters of related laws (obtained by modifying one or more factors in the protasis); and a propensity for specific scenarios. The contents, moreover, are introduced—and in the case of Deuteronomy, identified repeatedly—as "laws" or "judgments" in their broader literary contexts. It is therefore not surprising that these two units—or the larger blocks in which they are embedded, Exodus 20–23 and Deuteronomy 12–26—are regularly treated as Israelite/Judahite expressions of the Mesopotamian genre.[32] This assumption, however, requires a closer look.

30. It is worth noting, however, that the Middle Bronze Age city of Hazor also yielded two small fragments of Babylonian laws that echo the personal injury laws in LH. For an edition of the text, see Wayne Horowitz, Takayoshi Oshima, and Filip Vukosavović, "Hazor 18: Fragments of a Cuneiform Law Collection from Hazor," *IEJ* 62.2 (2012): 158–76. I treat this text at length in Chapters 1 and 4.

31. Here I am largely in line with Raymond Westbrook, who notes that there are only about sixty provisions within the Bible that pertain to what we would call law, with the most preserved in Exodus 21–22 and Deuteronomy 21–22, and a smattering preserved elsewhere in Deuteronomy 15–25, Leviticus, and Numbers ("The Laws of Biblical Israel," in *LTT* 2:317–18).

32. See, e.g., Westbrook's claim: "We are therefore justified in seeing in the clusters of everyday law in the Torah law codes of the same type as their Near Eastern and Mediterranean

THE PEDAGOGICAL ROOTS OF "BIBLICAL LAW"

Scholars have recognized, of course, that "biblical law" is unique in the context of the "other" Near Eastern law collections. They have observed that the biblical blocks are attributed to Yahweh, not a king; they intersperse civil and criminal laws with parenetic instructions and cultic regulations, often without transition; and they are embedded in a larger narrative context that recounts the Israelites' journey through the wilderness in the pre-monarchic period.[33] These differences, however, have not prompted a reclassification of the biblical content. Rather, the general consensus is that once-independent law collections or portions of such collections were taken up, adapted/supplemented, and reassigned to Israel's god.[34] In this light, the differences between biblical law and the Near Eastern collections are attributed to the Israelites'/Judahites' ingenuity in adapting the genre, whether for literary or even subversive political purposes. For Deuteronomy, this ingenuity is partly understood in

counterparts, notwithstanding their intermingling with sacral laws and ethical rules" ("Laws of Biblical Israel," 320).

33. On the novelty of ascribing divine revelation to laws, see Bernard M. Levinson, *Legal Revision and Religious Renewal in Ancient Israel* (New York: Cambridge University Press, 2008), 27–29. Specifically, Levinson states, "It was not the legal collection as a literary genre but the voicing of publicly revealed law as the personal will of God that was unique to ancient Israel" (27).

34. Building on the conclusions of Abraham Kuenen, Bruno Baentsch, Julius Wellhausen, and Julian Morgenstern, Martin Noth identified the Covenant Code (CC) as an independent book of law that was later inserted into the Pentateuchal narrative (see *Exodus: A Commentary* [London: SCM Press, 1962], 173). This position has since been upheld by others; see, e.g., Lothar Perlitt, *Bundestheologie im Alten Testament*, WMANT 36 (Neukirchen-Vluyn: Neukirchener-Verlag, 1969), 157–58; Hans Jochen Boecker, *Law and the Administration of Justice in the Old Testament and Ancient East*, trans. Jeremy Moiser (Minneapolis: Augsburg Publishing House, 1980), 136; and Otto Eissfeldt, *The Old Testament: An Introduction* (Oxford: Basil Blackwell, 1965), 218. Boecker, e.g., notes that "OT law" is inserted between the theophany in Exod 19:1–20:21 and the conclusion of the covenant in Exod 24:1–11, and in turn "is consequently understood as divinely given law" (136). In a related vein, others suggest that the casuistic content within CC ("*Mishpatim*") circulated as an independent "lawbook" (see, e.g., Ludger Schwienhorst-Schönberger, *Das Bundesbuch [Ex 20,22–23,33]: Studien zu seiner Entstehung und Theologie*, BZAW 188 [Berlin: De Gruyter, 1990], 1–2; Frank Crüsemann, *The Torah: Theology and Social*

the context of the scribes' bold reuse of Near Eastern treaty terminology to portray the Israelites' covenant with and loyalty to their deity.[35]

With this monograph, I propose that the law collection genre may not be the best analogue for the casuistic content in Exodus 21–22 and Deuteronomy 19–25. Rather, I contend that these units are closer in form and function to the Mesopotamian corpus of legal-pedagogical texts.[36] In addition to generating law collections, royal edicts, and documents of practice such as contracts and trial records, Mesopotamian scribes produced and copied a variety of legal-oriented pedagogical texts. As I outline in Chapter 1, this material included sample contracts ("model contracts"),

History of Old Testament Law, trans. Allan W. Mahnke [Minneapolis: Fortress Press, 1996], 165–66). Deuteronomy 12–26 (or parts of it) is then seen by some as representing a revision of CC, which was later supplemented at both ends (see, e.g., Bernard M. Levinson, *Deuteronomy and the Hermeneutics of Legal Innovation* [New York: Oxford University Press, 1997]; Norbert Lohfink, "Zur deuteronomischen Zentralisationsformel," *Bib* 65.3 [1984]: 297–329; and Eckart Otto, "Aspects of Legal Reforms and Reformulations in Ancient Cuneiform and Israelite Law," in *Theory and Method in Biblical and Cuneiform Law: Revision, Interpolation and Development*, ed. Bernard M. Levinson, reprint [Sheffield: Sheffield Phoenix Press, 2006], 192–96). Cf. John Van Seters, however, who argues for the reverse (*A Law Book for the Diaspora: Revision in the Study of the Covenant Code* [New York: Oxford University Press, 2003]). Alternatively, or in conjunction with this standpoint, a number of scholars contend that the family-oriented laws in Deuteronomy 21–25 originated as a once-independent collection prior to their inclusion in Deuteronomy; see Chapter 2 for further discussion.

35. This position is associated especially with Eckart Otto, who argues that Esarhaddon's Succession Treaty in particular served as the source for Deuteronomy; see Chapter 2 for discussion.

36. On the surface, this stance would seem to be in line with that of Otto ("Aspects of Legal Reforms," 160–62), who states matter-of-factly that the "predeuteronomistic" collections in Exodus 20–23 and Deuteronomy 12–26 are rooted in "scholarly-judicial traditions of scribal education" (160). Nonetheless, in my discussions of the content in Exodus and Deuteronomy, it will become clear that I diverge from Otto with respect to my understanding of the pedagogical roots of biblical law. While Otto attributes the casuistic content in Exodus 21–22 to disputes between clans (see, e.g., "Town and Rural Countryside in Ancient Israelite Law: Reception and Redaction in Cuneiform and Israelite Law," *JSOT* 57 [1993]: 3–22), I conclude that this material is rooted in a pedagogical exercise rooted in Babylonian law (see Chapter 4). Otto (along with others) takes the clusters of law in Deuteronomy 21–25 to belong to an old collection of family law, a position that I challenge in various ways (see Chapter 2, with ample references to Otto's oeuvre). I conclude, then, that while we both claim to perceive biblical law as rooted in pedagogical contexts, our notions of this concept are fundamentally different. Nonetheless, as is evident throughout this book (esp. Chapter 2), I appreciate many of Otto's insights on individual texts.

fictional court cases, extracts from law collections, independent sequences of casuistic laws, and legal phrasebooks with series of contractual clauses. The bulk of it is in Sumerian and dates to the early second millennium BCE in southern Mesopotamia, that is, the same geographical and chronological context that yielded the law collections. Some of this material, such as the model contracts, is amply represented and was integral to early education, while other text-types are far less attested. Nonetheless, these diverse texts exhibit numerous cross-references and evidently formed a kind of sub-corpus within their educational context. These texts also feature abundant ties to law beyond the educational sphere, including both the law collections and documents of practice. Provisions in the independent sequences echo provisions in the collections; clauses in the model contracts or the legal phrasebooks parallel clauses in actual contracts; and the fictional cases feature contractual clauses and scenarios that appear in the law collections.

Outside of the model contracts, the legal-pedagogical material has received only limited attention in the otherwise robust subfield of Mesopotamian scribal education.[37] Unfortunately, there is no sourcebook that gathers all of the evidence together, and a number of critical editions of texts remain scattered in various journals and volumes. In turn, the legal-pedagogical texts have been largely neglected by biblical scholars, despite the considerable interest in Mesopotamian scribal education in biblical studies over the last two decades. The stylistic, structural, and thematic parallels between this content and "biblical law" have thus been

37. The study of scribal education has yielded a number of important monographs in the last two decades. See esp. Paul Delnero, *The Textual Criticism of Sumerian Literature*, JCSSS 3 (Boston: American Schools of Oriental Research, 2012); Alexandra Kleinerman, *Education in Early 2nd Millennium BC Babylonia: The Sumerian Epistolary Miscellany*, CM 42 (Leiden: Brill, 2011); Eleanor Robson, *Mesopotamian Mathematics, 2100–1600 BC: Technical Constants in Bureaucracy and Education*, OECT 14 (Oxford: Oxford University Press, 1999); Niek Veldhuis, *Religion, Literature, and Scholarship: The Sumerian Composition of "Nanše and the Birds," With a Catalogue of Sumerian Bird Names*, CM 22 (Leiden: Brill, 2004); and Niek Veldhuis, *History of the Cuneiform Lexical Tradition*, GMTR 6 (Münster: Ugarit-Verlag, 2014). See Chapter 1 for discussion of the scholarship on the legal-pedagogical texts.

scarcely recognized. One exception is Clemens Locher's treatment of the "slandered bride" laws in Deut 22:13–21. Locher observed that the style of Deut 22:13–21 was similar to that of a Sumerian fictional case regarding the assault of a slave-girl.[38] Outside of this observation and its reiterations in scholarship, however, the potential of the Mesopotamian legal-pedagogical material to illuminate the origins of what we call biblical law has remained dormant.

Knowledge of the Mesopotamian legal-pedagogical content has the capacity to reshape our understanding of both the origins and trajectory of biblical law. In Chapter 2, I demonstrate that a set of casuistic laws in Exodus and Deuteronomy exhibit stylistic and thematic parallels to the colorful Mesopotamian pedagogical genre of fictional cases. These "Hebrew Legal Fictions" (HLFs) include Deut 19:4–6, the case of an accidental manslayer; Deut 21:15–17, the case of a man with two wives, one loved, the other hated; Deut 22:13–19, the case of a man who makes false accusations against his wife; Exod 22:15–16 and Deut 22:28–29, two cases of an assaulted virgin; Deut 24:1–4, the case of a two-time divorcee; Deut 25:5–10, the case of a widowed woman and her reluctant brother-in-law; and Exod 21:7–11, the case of a daughter sold as a slave-wife. With this argument, I thus diverge from scholars who claim that these texts and others once belonged to an old collection of "family law." Close examination of the HLFs indicates that all of them originated as independent texts. Only at a later point were most of the HLFs supplemented with "laws" of a fundamentally different nature and incorporated into what would become Deuteronomy. This development created the illusion of an old law collection in Deuteronomy, enabled by the use of the same methods of composition that are attested in the Near Eastern collections.

38. Clemens Locher, "Deuteronomium 22,13–21 vom Prozessprotokoll zum kasuistischen Gesetz," in *Das Deuteronomium: Entstehung, Gestalt und Botschaft*, ed. Norbert Lohfink, BETL 68 (Leuven: Leuven University Press, 1985), 298–303; see also Locher's more elaborate study, *Die Ehre einer Frau in Israel: Exegetische und rechtsvergleichende Studien zu Deuteronomium 22,13–21,* OBO 70 (Freiburg, Switzerland: Universitätsverlag / Göttingen: Vandenhoeck & Ruprecht, 1986), 93–109.

When the HLFs are isolated as a set, their unique and shared features come to light. One of these features, as detailed in Chapter 3, is the similarities between the HLFs and contracts from the ancient Near East. Although we lack access to whatever contracts the Israelites and Judahites may have produced, excavations in Syria and Iraq have yielded thousands of ancient contracts of all types, providing us with enormous insight into the terminology and format that such documents exhibited. Parallels between three of the HLFs and Late Bronze Age contracts from Emar (modern-day Tell Meskene, Syria) and Nuzi (Yorghan Tepe in northern Iraq) suggest that the scribes who composed the HLFs drew upon the terminology and format of analogous types of contracts and/or lists of contractual clauses. The case study for this hypothesis is Deut 25:5–10, a text that shares striking parallels with a set of wills from Emar. Two other HLFs (Exod 21:7–11 and Deut 21:15–17) also reflect the terminology and format that appear in other Near Eastern contracts. Given the parallels between the HLFs and the Mesopotamian fictional cases, I conclude that several of the HLFs were likewise composed with the aim of either teaching or practicing standard contractual clauses.

In Chapter 4, I demonstrate that Exod 21:18–22:16 is rooted in a different type of legal-pedagogical text: namely, a scribal exercise on the theme of physical and property damages. Toward this end, I profile the Mesopotamian legal-pedagogical practice of copying a limited sequence of laws, as attested, for example, in the exercises that Martha Roth has dubbed the "Laws about Rented Oxen" and the "Sumerian Laws Exercise Tablet."[39] Both of these exercises exhibit overlap with and divergence from laws in the collections, but neither one constitutes an "extract" per se.[40] Parallels between these exercises and Exod 21:18–22:16 suggest that a similar text-type lies behind the biblical block. This comparison helps account

39. Roth, *Law Collections from Mesopotamia.*

40. On the function of "extracts" (or "Type III" tablets) in Old Babylonian scribal education, see Paul Delnero, "Sumerian Extract Tablets and Scribal Education," *JCS* 62 (2010): 53–69. Delnero demonstrates persuasively that scribes would break down literary compositions into roughly four equal parts (or "extracts") and learn them in succession prior to copying the complete composition on a larger ("Type I") tablet.

not only for the limited focus of Exod 21:18–22:16 on physical and property damages, but also for its disjointedness, ambiguities, and errors. It also accounts for the fact that the units in Exod 21:18–22:16 overlap with provisions known from LH but also diverge from them in substantial ways. Rather than presume that the Israelites/Judahites omitted large swaths of content from LH, selecting only the material on damages, I propose that they had access to a legal-pedagogical exercise on this topic alone. Only at a later point was this pedagogical exercise repackaged—evidently with minimal internal adjustment—as (divine) law.

As I conclude in Chapter 5, the trajectories of the HLFs and Exod 21:18–22:16 were both similar and distinct. While the scribes responsible for Exodus 20–23 preserved the old exercise (Exod 21:18–22:16) intact and framed it at both ends, those who preserved certain HLFs in Deuteronomy supplemented them with a set of additional "laws" that repeatedly prescribed the death penalty for civil, criminal, and theological offenses. In certain cases, these additional units were standalone, while in others, the scribes modified factors in the HLFs in order to produce ostensible counter-cases. Although both blocks of material are each presented as "the laws/judgments" that Yahweh gave to the people, such claims do not automatically render these blocks law collections in the Near Eastern sense of the term. I conclude that the genre of the law collection not only originated in southern Mesopotamia but remained a Mesopotamian/Greater Mesopotamian phenomenon for the duration of its use in the ancient Near East.

I thus propose that the starting point for what we call "biblical law" is a set of legal-pedagogical exercises that played a role in scribal education. Of course, because the Israelites and Judahites wrote on perishable materials in an unforgiving climate, we lack hard evidence of such scribal exercises. In contrast, the Mesopotamians' proclivity for the more durable medium of clay tablets enables us to take stock of a robust Near Eastern corpus of legal-pedagogical texts. Although not all of this material had parallels in ancient Israel and Judah, it nonetheless provides a crucial foundation for reassessing the pedagogical roots of "biblical law." It is to this content that we now turn.

1

The Role of Legal Texts in Mesopotamian Scribal Education

This is truly a case of law school before lawyers.

—William Hallo

Over the past twenty years, Assyriologists have made substantial progress in reconstructing the contours of scribal education, especially for the Old Babylonian (OB) period (2000–1595 BCE), for which there is considerable evidence.[1] Within this subset of robust scholarship, however, the role of law and legal-pedagogical texts in scribal education has received only subsidiary attention. There are indeed exceptions to the rule, particularly in the area of "model contracts," that is, sample contracts that were copied at an early phase in OB education.[2] In terms of broader overviews,

1. The quotation in the epigraph derives from William W. Hallo's Foreword to Walter R. Bodine's monograph, *How Mesopotamian Scribes Learned to Write Legal Documents: A Study of the Sumerian Model Contracts in the Babylonian Collection at Yale University* (Lewiston, NY: Edwin Mellen Press, 2014), ii. The statement is a bit of an exaggeration, but the evidence certainly points to the presence of law *in* school, if not law school.

2. Two recent volumes provide fresh insight into this important pedagogical genre: Gabriella Spada's *Sumerian Model Contracts from the Old Babylonian Period in the Hilprecht Collection Jena*, Texte und Materialien der Frau Professor Hilprecht Collection of Babylonian Antiquities im Eigentum der Friedrich-Schiller-Universität Jena XI (Wiesbaden: Harrassowitz, 2018); and Bodine's *How Mesopotamian Scribes Learned*. In addition, Spada has edited twenty-five prisms and tablets with model contracts from the Schøyen collection in a volume that also includes editions of literary letters, a handful of fictional cases, and several other legal-pedagogical

Making a Case. Sara J. Milstein, Oxford University Press. © Oxford University Press 2021.
DOI: 10.1093/oso/9780190911805.003.0002

however, the most thorough treatment of law in scribal education remains that of Martha T. Roth's unpublished 1979 dissertation on the OB prism that she later dubbed the Sumerian Laws Handbook of Forms (SLHF).[3] Stephen Lieberman had planned to publish all of the available legal-pedagogical material before his untimely death; unfortunately, no volume has since filled the void. The lack of a single sourcebook has made it difficult to take stock of the function of legal texts in Mesopotamian scribal education and of their relationship to law beyond the pedagogical sphere. In turn, it is not surprising that biblical scholars who otherwise have drawn liberally on data for Mesopotamian education in their reconstructions of Israelite scribal training have paid scant attention to the legal-pedagogical texts.[4] Although not all Mesopotamian scribes would have been exposed to the full gamut of these texts, it is thus worth profiling the range of legal-pedagogical texts that were in circulation, the potential role(s) that these texts served, and their links to law more broadly.

AN OVERVIEW OF MESOPOTAMIAN LEGAL-PEDAGOGICAL TEXTS

While legal-pedagogical texts were learned somewhat less widely than other pedagogical genres, at least some scribes in the OB period and beyond

texts ("Old Babylonian Model Contracts and Related Texts," in Andrew R. George and Gabriella Spada, *Old Babylonian Texts in the Schøyen Collection, Part Two: School Letters, Model Contracts, and Related Texts*, CUSAS 43 [University Park, PA: Eisenbrauns, 2019], 73–145).

3. Martha T. Roth, "Scholastic Tradition and Mesopotamian Law: A Study of FLP 1287, a Prism in the Collection of the Free Library of Philadelphia" (PhD diss., University of Pennsylvania, 1979).

4. See, e.g. Karel van der Toorn, *Scribal Culture and the Making of the Hebrew Bible* (Cambridge, MA: Harvard University Press, 2009); David M. Carr, *Writing on the Tablet of the Heart: Origins of Scripture and Literature* (New York: Oxford University Press, 2005); Christopher Rollston, *Writing and Literacy in the World of Ancient Israel: Epigraphic Evidence from the Iron Age*, ABS 11 (Atlanta: SBL Press, 2010); and most recently, William M. Schniedewind, *The Finger of the Scribe: How Scribes Learned to Write the Bible* (New York: Oxford University Press, 2019).

were exposed to a rich and varied assortment of such texts. Although the "unusable" aspects of OB scribal education have been emphasized, it is important to note that some of the legal-pedagogical content was tied to practical application.[5] The Sumerian model contracts, for example, exhibit much overlap with the content and form of actual contracts, some of which continued to be written in Sumerian in the OB period. OB legal phrasebooks and certain fictional cases include Sumerian contractual clauses and terms that likewise mirror those used in actual OB contracts. An exercise with laws and related clauses on the topic of rented oxen exhibits parallels both with actual contracts of hire and laws in the collections.[6] When this diverse content is examined as a whole, it becomes apparent that the legal texts reflect a cultural matrix unto themselves, with copious cross-references and abundant links to law beyond the educational sphere.

One caveat is in order. The conceptual categories profiled later (e.g., "model contracts," "fictional cases") do not always constitute separate sources. Certain texts, such as SLHF, feature a combination of verbal paradigms, contractual clauses, model contracts, and laws. On several occasions, model contracts, contractual clauses, and/or fictional cases were copied on the same compilation tablet, or Sammeltafel. In other cases, model contracts were copied together with non-legal pedagogical texts, such as proverbs or lexical lists. The occasional combination of these different text-types in a single document indicates that the scribes must have viewed them as part of the same educational package—and as such, so should we.

Model Contracts

Although not all ancient legal transactions would have required documentation, thousands of texts from Mesopotamia indicate that scribes from the

5. See, e.g., Piotr Michalowski's comments in "The Libraries of Babel: Text, Authority, and Tradition in Ancient Mesopotamia," in *Cultural Repertoires: Structure, Function, and Dynamics*, ed. Gillis J. Dorleijn and Herman L. J. Vanstiphout, GSCC 3 (Leuven: Peeters, 2003), 105–29: "Once they graduated, the newly minted scribes would have little use for their Sumerian, as they would be working mostly with the more familiar Akkadian language" (110–11).

6. Roth, "Scholastic Tradition," 15.

third millennium BCE on were employed to produce all types of written contracts: marriage and divorce contracts, adoptions, loans, hires, sales, rentals, wills, and so on. It is thus logical that model contracts were an integral part of OB elementary education, for they provided scribes with the skills for drawing up a range of functional contracts.[7] Indeed, in one text, a scribe boasts of his ability to write "contracts for formalizing marriages and for business partnerships; for selling houses, fields, and slaves; for deposits of silver; for leasing cultivation fields or palm-groves; and tablets for contracts of adoption."[8] About 350 model contracts are known, though only a limited number have been published. Not all of the published texts are provenanced, but the ones that are demonstrate ties to Nippur, Larsa, Isin, Ur, Tulul Khattab, and Sippar.[9] The sources are varied and include Types I, II, III, and IV tablets; prisms; and cylinders.[10] In certain instances,

7. Stephen Lieberman identified two modes of instruction: the "paradigmatic" approach, in which one learned a series of words, phrases and clauses; and "pattern practice," when a student copied a series of sample legal and administrative records. The model contracts would fall under the latter category ("Nippur: City of Decisions," in *Nippur at the Centennial: Papers Read at the 35e Rencontre Assyriologique Internationale, Philadelphia 1988*, ed. Maria deJong Ellis, Occasional Publications of the Samuel Noah Kramer Fund 14 [Philadelphia: University Museum, 1992], 129–30).

8. Charpin, *Hammurabi of Babylon*, 14. The citation is from the composition "Edubba D," also known as "Scribal Activities" or "The Dialogue between an Examiner and a Student."

9. Spada notes that the model contracts in the Hilprecht Collection are almost entirely from Nippur (*Sumerian Model Contracts*, 3). Bodine does not specify the provenance of the tablets he translates, but notes that a large quantity of model contracts were found at House F in Nippur, a rich site that has yielded fourteen hundred tablets alone (*How Mesopotamian Scribes Learned*, 7; on House F, see Eleanor Robson, "The Tablet House: A Scribal School in Old Babylonian Nippur," *RA* 95.1 [2001]: 39–66). The tablets in the Schøyen collection are mostly without archaeological provenance, but on the basis of the texts themselves, Martin Schøyen estimates that about 90% of the OB tablets come from Larsa ("Statement of Provenance," in George and Spada, *Old Babylonian Texts*, viii). In "Two Old Babylonian Model Contracts," *CDLJ* 2 (2014), Gabriella Spada provides a list of published model contracts with their provenance (1 n. 6); see also Spada, "I modelli di contratto nell'edubba paleo-babilonese: un esempio di contratto di adozione," *AION* 72 (2012): 133–48, and "I Want to Break Free: Model Contracts Recording Slave Self-Emancipation," in *^{d}Nisaba za3-mi2: Ancient Near Eastern Studies in Honor of Francesco Pomponio*, ed. Palmiro Notizia, Annunziata Rositani, and Lorenzo Verderame, dubsar 19 (Münster: Zaphon, 2021).

10. As is typical, the prisms that Spada surveys have a hollow central axis so that they could either be handled on a stick or suspended from the ceiling and turned horizontally (*Sumerian Model Contracts*, 74). Miguel Civil analyzed collections of lexical tablets and categorized them into four formats, Types I–IV. Type I tablets are large, multi-columned tablets that were copied

only one model contract is preserved on a tablet.[11] In other cases, multiple model contracts are preserved on a tablet or prism, either on their own (Fig. 1.1) or on the same tablet with proverbs or lexical lists.[12] Others appear with fictional cases or together with legal provisions.[13] The eclectic OB prism SLHF includes six model contracts together with verbal paradigms, contractual clauses, and a handful of laws.[14]

Unlike actual contracts, model contracts typically lack witnesses, seals, and dates. Some model contracts refer to the omitted witnesses with generic statements ("the witnesses, its month, and its year").[15] Bodine points to a number of other potential indicators of their pedagogical Sitz im

by advanced students. Type II are large "teacher-student copies," with different exercises typically written on the obverse and reverse. The obverse ("II/1") featured a model composition written in the left column by the teacher, with room in the right column(s) for the student to copy it multiple times. The student then used the reverse ("II/2") to copy a text that he had previously learned. Type III are single-column extracts of compositions, and Type IV are lenticular-shaped tablets that consist of two to four lines of composition and show signs of inscription by teachers and students ("Old Babylonian Proto-Lu: Types of Sources," in *The Series lú = ša and Related Texts*, ed. Miguel Civil and Erica Reiner, MSL 12 [Rome: Pontificium Institutum Biblicum, 1969], 27–28; *Ea A = nâqu, Aa A = nâqu, with Their Forerunners and Related Texts*, ed. Miguel Civil, with the collaboration of Wilfred G. Lambert and Margaret W. Green, MSL 14 [Rome: Pontificium Institutum Biblicum, 1979], 5–7; and with the identification of additional tablet types for later periods, Miguel Civil, "Ancient Mesopotamian Lexicography," *CANE* 4: 2308). Civil classified prisms as Type I tablets; Steve Tinney later identified prisms as a separate category ("On the Curricular Setting of Sumerian Literature," *Iraq* 61 [1999]: 159–72).

11. For example, NBC 8630 and YBC 12074; see Bodine, *How Mesopotamian Scribes Learned*, 41–44.

12. The combination of model contracts and proverbs or lexical lists is attested on Type II tablets, typically with one genre occupying the obverse and the other occupying the reverse. Regarding tablets that combine model contracts with lexical lists, see Spada, *Sumerian Model Contracts*, 60.

13. MS3176/5 combines model contracts with four fictional cases (Spada, "Old Babylonian Model Contracts and Related Texts," 95–106). The combination of model contracts and legal provisions (specifically from the exercise known as Laws about Rented Oxen, to be discussed later) is attested only in N963 and the school prism CUNES 52-10-148; see Spada, "A New Fragment of the 'Laws about Rented Oxen' and the Sumerian Verb bu-us2," *RSO* 91 (2018): 11–18.

14. The text is of unknown provenance, but Roth surmises that it may have originated in southern Babylonia ("Scholastic Tradition," 25).

15. Bodine, *How Mesopotamian Scribes Learned*, 161. There are exceptions to the rule, however. Some model contracts include a date but no witnesses (Bodine, 162) and a prism with seventeen model contracts lists a date (month and year name) with one to three witnesses at the end of each contract; one of the witnesses is often the scribe (Spada, "Old Babylonian Model Contracts and Related Texts," 75).

Figure 1.1 The reverse of NBC 7800, an OB tablet preserving eighteen model contracts of various types. Courtesy of the Yale Babylonian Collection; photograph by Klaus Wagensonner.

Leben: the existence of duplicates; the appearance of multiple contracts on the same tablet; the appearance of model contracts together with other pedagogical texts; the inclusion of unusual features or dramatic details; the anonymity of the parties; the emphasis on grammar; the repetition of formulas in various forms; the dedication of the text to Nisaba, the patron goddess of scribes; the inclusion of blank spaces; and careless writing.[16] Some of these features are definitive markers in and of themselves (e.g., the dedication to Nisaba; the inclusion of blank spaces) while others are occasionally associated with functional contracts as well (e.g., unusual features; a series of contracts on a single tablet).[17] It is worth adding that the fragmentary nature of some tablets can sometimes make it difficult to determine whether or not a particular factor is present. In any case, the pedagogical function of the source becomes more certain when more of these factors are present in combination.

The model contracts share numerous parallels in content, format, and terminology with functional contracts, legal phrasebooks, and precepts from the law collections. First of all, the model contracts cover a range of situations similar to that in the functional contracts: sales and

16. Bodine, *How Mesopotamian Scribes Learned*, 160–79. For further discussion, see Gabriella Spada's thorough assessment, Review of Walter Ray Bodine, *How Mesopotamian Scribes Learned to Write Legal Documents: A Study of the Sumerian Model Contracts in the Babylonian Collection at Yale University* (Lewiston/Lampeter: Edwin Mellen Press, 2014)," *ZA* 107 (2017): 290–307. To Bodine's list, Spada adds the presence of catch-lines, the appearance of colophons with "paratextual information," and the range of formats that were employed (Type I, II, III, IV, and prisms) (293). See also Dominique Charpin's critique of Bodine's list in his review ("Chroniques bibliographiques 20: Pour une diplomatique des documents paléo-babyloniens," *RA* 111 [2017]: 155–78). As Charpin remarks, certain items on Bodine's list are also characteristic of drafts as opposed to exercises (161).

17. Similar challenges arise with respect to distinguishing Akkadian "model letters" from actual missives. About seventy Akkadian school letters have been found throughout Babylonia, at Nippur, Uruk, Kish, Sippar, and Adab (Andrew R. George, "Old Babylonian School Letters," in George and Spada, *Old Babylonian Texts*, 47). As with the model contracts, the Akkadian school letters appear to have been used to teach scribes the epistolary format (yet cf. Walther Sallaberger, who questions the applicable nature of the "model letters," given the differences between them and contemporaneous letters [*"Wenn Du mein Bruder bist, . . .": Interaktion und Textgestaltung in altbabylonischen Alltagsbriefen*, CM 16 [Groningen: Styx, 1999], 153). Fritz R. Kraus, the first to study this corpus, identified four possible markers of pedagogical origins: distorted tablets, poor script, mistakes in execution, and the presence of duplicates or duplicated content in other letters ("Briefschreibübungen im altbabylonischen Schulunterricht," *JEOL* 16 [1964]: 16–39, cited in George, "Old Babylonian School Letters," 10–12). He later considered the possibility, however, that some of these letters were in fact rough drafts for actual letters. More recently, George has identified additional markers of the pedagogical function of these texts, including the appearance of double rulings after the letters, the use of round numbers, the heavy use of formulaic clauses, and the presence of technical terms that would be useful in practical contexts ("Old Babylonian School Letters," 54–55).

leases, hires, adoptions, manumissions, pledges, and loans.[18] In a number of cases, clauses in the model contracts are repeated verbatim in functional contracts. Thus, for example, manumission model contracts refer to "clearing the forehead and smashing the pot," symbolic acts that are also attested in functional contracts.[19] Parallel no-contest clauses and instructions to destroy lost tablets if they are found are attested in the model contracts and in a number of functional contracts.[20] Similar no-flight clauses are preserved in slave hire model contracts and in functional pledge and hiring contracts.[21] As Aaron Skaist notes, model contracts and functional contracts for barley loans include similar clauses that specify the location where the loan is to be repaid.[22] While it is not possible to determine whether or not some of the model contracts are based on actual contracts, the close relationship between the two is undeniable. The model contracts also demonstrate considerable overlap with the contractual clauses in the legal phrasebook *ana ittišu* (Ai) and in ḪAR-ra = *ḫubullu* (Ḫḫ) I and II, both of which have OB antecedents. The aforementioned symbolic acts associated with manumission, for example, also appear in the phrasebooks.[23] In terms of law, a reward clause for finding a lost slave in a model contract is paralleled in Laws of Ur-Namma (LU) §17; and the same interest rates—20% for silver loans, 33% for barley or grain loans—also occur in the model contracts, functional contracts, and the law collections.[24] It thus

18. Spada, *Sumerian Model Contracts*, 3.

19. Roth, "Scholastic Tradition," 106; see also Spada, *Sumerian Model Contracts*, 21. The model contracts exhibit parallels to both Ur III and OB functional contracts.

20. See, e.g., Bodine, *How Mesopotamian Scribes Learned*, 60–61. In the case of destroying a lost tablet that is found, this directive is found in numerous Ur III texts (Spada, *Sumerian Model Contracts*, 47).

21. Spada, *Sumerian Model Contracts*, 33.

22. Aaron J. Skaist, *The Old Babylonian Loan Contract: Its History and Geography*, Bar-Ilan Studies in Near Eastern Languages and Culture (Ramat Gan: Bar-Ilan University Press, 1994), 190–91.

23. See Spada, *Sumerian Model Contracts*, 21. Although Ai postdates the OB period, it is based on an OB forerunner from Nippur (Spada, *Sumerian Model Contracts*, 3).

24. Spada, *Sumerian Model Contracts*, 35, 46, and 50–51.

appears that copying model contracts not only contributed to the scribes' acquisition of Sumerian but also had practical applicability with respect to the drafting of actual contracts.

Fictional Cases

Fictional cases, or what scholars have called "model (court) cases," are also attested for the OB period.[25] These Sumerian texts provide accounts of (fictional) court cases yet are evidently not *actual* trial records, as indicated by the fact that they lack witnesses, seals, and dates. The limited "corpus" includes a homicide case (the famous "Nippur Homicide Trial," henceforth, NHT), two cases of adultery, three inheritance disputes (see, for example, Fig. 1.2), a case regarding the rape of a slave-girl, an unpublished dispute over heirs to a slave-girl, another unpublished dispute over office, two cases about a barley loan, two cases concerning a burgled house, a case of slander, and possibly several others.[26] Scholars have generally assumed

25. For discussion of the genre, see Martha T. Roth, "The Slave and the Scoundrel: CBS 10467, A Sumerian Morality Tale?," *JAOS* 103.1 (1983): 279; and William W. Hallo, "A Model Court Case Concerning Inheritance," in *Riches Hidden in Secret Places: Ancient Near Eastern Studies in Memory of Thorkild Jacobsen*, ed. Tzvi Abusch (Winona Lake, IN: Eisenbrauns, 2002), 142–43. Hallo surveys the various names that have been assigned to these texts: "a literary collection of legal decisions by the kings of Isin," "'literary' legal decisions," and "literarisches ditilla."

26. The classic edition of NHT is that of Thorkild Jacobsen, "An Ancient Mesopotamian Trial for Homicide," in *Toward the Image of Tammuz and Other Essays on Mesopotamian History and Culture*, ed. William Moran, HSS 21 (Cambridge, MA: Harvard University Press, 1970), 193–215; more recently, see the translation and discussion by Martha T. Roth, "Gender and Law: A Case Study from Ancient Mesopotamia," in *Gender and Law in the Hebrew Bible and the Ancient Near East*, ed. Bernard Levinson, Tikva Frymer-Kensky, and Victor H. Matthews, JSOTSup 262 (Sheffield: Sheffield Academic Press, 1998), 173–84. On the two adultery cases, see Samuel Greengus, "A Textbook Case of Adultery in Ancient Mesopotamia," *HUCA* 40–41 (1969–70): 33–44; and Raymond Westbrook, *Old Babylonian Marriage Law*, AfOB 23 (Horn: Verlag Ferdinand Berger & Söhne, 1988), 133; henceforth, *OBML*. On the inheritance disputes, see Hallo, "Model Court Case"; and Jacob Klein and Tonia Sharlach, "A Collection of Model Court Cases from Old Babylonian Nippur (CBS 11324)," *ZA* 97.1 (2007): 1–25. On the rape of the slave-girl, see J. J. Finkelstein, "Sex Offenses in Sumerian Laws," *JAOS* 86.4 (1966): 359–60. The cases regarding the barley loan and burgled houses are in Spada, "Old Babylonian Model Contracts and Related Texts," 100–101. Spada also includes a fragmentary text that could be either a collection of actual contracts and legal cases or a school collection used for training scribes in Sumerian formularies (121–23).

Figure 1.2 A fictional court case involving an inheritance dispute that a man brought against his nephews (YBC 9839). Courtesy of the Yale Babylonian Collection; photograph by Klaus Wagensonner.

that the fictional cases are based on actual cases that were adapted for use in the educational sphere.[27] For Martha Roth, the "model court records" likely served to expose scribes to the form of trial records.[28] Their function would thus appear to mirror that of the model contracts: hence, the analogous name.[29]

It is important to note, however, that the evidence for the two text-types differs in key ways. Most significantly, the model contracts were integral to the elementary scribal curriculum, while the fictional cases were not. As such, the fictional cases are attested in far fewer copies, with a number of them known from only a single attestation. In addition, the stylistic relationship between the fictional cases and actual trial records is not nearly as close as that of the contracts. This discrepancy is due to the nature of OB trial records in general, which do not follow a template like the contracts do.[30] Thus, although it is possible that the fictional cases were used to train scribes in the format of trial records, the available data do not merit this conclusion in the same way that the model contracts do.

Nonetheless, the fictional cases do exhibit certain pedagogical indicators. As noted above, like the model contracts, they uniformly lack witnesses, seals, and dates. On a few occasions, several cases were copied in succession on a Sammeltafel, a phenomenon that is also associated with

27. See, for example, Roth, "Slave and the Scoundrel," *JAOS* 103.1 (1983): 282. Greengus' statement is paradigmatic of this stance: "[T]he literary legal decisions appear to be records of such real cases from which general principles of adjudication could have been extracted" ("Textbook Case of Adultery," 43–44); see also Finkelstein, "Sex Offenses," 360. Until recently, there was no evidence to support this position, yet Spada refers to one instance in which a real case was recopied with some variations by a student ("Old Babylonian Model Contracts and Related Texts," 119–20). This instance need not indicate that all of the fictional cases are rooted in actual documents or trials, however.

28. Roth, "Slave and the Scoundrel," 282.

29. Indeed, Hallo, following Stephen Lieberman, stresses the relationship between the two ("Model Court Case," 143).

30. Outside of concluding with a list of witnesses and the date, the OB records are fairly heterogeneous. This is apparent from the collection of OB trial records in Dominique Charpin, "Lettres et procès paléo-babyloniens," in *Rendre la justice en Mésopotamie: Archives judiciaires du Proche-Orient ancien (IIIe–Ier millénaires avant J.-C)*, ed. Francis Joannès, Temps et espaces (Saint-Denis: Presses universitaires de Vincennes, 2000), 69–111.

pedagogical texts.[31] Again, as noted in the previous section, one tablet preserves a set of fictional cases together with model contracts. The fictional cases are also tied to Nippur, a site that is known for its associations with OB scribal education. In addition to the fact that most of the provenanced copies were found at Nippur, at least five refer directly to "the Nippur assembly," and one case features Nippurean personages as the legal parties.[32] As with the model contracts, several of the fictional records are also peppered with colorful literary flourishes, a feature that scholars associate with pedagogical texts.[33] In the adultery case edited by Samuel Greengus, for example, a married woman is said to be guilty of three transgressions: "In the first place, she burglarized [her husband's] storeroom; in the second place, in his oil jar she made an opening and covered it up with a cloth. In the third place, [her husband] caught her upon a man." The cuckolded husband then ties his wife and her lover to the bed and carries the bed

31. The aforementioned tablet edited by Klein and Sharlach (CBS 11324) preserves a series of three fictional cases, though the first can be said to blur the line between model contract and fictional case ("Collection of Model Court Cases"). According to Jacobsen, the series of NHT, a dispute over office, and the rape of slave-girl is also attested on at least three Sammeltafeln ("Ancient Mesopotamian Trial," 196–97), though Hallo cites four ("Model Court Case," 141).

32. See Roth, "Slave and the Scoundrel," 282. NHT is forwarded by King Ur-Ninurta to the assembly at Nippur and closes with the subscript "Case accepted for trial in the Assembly of Nippur." Another case on the same Sammeltafel as NHT is forwarded to the Assembly of Nippur, as is Finkelstein's case of the raped slave-girl ("Sex Offenses"). Greengus's adultery case does not reference Nippur but does refer to the "assembly" ("Textbook Case of Adultery"). CBS 11324 is from Nippur; and in one case, the king Išme-Dagan orders the Assembly of Nippur and its judges to gather and judge the case in the Ubšu-ukkina, a site in Nippur that is associated with the divine assembly. An unpublished case cited by Roth likewise refers to the Assembly of Nippur ("Slave and the Scoundrel," 282), as does Hallo's inheritance case. In addition, Hallo's case references the "anointed priest of Ninlil" and "the elder," two offices that existed only at Nippur. Moreover, the names of two of the parties in the model case, Aabba-kalla and his son Enlil-mašzu, are both referenced as holding these roles in external evidence dating to the mid-nineteenth century BCE. The involvement of Ninurta in the case also ties it to Nippur (Hallo, "Model Court Case," 144–45).

33. For Hallo, these flourishes were an indicator of the pedagogical function of these texts ("Model Court Case," 150–51). For a similar argument, see Piotr Steinkeller's discussion of a model contract pertaining to the loss of a seal text ("Seal Practice in the Ur III Period," in *Seals and Sealing in the Ancient Near East*, ed. McGuire Gibson and Robert D. Biggs, BibMes 6 [Malibu: Undena, 1977], 41–53, here, 49); see also Klein and Sharlach, "Collection of Model

to the assembly, a trope that anticipates Hephaestus's capture of his wife Aphrodite with Ares.[34]

NHT (Fig. 1.3) is singular among the fictional cases, both with respect to its length and literary flair (see the appendix). In this text, the *nešakku*-priest Lu-Inanna is said to be murdered by three male assailants. When his wife Nin-Dada was informed of her husband's murder, she is said to have "not open[ed] her mouth; she covered it with a cloth."[35] This subtle indication of Nin-Dada's guilt recalls the "cloth cover-up" in the adultery case and may point to a direct relationship between the two texts.[36]

The case is taken to the assembly at Nippur, which comprises a colorful cast of characters: Dudu the bird-catcher; Šeš-kalla, the potter; Lugala-kam, the gardener; and curiously, a man who has the same patronym as one of the assailants. The men then engage in a debate regarding Nin-Dada's culpability. The majority contingent speaks first and states that Nin-Dada should be killed together with the three men. A minority contingent retorts that Nin-Dada cannot be responsible because she is a woman. The majority then returns with a subtler argument, now couched in generalized terms. They state, "A woman who does not value her husband might surely *know* his enemy; he might kill her husband; he might then inform her that her husband has been killed. Why should he not make her keep her mouth shut about him?" In other words, the majority

Court Cases," 2; and Roth, "Slave and the Scoundrel," 279 ("That which is unusual is interesting, and makes excellent teaching material").

34. Greengus, "Textbook Case of Adultery," 37. Greengus's translation and interpretation served as an important correction to J. Van Dijk's earlier understanding of this text as a man whose wife catches him in flagrante with another man (37–38). As Greengus points out, the ambiguity stems from the absence of gender determination in Sumerian, making it difficult to determine the identity of the plaintiff and defendant. He nonetheless makes a persuasive case that the guilty party is the wife, not the husband. My references rely on Greengus's translation and interpretation.

35. My translations throughout this section rely on Roth, "Gender and Law."

36. While the detail in the adultery case is literal, in NHT it functions in a metaphorical sense and highlights Nin-Dada's failure to report her husband's murder to the authorities. Given the literal function of the detail in the adultery case, I am inclined to suggest that it originated there.

Figure 1.3 A copy of the "Nippur Homicide Trial" (A30240, joined to Penn Museum UM 55-21-436), a Sumerian fictional case. Courtesy of the Oriental Institute of the University of Chicago and the Penn Museum; photograph by Susanne Paulus.

contingent insinuates that Nin-Dada was informed by the manslayers themselves, possibly because she was having an affair with one of them, as Martha Roth argues.[37] While this line of legal reasoning may seem preposterous, it nonetheless proceeds from the one known "fact" stated at the outset: Nin-Dada did not report her husband's death to the authorities. In turn, the assembly members reconstruct a plausible series of events based

37. For Roth, this reflects "an increasingly paranoid fantasy" ("Gender and Law," 180).

on the paltry evidence that they do possess. On the basis of this claim, the judges render a verdict, and Nin-Dada is sentenced to death along with the three men.[38]

Another fictional case likewise includes a colorful, if not strange, flourish. The text is the first of three fictional cases on CBS 11324, an OB tablet edited by Jacob Klein and Tonia Sharlach. The case pertains to a child who is adopted by a woman and launches with a string of adoption-oriented formulas known from the legal phrasebook Ai: "A suckling male child, found in a well, saved from the mouth of a dog, having no mother, having no sister, having no brother, and having no stepbrother . . . ." The text then outlines consequences if someone should make a claim on the baby. The "fee," however, is utterly bizarre, as Klein and Sharlach note: the biological parent is to bring the foster parent a twenty-liter jar of human milk as compensation! The authors suggest that the fanciful detail might be used to indicate that the claimant is supposed to cover all of the expenses of the foster mother, down to "the last penny."[39]

It is important to emphasize that none of these features—the reference to specific assembly members by name and profession, colorful literary flourishes, debates, and generalizations—is found in the contemporaneous OB trial records or in the Ur III collections of verdicts known as ditilla ("case completed") texts.[40] The fictional cases are also far more

38. Roth, "Gender and Law," 177.

39. Klein and Sharlach, "Collection of Model Court Cases," 9.

40. I am not aware of a single trial record from any period that includes a judicial debate. See Joannès, *Rendre la justice en Mésopotamie*, for translations of the most comprehensive set of trial records available for all of the major periods in Mesopotamian history. On the Neo-Assyrian records, see Remko Jas, *Neo-Assyrian Judicial Procedures*, SAAS 5 (Helsinki: Neo-Assyrian Text Corpus Project, 1996); on the Neo-Babylonian records, see Shalom Holtz, *Neo-Babylonian Trial Records*, WAW 35 (Atlanta: SBL Press, 2014); and F. Rachel Magdalene, Cornelia Wunsch, and Bruce Wells, *Fault, Responsibility, and Administrative Law in Late Babylonian Legal Texts*, MC 23 (University Park, PA: Eisenbrauns, 2019). A trilingual (Sumerian/Akkadian/English) edition of select trial records, to be published by SBL Press and edited by Daniel Fleming, is currently in the works. The ditilla texts preserve only an extremely brief account of the trial proceedings and in some cases do not even include the decision (Bertrand Lafont and Raymond Westbrook, "Mesopotamia: Neo-Sumerian Period [Ur III]," *HANEL* 1:184).

straightforward than actual OB records, which tend to preserve only the bare bones of the case.[41] This latter inclination toward brevity reflects the purpose of the record itself, which was apparently to confirm the judge's decision in the face of later appeals or failures to comply. The scribe was thus not a court transcriber but rather played a role in shaping the narrative of the legal victor.[42] In this light, it is again difficult to envision how the fictional cases would have prepared scribes for the task of writing trial records, even if they appear to cover similar territory.

Another recurring feature in the fictional cases may point to a different function. Six of the fictional cases include common contractual phrases known from contracts and legal phrasebooks. As emphasized by Klein and Sharlach, the three cases in CBS 11324 exhibit numerous parallels to Ai and to Ḫḫ.[43] The inheritance case edited by William Hallo includes a variation on the ubiquitous contractual clause, "His heart was satisfied with the money."[44] Greengus's adultery case opens with a formula that is similar to the opening formulas of some contemporaneous marriage contracts: "Eštar-ummī, daughter of Ilī-asû, did Irra-malik take in marriage."[45] The fictional case about a barley loan, edited by Gabriella Spada, includes an expression known from six unpublished model contracts and Ai.[46] A similar phenomenon is attested in other pedagogical text-types.

41. George notes a similar phenomenon for the Akkadian model letters vis-à-vis actual letters, in that the latter "often presume a level of knowledge that leaves a third party in the dark" ("Old Babylonian School Letters," 15).

42. This point is eloquently articulated by Martha T. Roth in "Reading Mesopotamian Law Cases PBS 5 100: A Question of Filiation," *JESHO* 44.3 (2001): 243–92. The trial record that Roth profiles is an exception to the rule of brevity.

43. Klein and Sharlach, "Collection of Model Court Cases," 2–3 and 23–25.

44. Hallo, "Model Court Case," 147.

45. A contract from Nippur, for example, reads, "Awilia, son of Warad-Sin, has taken Naramtum, daughter of Sinatum, for marriage." Another reads, "Warad-Šamaš has taken TaramSagila and Iltani, daughter of Sinabušu, for marriage" (Westbrook, *OBML*, 115–16). Although the fictional case fronts the woman's name—anticipating, perhaps, the crucial role she will play in the "plotline"—the wording is virtually the same.

46. Spada, "Old Babylonian Model Contracts and Related Texts," 100.

In his discussion of Akkadian model letters, Andrew George notes that while scribes copied letters closely at early stages, advanced scribes occasionally appear to have drawn on stock phrases to create their own improvisations.[47] In a similar vein, the first-millennium BCE text known alternatively as "The Illiterate Doctor of Isin" or "Why Do You Curse Me?" includes a set of names that appear in bilingual lexical lists. In this case, the ties between the text and scribal schooling are evident by the colophon, which reads "Text written for the recitation of the young scribes." Franco D'Agostino suggests that a teacher wrote the text in order to help his students master some of the unwieldy personal names, a known crux for scribes.[48] In addition as D'Agostino emphasizes, the teacher evidently employed humor toward pedagogical ends, namely, as a clever strategy for helping his students learn the names in a playful way.

Just as the letters and "Why Do You Curse Me?" reflect the creative efforts of scribes either to master or teach their students recurring names or phrases, the inclusion of contractual clauses in the context of fictional cases appears to reflect a parallel pedagogical aim.[49] The choice to embed contractual clauses in the context of these fictional court cases is logical. Near Eastern contracts regularly include clauses that anticipate one or more parties breaking the terms of the agreement and prescribe penalties for such a breach. Court cases would then reflect the formal proceedings that might transpire in the wake of a broken agreement. It thus appears that at least some of the fictional cases were composed with a similar aim to that of the model contracts, albeit in a more creative, playful way: namely, to teach or practice standard contractual clauses.

Practicing contractual clauses may not have been the only purpose of the fictional cases, however. At least two of the fictional cases deal with

47. George, "Old Babylonian School Letters," 50.

48. Franco D'Agostino, "Some Considerations on Humour in Mesopotamia," *RSO* 72 (1998): 276.

49. Klein and Sharlach likewise suggest that their tablet was composed either by a teacher or an advanced student ("Collection of Model Court Cases," 3). For a similar argument regarding the Sumerian literary letters, see Kleinerman, *Education in Early 2nd Millennium BC Babylonia*, 85.

what might be called "interesting points of law," to use Hallo's phrase. Hallo's inheritance case concerns a unique situation: ten years after the death of Ur-Suena, the elder of two brothers, his brother Anna-babdu sues Ur-Suena's heirs, claiming that he never received his share of the inheritance. As Hallo points out, this case thus appears to rule out what we might call a "statute of limitations."[50] NHT, as discussed above, likewise deals with another intriguing legal quandary concerning what today would be called an accessory to murder. Nin-Dada is never accused of having committed her husband's murder herself, but the possibility that she helped orchestrate it and/or failed to report it leads to her conviction. Perhaps, at least these two cases were designed to incite discussion regarding complex legal quandaries.

It is finally worth adding that the fictional cases exhibit another common feature: a number of them exhibit parallels to certain Mesopotamian laws. As Thorkild Jacobsen notes, the reasoning in NHT evokes the Laws of Hammurabi (LH) §153. The law stipulates that if a woman has her husband killed on account of another man, she should be put to death.[51] This precept is thus similar to the hypothetical scenario posited by the majority contingent, namely, that a woman who "knows" her husband's enemy might be involved in his death. Greengus makes a similar observation, noting that his adultery case exhibits parallels to LH §§141–43, in that both feature wives committing three crimes of appropriating goods, squandering household possessions, and being wayward.[52] Although the penalty is not identical, the unique combination of household infractions and adultery is represented in both the fictional case and LH §§141–43. Similar observations have been made about some of the other cases. As Raymond Westbrook observes, another adultery fictional case bears a resemblance

50. Hallo, "Model Court Case Concerning Inheritance," 151. The second case on Klein and Sharlach's tablet likewise concerns a dispute between an uncle and his nephew, also after ten years, though in this case, the nephew is the plaintiff and wins the case.

51. Jacobsen, "Ancient Mesopotamian Trial," 212–13.

52. Greengus, "Textbook Case of Adultery," 37–38.

to LH §129.[53] In addition, J. J. Finkelstein notes that the slave-girl fictional case corresponds to the Laws of Eshnunna (LE) §31.[54] This instance is the closest parallel of all: in both texts, if a man assaults the slave-woman of another man, he is to pay a fixed amount (twenty shekels in LE §31; thirty in the fictional case).

There are different ways to account for these parallels. First, the "links" could be more illusory than real. While this stance is worth considering, the closeness of some of the parallels, the recognition of parallels in four cases, the repetition of certain unusual details (e.g., a woman arranging for her husband to be killed), and the scribal context for the generation of both genres speak against it. Second, actual cases or records could have spawned both the laws *and* the fictional cases. This proposal is not possible to prove but remains feasible and could account for some of the divergences in detail. Third, the fictional cases could have served as fodder for the laws. This suggestion is also difficult to prove, for in most cases, the content is contemporaneous. It would, however, be in line with the theory that the law collections are rooted in actual cases that were stripped of their particulars and generalized into law.[55] Fourth, the *laws* could have preceded and generated the fictional cases. To further complicate matters, the process may not have been the same in each case. Nonetheless, what can be said is that the fictional cases belonged to the same legal-pedagogical matrix as the phrasebooks, model contracts, and law collections. Even if this text-type was not as central to scribal training as the model contracts, it was somehow thought to be connected to this corpus, as suggested by the occasional combination of fictional cases and model contracts on the same tablet and by certain overlapping aims and features.

53. In this fictional case, the husband is said to have caught his wife "in the lap" of her lover; the king then puts both the woman and her lover to the stake (Westbrook, *OBML*, 133). LH §129 also involves the king but allows for a variable punishment: the woman and her sexual partner are to be cast into the water, but if the husband allows his wife to live, the king will do the same for the other man.

54. Finkelstein, "Sex Offenses," 360.

55. See Bottéro, "'Code' of Ḫammurabi," 156–84.

Extracts from Law Collections and Related Exercises

In addition to copying and composing texts related to documents of practice and legal protocol, scribes in educational contexts also occasionally copied a short series of laws.[56] The sources for this include (a) laws copied together with contractual clauses and model contracts, (b) actual excerpts drawn from the law collections, or "extracts," and (c) related exercises with precepts that are similar but not identical to those in the law collections. Regarding the first category, SLHF includes a handful of laws on boat mishaps and rented oxen, topics that are also covered in LH. As for the second category, the copying of extracts from collections is attested for the OB period and beyond. An exercise from Tell Haddad with an extract from LE and a handful of extracts from LH have been discovered.[57] The LH extracts date from the early second through the late first millennium BCE. According to David Wright, three apparent OB extracts preserve LH §§45–47, §§153–58, and §§273–77; two Middle Babylonian extracts appear to preserve only LH §7 and LH §1; and a Neo-Babylonian extract appears to preserve LH §§275–77.[58]

The third category is then best represented by the texts that Roth dubbed "A Sumerian Laws Exercise Tablet" (SLEx) and the "Laws about Rented Oxen" (LOx).[59] The former is of unknown provenance and the

56. This phenomenon is in addition to the robust practice of producing complete copies of LH in particular, an activity that started in the early second millennium and continued through the late first millennium BCE (David P. Wright, *Inventing God's Law: How the Covenant Code of the Bible Used and Revised the Laws of Hammurabi* [New York: Oxford University Press, 2009], 106–10, 118–20).

57. Roth, *Law Collections from Mesopotamia*, 58. The laws on the LE extract correspond to LE §§44–47A (Roth, 66).

58. Wright, *Inventing God's Law*, 118–20. The extracts are to be distinguished from tablets that belong to a series, though it is difficult in some cases to determine the difference. The existence of a colophon aids in identifying it as part of a series, but unfortunately, the colophon is not always preserved.

59. Roth, *Law Collections from Mesopotamia*, 40–45. More recently, see also Spada's publication of a fragmentary prism belonging to the Rosen Collection ("New Fragment," 11–18; and Spada, "Addenda et corrigenda to G. Spada, 'A New Fragment of the 'Laws about Rented Oxen' and the Sumerian Verb bu-us2,' *RSO* 91 [2018]: 11–18," *Nouvelles Assyriologiques Brèves et Utilitaires* (2019): 22–23. SLEx is also known as YOS I 28. I discuss these texts in further detail in Chapter 4.

latter is known mostly from Nippur.[60] SLEx is attested in only a single copy.[61] Ten legal provisions, largely organized in pairs, are visible on the reverse; the unpublished and fragmentary obverse apparently included additional provisions and/or contractual clauses.[62] The colophon indicates that the tablet originally included 190 lines and was copied by the scribe Bēlšunu. The dedication to Nisaba and the presence of multiple mistakes provide confirmation of its nature as a school exercise. SLEx covers a range of topics that also appear in the law collections: an induced miscarriage, negligence regarding boats, failure to fulfill obligations in adoption agreements, assault, and liabilities concerning rented oxen. It is important to note, however, that SLEx is not an extract per se, as its contents do not overlap directly with any one section in the collections. Rather, it is more like a mash-up of classic laws. LOx is then known from six exercises and preserves about nine laws. One attestation features three provisions of LOx on the obverse and an extract from Proto-Ea on the reverse. As noted

60. The provenance of the provisions of LOx on the prism belonging to the Rosen Collection is unknown (Spada, "New Fragment").

61. Finkelstein, who was the first to publish part of this text, identified it as a school exercise and a "forerunner of sorts to Ai." In his nomenclature, the text is YBT I 28 (= YOS I 28) ("Sex Offenses," 357–58).

62. The distinction between casuistic contractual clauses and laws is not always apparent. Thus, for example, the three units featuring penalties for the repudiation of adoption in SLEx §§4′–6′ (in Roth, *Law Collections from Mesopotamia*, 44) could be construed either as legal provisions or as casuistic contractual clauses. The terminology in these units is frequently attested in adoption contracts, yet certain laws (e.g., LL §31 and LH §192) preserve similar formulas. This instance illustrates well the blurred boundaries in some cases between contractual clauses, which are typically formulated in casuistic terms, and laws that deal with topics similar to those covered in the contracts. The matter is compounded by the fact that certain laws may have their origins in contracts. A number of laws, for example, fix the prices for certain items or establish the cost for hiring various specialists: i.e., concerns that one would associate first with contracts (LE §§1, 2, 3, 7–11, 14; LH §§234–39, 257–58, 261, and 268–77). LE §§20–21 deal with lending and interest rates. LE §28 includes a clause that is identical to that which appears in numerous OB marriage contracts. LH §60 presents a standard agreement between a man and a gardener: a man is to cultivate the field for four years and divide the yield with the owner in the fifth; LH §§61–65 then consider various cases in which the gardener does not fulfill the agreement. This progression in LH §§60–65 from an agreement to the potential infringement of that agreement corresponds closely to the structure of contracts.

earlier, there are two attested combinations of model contracts with provisions from LOx.[63] Unlike SLEx, it is devoted entirely to one topic: mishaps related to rented oxen. As Spada points out, this exercise would have helped familiarize scribes with common terminology in animal rental contracts and with legal protocol related to animal rentals.[64] The laws overlap most closely with LL §§34–37, but even in this case, the order of the laws differs, the penalty varies in at least one case, and LOx preserves several additional provisions. It thus appears that LOx is better characterized as a thematic exercise than an extract from LL or any other collection. Most importantly, both SLEx and LOx indicate that "laws" could be generated and copied outside of the law collections proper.

There may be a Canaanite parallel that is comparable to these Mesopotamian exercises. Two Middle Bronze Age fragments preserving parts of seven Akkadian laws were found in Hazor, a major political center in the southern Levant in the second millennium BCE (Figure 1.4).[65] The fragments were edited and published by Wayne Horowitz, Takayoshi Oshima, and Filip Vukosavović in 2012.[66] This find is one of a number of objects inscribed with cuneiform that have been discovered throughout Canaan, a phenomenon that is attested elsewhere in the ancient Near East in the middle to late second millennium BCE, when Akkadian served as the common language of communication in the region. Several Canaanite sites, such as Hazor, Aphek, Ashqelon, and Beth Shemesh, have yielded cuneiform school-texts dating to the Middle and Late Bronze Ages.[67]

63. Spada, "New Fragment," 12. Another text, MS 4287, also preserves a legal phrasebook together with a few provisions regarding oxen (George and Spada, *Old Babylonian Texts*, 147–53).

64. Spada, "New Fragment," 11.

65. The city is mentioned numerous times in the Mari evidence and is also the only locale in Canaan to be referenced in Mesopotamian omens and geographical lists (Wayne Horowitz and Takayoshi Oshima, *Cuneiform in Canaan: Cuneiform Sources from the Land of Israel in Ancient Times*; *Alphabetic Cuneiform Texts*, by Seth Sanders [Jerusalem: Israel Exploration Society and the Hebrew University of Jerusalem, 2006], 65).

66. Horowitz, Oshima, and Vukosavović, "Hazor 18."

67. *Cuneiform in Canaan* (see n. 65) includes a total of ninety-one objects from twenty-eight different sites in Canaan dating from the mid-second millennium through the late first

Figure 1.4 The obverse and reverse of Middle Bronze Age Fragment A of Hazor 18. Courtesy of the Israel Exploration Society; photographs by Wayne Horowitz.

Outside of Canaan, sites such as Ugarit (Ras Shamra, Syria), Tell el-Amarna, Egypt, and Emar (Tell Meskene, Syria) have yielded a variety of Akkadian school-texts dating to the Late Bronze Age, testifying to the proliferation of Babylonian education beyond the confines of Babylonia proper.[68] While there is some overlap among these school-texts, others constitute sole attestations of particular texts: for example, the Tell el-Amarna version of the myth known as "Adapa" constitutes the only known school-text that preserves the myth, both within and outside of Babylonia. The Hazor find likewise is the only known cuneiform attestation of Babylonian laws in the "west."

The two fragments that constitute "Hazor 18" ("A" and "B," in the editors' nomenclature) have the same chemical composition and apparently once belonged to the same tablet. Fragment A preserves the opening signs of nine lines that pertain to five laws, while Fragment B preserves only seven signs that belong to two laws. All of the laws refer to penalties for injury. The editors suggest that the fragments belonged to a larger tablet that might have contained as many as twenty or thirty additional laws, but also suggest that the number was "most likely fewer."[69] They note further that it is not possible to determine whether the original tablet was once part of a series or was an extract from a larger collection. It is important to emphasize that the material is extremely fragmentary, with no law preserved in full, and thus any conclusions about the original content and/or function of this tablet must remain tentative. I base my translation on the

millennium BCE, with fifty-seven dating to the Middle and Late Bronze Ages. The sources include fragments of royal stelae, cylinder seals, clay liver models, letters, administrative texts, lexical lists, and school exercises of various types. More than one-third of the sources come from three sites: Taanach, Hazor, and Aphek (4). The publication includes fifteen texts from Hazor, including an excerpt from Ḫḫ II and a four-sided prism with multiplication tables (65–87). Cuneiform lexical texts dating to the Middle or Late Bronze Ages have also been found at Aphek, Ashqelon, and Beth Shemesh.

68. On the school-texts at Tell el-Amarna, see Shlomo Izre'el, *The Amarna Scholarly Tablets*, CM 9 (Groningen: Styx, 1997). On the school-texts at Emar, see Matthew Rutz, *Bodies of Knowledge in Ancient Mesopotamia: The Diviners of Late Bronze Age Emar and Their Tablet Collection*, AMD 9 (Leiden: Brill, 2013).

69. Horowitz, Oshima, and Vukosavović, "Hazor 18," 159.

editors' transliterated Akkadian.[70] While I take their reconstructions to be highly plausible and I urge the reader to consult their edition, I have opted to provide only what is actually visible on the tablets.

Like SLEx and LOx, Hazor 18 includes content similar to certain sections of the known law collections, but it is not a direct replica of any one section. LU, LE, and LH all deal with penalties for injury. The sequence in LH §§196–205 is the most developed, with laws pertaining to the injury of an *awīlum*, or "free man" (§§196–97, 200, 202, and 205), a commoner (§§198, 201, and 204), and a slave (§199). The visible content of Hazor 18 both parallels the content in LU, LE, and LH and diverges from it. As is evident in Table 1.1, the most striking difference is that all of the legible laws in Hazor 18 involve *three* parties: namely, they deal with an *awīlum* who has injured the slave of another man.

The implication in the Hazor sequence is that if an *awīlum* hires a slave from his owner for work and then injures that slave, he must compensate the owner. The only law in LH that likewise pertains to the same three parties is §199, though unlike Hazor 18, LH §199 does not refer directly to the slave's owner (*bēl wardim*) and also combines eye and bone in a single law. LE and LU only concern injuries by a free man to a free man. Hazor 18 is thus unique in its elaboration of what appear to be at least five laws pertaining to an injured slave.[71] In addition, the sequence of body parts in Hazor 18 differs from that preserved in LH, LU, and LE.[72] Hazor 18 also prescribes substantially lesser penalties of twelve shekels (apparently) for

70. Likewise, my translation of the sequence in LH proceeds from Roth's transliterated Akkadian in *Law Collections from Mesopotamia*, 121.

71. Although the slave and owner are not visible in A§1, the fact that the penalty is both pecuniary and comparable to the penalty in the following law suggests that the injured party is likewise a slave in this law. B§1 also appears to refer to an owner, but it is too fragmentary to determine its contents.

72. See the comparative chart in Horowitz, Oshima, and Vukosavović, "Hazor 18," 170. Hazor 18 proceeds from something (most likely, the eye) to nose to tooth to cheek. LH proceeds from eye to bone to tooth to cheek, with no reference to nose. LE lists penalties for nose, eye, tooth, ear, and a slap to the cheek. LU is the most distinct: it shifts from the foot to bone to nose to something to tooth; it also makes reference to the weapon that is used.

Table 1.1 Hazor 18, Fragments A and B versus LH §§196–201

Hazor 18	LH
A §1 (obv.) [If . . . twelve shekels of [silver to the . . .	§196 If an *awīlum* has blinded the eye of another *awīlum*, they shall blind his eye.[a]
A §2 If the n[ose . . .[b] ten to the owner of the sla[ve . . .	§197 If he has broken the bone of another *awīlum*, they shall break his bone.
A §3 If the too[th . . . three shekels of silver t[o . . .	§198 If he has blinded the eye of a commoner or broken the bone of a commoner, he shall pay (lit. "weigh") one *mina* of silver (sixty shekels of silver).
A §4 (rev.) If the cheek . . . and the slave to the owner of the s[lave . . .	§199 If he has blinded the eye of an *awīlum*'s slave or broken the bone of an *awīlum*'s slave, he shall pay one-half of his purchase price.
A §5 If a man, the e[ar . . . and the slave [. . .	§200 If an *awīlum* has knocked out the tooth of an *awīlum* of equal status, they shall knock out his tooth.
B §1 . . .] . . . [. . . . . .] to the own[er . . .	§201 If he has knocked out the tooth of a commoner, he shall pay one-third *mina* (twenty shekels of silver).

[a] For *ḫuppudu* v., the *CAD* Ḫ (vol. 6) lists "to cause an eye injury, perhaps to blind," noting that the OB term is limited to use in LH (240). The verb appears also in LH §218 (involving malpractice) and LH §247 (involving a man who destroys the eye of a rented ox).
[b] Most likely a verb denoting injury would have followed each body part, and thus would precede the body part in the English translation (e.g., "If he has . . . the nose"), but given that the verbs are not visible, I have opted to leave the Akkadian word order intact.

a slave's eye, ten shekels for injury to a slave's nose, and three shekels for knocking out a slave's tooth.[73]

How does one account for the origins or function of the text represented by Hazor 18? Horowitz, Oshima, and Vukosavović propose that Hazor 18 points to the existence of an independent "Code of Hazor" that was promulgated by the king of Hazor. To their minds, this evidence for the existence of a local set of laws confirms that Hazor was "one of the leading cities of the world of its time." In turn, they dismiss the idea that Hazor 18 could be a school tablet, due to the fact that it is well formed, the signs are well written, and the content on the tablet is carefully structured.[74] These features, however, need not rule out the possibility of a school-text, for as discussed earlier, some pedagogical texts were produced by teachers or advanced students and thus manifest such features.[75] In addition, although the laws are only partially preserved, there may be some indication of error. Fragment A §§1–3 all appear to have the protasis on one line and the apodosis on the second, with the monetary payment constituting the first signs. On the reverse of Fragment A, however, the apodosis of §4 inexplicably reads *ù* ÌR *a-na be-el* Ì[R . . .], or "*and the slave* to the owner of the sl[ave . . .]." The apodosis of A §5 also appears to start with *ù* ÌR ("and the slave") and then reads *i*[*m*- . . .], what may be the beginning of a third-person preterite form (possibly *imḫaṣ*, "he struck"). In addition, unlike A §§1–4, the protasis of A §5 includes the term "LÙ" ("a man") before the body part: LÙ GIŠ.P[I.TUG . . . ("If a man, the ear . . .").

73. In contrast, LE prescribes sixty shekels for injury to nose or eye and thirty shekels for knocking out another's tooth. LH prescribes talionic retribution for injuries by an *awīlum* to an *awīlum* for eye, bone, and tooth. As for blinding the eye of a slave or breaking the bone of a slave, the striker must pay one-half of the slave's value, evidently to the owner. The case of an *awīlum* knocking out the tooth of another man's slave is omitted from the sequence in LH, most likely because it would not have been regarded as having an impact on the owner. Horowitz, Oshima, and Vukosavović suggest that the different penalties in Hazor 18 could be due to the different economic standards in operation at Hazor vis-à-vis southern Mesopotamia ("Hazor 18," 171).

74. Horowitz, Oshima, and Vukosavović, "Hazor 18," 174.

75. With regard to the Akkadian model letters, e.g., see George, "Old Babylonian School Letters," 14 and 16.

This construction is unexpected, given that A §§1–4 all read *šumma* + body part, and A §5 is again dealing with injury to a slave, as is clear from the apodosis. While the fragmentary nature of both laws makes it difficult to determine whether or not these are mistakes, what can be said is that A §§4 and 5 both diverge from the format of A §§1–3.

Given that Hazor 18 was found alongside two other school-texts, in addition to the fact that Akkadian school-texts have been elsewhere attested in Canaan in the mid-second millennium BCE and thereafter, the identification of Hazor 18 as a school-text should not be ruled out. What is visible of the text reflects Babylonian origins, with the regular use of Sumerograms, common terms for Babylonian social status (*awīlum*, *wardum*), and no apparent West Semiticisms. Although the fragmentary content makes it difficult to draw firm conclusions, what is evident points to a limited set of laws on a single topic. The laws in Hazor 18 also overlap with known content from the law collections yet diverge from it. These two features—a (potentially) limited composition and the combination of parallels to and variations from "codified" law—are likewise characteristic of the school exercises SLEx and LOx.

In the light of the data that are available, I propose that Hazor 18 is most similar in form to the pedagogical genre represented by SLEx and LOx: a series of provisions selected for copying that echo the format and content of Mesopotamian laws. Just as other non-Babylonian scribes in the second millennium BCE had access to portions of Babylonian texts for copying, it appears that the scribes at Hazor possessed a short series of sample Babylonian laws. Moreover, while they may have known this particular series, there is no indication that they had access to or knowledge of LH in its entirety. One can compare the Middle Babylonian fragments of Gilgamesh school-texts that were discovered at Megiddo, Emar, and Ugarit: there is likewise no reason in these cases to assume that these non-Babylonian scribes had access to or even knowledge of the entirety of the Gilgamesh Epic in written form.[76] This phenomenon of possessing what

76. On the Gilgamesh fragments found at Ugarit, see Daniel Arnaud, *Corpus des texts de bibliothèque de Ras Shamra-Ougarit (1936–2000) en sumérien, babylonien et assyrien*, Aula Orientalis Supplementa 23 (Sabadell: Editorial Ausa, 2007); and Andrew R. George, "The Gilgameš Epic at Ugarit," *AuOr* 25.2 (2007): 237–54.

we might call "partial texts" resonates with the patterns of evidence for literary texts in royal, temple, and private libraries in the first millennium BCE. As Piotr Michalowski observes, literary texts such as the Gilgamesh Epic, Etana, and Enuma Elish are rarely preserved in complete form in these collections.[77] If this pattern is not attributable to the luck of the finds, it indicates that at least in some cases, it would have been sufficient for collectors to acquire only a portion of a "classic" work. A similar principle—albeit for different reasons—appears to have been at work in pedagogical contexts.

Legal Phrasebooks and Sequences of Contractual Clauses

A number of local Sumerian legal phrasebooks were also in circulation during the OB period. As Niek Veldhuis notes, two of these phrasebooks were standardized and continued to be copied after the OB period: the "northern version," primarily known from Sippar, and the Nippur version.[78] The Nippur phrasebook is known by its incipit, *Ki-ulutin-bi-še*$_3$ ("At the agreed upon time"), and includes verbal paradigms and series of Sumerian contractual words or phrases in combination with other words or phrases. Thus, for example, the opening sequence reads: "At the established time it is there for him, at the established time he gave it to him,

77. Michalowski, "Libraries of Babel," 118. Ulla Koch-Westenholz similarly points out that in the acquisition lists from Nineveh, no complete edition of the famous divinatory series *Enūma Anu Enlil* is mentioned. Complete editions, however, were prepared at Nineveh especially for the library (*Mesopotamian Astrology: An Introduction to Babylonian and Assyrian Celestial Divination*, CNIP 19 [Copenhagen: Carsten Niebuhr Institute of Near Eastern Studies, Museum Tusculanum Press, University of Copenhagen, 1995], 79).

78. Veldhuis, *Cuneiform Lexical Tradition*, 188–90. Other independent phrasebooks were found at Larsa and Tell Dhiba'i near Baghdad (194). See also Spada for an edition of a damaged fragment that appears to belong to one of the local phrasebooks ("Old Babylonian Model Contracts and Related Texts," 123–24). In addition, within George and Spada's volume, an anonymous author provides editions of MS 4287, a large, six-column tablet with a collection of legal phrases dubbed "A Compendium of Legal Forms"; and MS 4507, a text with legal clauses that is called "A Tablet of Legal Prescriptions" (*Old Babylonian Texts*, 147–54).

at the established time he paid him, at the established time he hired for him, at the established time he will measure out, at the established time he will pay," and so on.[79] Other sequences in *Ki-ulutin-bi-še₃* include series of verbs that might come up in contracts or trial records, for example, "he divorced, and then she gave birth, he wrote, he brought in . . . he broke (the tablet), he violated," and so on. Certain phrases overlap with content in the model contracts and in a few of the fictional cases (e.g., "rescued from a well, brought in from the street, from the mouth of a dog," "the status of heir," "the inheritance of their father"). In some instances, both the obverse and the reverse of the tablet are occupied with the phrasebook, while in other instances, the phrasebook is paired with other pedagogical texts on the reverse, such as mathematical texts, metrological tables, or god lists. As Veldhuis notes, *Ki-ulutin-bi-še₃* eventually developed into *ana ittišu* (Ai), a seven-tablet bilingual (Sumerian/Akkadian) composition with eighteen hundred entries that is attested only at Middle Assyrian Assur and Neo-Assyrian Nineveh.[80] Like its OB antecedents, Ai includes verbal paradigms and contractual clauses; it also includes some laws. The Sippar phrasebook took a rather different trajectory, however: it was later affixed to the front of the thematic lexical list Ḫḫ and was widely copied in scribal centers from the Middle Babylonian period on.[81] The Sippar phrasebook likewise includes series of contractual clauses (e.g., "he hired, they will hire"), phrases that would potentially appear in trial records (e.g., "elder of the city, elder of the judge, before the elders of the city"), and verbal paradigms. It also features several model contracts in

79. All of the excerpts from the legal phrasebooks in this section derive from the Digital Corpus of Cuneiform Lexical Texts, available at http://oracc.org/dcclt/pager.

80. The only available edition of Ai remains that of Benno Landsberger, *Die Serie ana ittišu*, MSL 1 (Rome: Pontificium Institutum Biblicum, 1937).

81. Both unilingual and bilingual copies of Ḫḫ are attested after the OB period. For a detailed discussion of the attestations of Ḫḫ at Emar, see Rutz, *Bodies of Knowledge*, 172–209. According to Rutz, with the exception of Tell el-Amarna, Egypt, copies of Ḫḫ have been found at virtually every site that has yielded lexical texts from the OB period on (172). He adds that a few of the Sumerian expressions from Ḫḫ I–II are also represented in legal documents found at Emar (173, 175).

their entirety, but as Veldhuis notes, these were eliminated in the first-millennium counterparts.[82]

The combination of contractual phrases and model contracts is likewise attested in SLHF. SLHF features forty-eight contractual and other legal clauses, some of which overlap with content in the model contracts; six model contracts; and a handful of laws that overlap with laws from the collections. The contractual clauses in SLHF relate to a wide range of legal scenarios, including inheritance, marriage and divorce, adoption, apprenticeship, and field and boat rentals.[83] As with the model contracts and phrasebooks, the phraseology in the model contracts and contractual clauses in SLHF parallels that of documents of practice and shares numerous parallels with Ai and Ḫḫ I–II.[84] The presence of laws alongside contractual clauses and model contracts in SLHF then highlights the degree to which these different text-types belonged to the same domain. Indeed, both contracts and laws have the capacity to deal with the problem of broken agreements, but while contracts are designed to anticipate and thwart such scenarios, the laws (grammatically) contend with breaches that have already transpired.

CONCLUSION

This overview indicates that Mesopotamian legal-pedagogical texts were not only interconnected but were also directly tied to law "on the ground." The interrelated nature of the legal-pedagogical texts is indicated first of all by the constitution of the tablets themselves. Texts such as the legal phrasebooks, SLHF, and others freely combine contractual clauses, model

82. Veldhuis, *Cuneiform Lexical Tradition*, 190.

83. Several of the clauses, however, appear to correspond to phrases that would appear in trial records (e.g., "He deflowered her. After he deflowered her," or "They handed him over to swear an assertory oath").

84. Roth observes that thirty-three of the forty-eight contractual clauses in SLHF have "exact or approximate correspondences" in Ai, and at least nine of the forty-eight clauses correspond to entries in Ḫḫ ("Scholastic Tradition," 250).

contracts, fictional cases, and/or laws. These "multi-genre" works demonstrate that in the scribes' estimation, this material belonged together and likely was learned at similar phases in training. Moreover, the legal-pedagogical texts frequently exhibit overlapping phraseology. Regarding links to law beyond the educational sphere, the model contracts and contractual clauses dovetail with actual documents of practice, and the model contracts and fictional cases both exhibit parallels to laws in the collections. In addition, scribes produced series of laws that were either drawn directly from the collections or were broadly related to them in format and content.[85] Although not all legal-pedagogical texts would have had practical application, it is evident that at least for certain text-types, pragmatics were at play.

It is important to reiterate that not every scribe would have been exposed to the full slate of texts profiled here. While the model contracts belonged to a standard phase of the OB curriculum and the legal phrasebooks likewise enjoyed a long and widespread circulation, the limited attestations of some of the other texts suggest that they were not studied widely—and in some cases, may have been one-offs. Only a few of the fictional cases are available in multiple copies, for example, and this text-type appears to have been associated primarily with Nippur. SLHF is known from one complete copy. LOx—another work tied to Nippur—is known from only six copies, in comparison with the 350 extant model contracts. Certain unica, such as CBS 11324, appear to represent the products of teachers or advanced students who drew on legal phrasebooks as building blocks to compose new works. It is possible that the scribes who were exposed to a wider range of legal-pedagogical material or asked to produce it themselves were being groomed for legal activities beyond the

85. While the extracts clearly derive from the law collections, the exercises may point to a more complex scenario. It is possible, for example, that laws in an exercise could derive from one collection but then could have served as fodder for the development of laws in another collection. E.g., the two laws in SLEx concerning penalties for jostling/striking a pregnant woman have parallels in both LL and LH. Theoretically, this section of the exercise could have drawn on LL §§d–f and then have been adapted by the scribes who composed LH §§209–14. The appearance of this particular problem in a number of the law collections may reflect the fact that scribes were exposed to it in the course of their education. See Chapter 4 for further discussion.

writing of contracts, such as the composition of trial records. In special cases, some scribes may have even been tapped to compose actual law collections. The limited nature of the evidence, however, makes it difficult to determine the nature of the relationship between scribal training and the wider world of legal professionals.

My aim in showcasing the diverse legal-pedagogical texts that were produced in Mesopotamia is to suggest neither that ancient Israelite/Judahite scribes had firsthand knowledge of this content nor that versions of all of these text-types were developed in Israel/Judah. There is no evidence, for example, that the Israelites/Judahites developed model contracts, and the obligation of Mesopotamian scribes in the early second millennium BCE to master Sumerian was obviously irrelevant to Israelite/Judahite education. At the same time, the Mesopotamian evidence gives us a sense of the legal-pedagogical content that was actually attested in the ancient Near East and of the training that at least some scribes underwent. It gives us a blueprint, a model for what might have been. The notion that legal texts also played a role in Israelite/Judahite scribal education is indeed plausible, given the practical need for scribes to draft legal documents and arguably even the very existence of "law" in the Bible itself. In the subsequent chapters, I aim to show what might be gained if we reassess the roots of biblical law from the vantage point of scribal education. In the following chapter, I explore how knowledge of the Mesopotamian fictional cases in particular can offer fresh insight into the origins of a set of laws that are now mostly preserved in Deuteronomy.

2

Hebrew Legal Fictions and the Development of Deuteronomy

Poetry is the art of creating imaginary gardens with real toads.

—MARIANNE MOORE

AWARENESS OF THE Mesopotamian legal-pedagogical text-type of fictional cases has the potential to shed fresh light on the origins of a particular set of biblical laws, most of which are now concentrated in Deuteronomy 19–25.[1] These texts—Deut 19:4–6, the case of an accidental manslayer; Deut 21:15–17, the case of a man with two wives, one loved, the other hated; Deut 22:13–19, the case of a man who makes false accusations against his wife; Exod 22:15–16 and Deut 22:28–29, two cases of an assaulted virgin; Deut 24:1–4, the case of a two-time divorcee; Deut 25:5–10, the case of a widowed woman and her negligent in-law; and Exod 21:7–11, the case of a daughter sold as a slave-wife—are bound together by a variety of distinct features, including colorful flourishes, recurring terminology, the use of contractual language, and a preoccupation with vulnerable individuals. The Mesopotamian genre of fictional cases offers the closest parallel

1. A "legal fiction" is "an assumption that something occurred or that someone or something exists which is not the case, but that is made in the law to enable a court to equitably resolve a matter before it" (s.v. "legal fiction," in *West's Encyclopedia of American Law*, 2nd ed., ed. Jeffrey Lehman and Shirelle Phelps [2008], http://legal-dictionary.thefreedictionary.com/legal+fiction). My use of the term here reflects a play on the idiom but without the attendant connotations. Rather, I intend to convey both the legal orientation of these texts and their inherent literary qualities.

Making a Case. Sara J. Milstein, Oxford University Press. © Oxford University Press 2021.
DOI: 10.1093/oso/9780190911805.003.0003

to this set with respect to content, style, and function. This proposal in turn has major implications for our understanding of the development of Deuteronomy. The reader is encouraged to consult the appendix while reading this chapter.

"FAMILY LAW COLLECTION" OR HEBREW LEGAL FICTIONS?

Although Deuteronomy 12–26 is traditionally demarcated as a unit, scholars recognize that the block itself reflects a complex literary history.[2] The first half includes regulations regarding worship and the cult (mostly in Deuteronomy 12, 14, 15, 16, and 17:8–10) as well as harsh stipulations prescribing the death penalty for those who fail to worship Yahweh exclusively (Deut 13:2–19, 17:2–7).[3] The latter half then preserves a smattering

2. Already in the nineteenth century, scholars identified Deuteronomy 12–26 as a "core" vis-à-vis Deuteronomy 1–11 and 27–34. More recently, scholars have made efforts to reconstruct the complex literary history of Deuteronomy 12–26 itself. See, first of all, Christoph Levin, who specifies that the pre-Covenant Code Ur-Deuteronomium consists of Deut 16:18–21:9 (*Die Verheissung des neuen Bundes in ihrem theologiegeschichtlichen Zusammenhang ausgelegt*, FRLANT 137 [Göttingen: Vandenhoeck & Ruprecht, 1985], 85–88). See also Timo Veijola, *Das fünfte Buch Mose (Deuteronomium) Kapitel 1,1–16,17*, ATD 8/1 (Göttingen: Vandenhoeck & Ruprecht, 2004), 262–79; Norbert Lohfink, "Distribution of the Functions of Power: The Laws Concerning Public Offices in Deuteronomy 16:18–18:22," in *A Song of Power and the Power of Song: Essays on the Book of Deuteronomy*, ed. Duane L. Christensen, Sources for Biblical and Theological Study 3 (Winona Lake, IN: Eisenbrauns, 1993), 336–52; Reinhard Kratz, *The Composition of the Narrative Books of the Old Testament*, trans. John Bowden (London: T&T Clark, 2005), 117–23; and Eckart Otto, *Deuteronomium 1–11: Erster Teilband 1,1–4,43*, HThKAT (Freiburg: Herder, 2012), 237 and *passim*. Kratz limits the Ur-Deuteronomium to Deut 12:13–18, 14:22–26, 15:19–23, 16:16, 16:18 + 17:8–10, and 19:1–12 while Otto includes much more of Deuteronomy 12–26 in his reconstruction (Deut 12:13–27, 13:2–12, 14:22–15:23, 16:1–17, 16:18–18:5, 19:2–13*, 19:15–21:23, 22:1–12*, 22:13–29, 23:16–26, 24:1–4, 24:6–25:4*, 25:5–10, 25:11–12, 26:2–13, 28:(15)20–44*). In contrast to Kratz, then, Otto's Ur-Deuteronomium already includes portions of chs. 13 and 28 and the family-oriented laws.

3. A number of scholars have recognized parallel terminology between Deuteronomy 13 and 28 and Near Eastern treaties. There is debate, however, concerning the nature of the source (i.e., whether it is Esarhaddon's Succession Treaty and/or other sources), and by extension, the chronological context of the access to such a source (i.e., the Neo-Assyrian period or the post-monarchic period). For an overview of the various perspectives, see the nuanced discussions in

of casuistic units on "classic" legal themes, such as inheritance, marriage, and assault (Deut 21:15–17, 21:18–21, 22:13–21, 22:22, 22:23–29, 24:1–4, and 25:5–10). These units are interspersed with ethical precepts and other cultic regulations. Unlike much of the other content in Deuteronomy 12–26, these units deal solely with interpersonal matters and exhibit no explicit interest in the cult or monolatry. Moreover, as a general rule, they do not correspond to laws in Exodus 20–23; as such, they resist straightforward classification as revisions to the Covenant Code.[4] Given the unique profile of these units, combined with the parallels in terminology and protocol among them, a number of scholars contend that they had origins as

Juha Pakkala, "The Influence of Treaties on Deuteronomy, Exclusive Monolatry, and Covenant Theology," *HeBAI* 8 (2019): 159–68; and William Morrow, "Have Attempts to Establish the Dependency of Deuteronomy on the Esarhaddon Succession Treaty (EST) Failed?" *HeBAI* 8 (2019): 133–35. Morrow suggests that Deuteronomy 13 and 28 is rooted in a loyalty oath to Judah's monarch that was adapted both from EST and West Asian treaty traditions; only at a later point was it adapted to suit loyalty to Yahweh. This loyalty oath to the king originally would have stood together as a single composition (156–57). Given the chronological distance between the adaptation of Deuteronomy 13 and 28 and their incorporation into Deuteronomy, Morrow rejects the thesis that this adaptation of the old loyalty oath was designed to subvert Neo-Assyrian hegemony over Judah (158).

4. The one possible exception is Deut 22:28–29, though here I concur with Carolyn Pressler that Deut 22:28–29 and Exod 22:15–16 are better understood as variants of the same case as opposed to revision (*The View of Women Found in the Deuteronomic Family Laws*, BZAW 216 [Berlin: De Gruyter, 1993], 36). On the general notion that Deuteronomy 12–26 represents a revision of the Covenant Code (CC), see especially Levinson, *Deuteronomy*; Norbert Lohfink, *Studien zum Deuteronomium und zur deuteronomistischen Literatur II* (Stuttgart: Verlag Katholisches Bibelwerk, 1991), 147–77 (see the helpful chart on p. 174, with reference also to Exod 34:10–26); and Eckart Otto, "Vom Bundesbuch zum Deuteronomium: Die deuteronomische Redaktion in Dtn 12–26," in *Biblische Theologie und gesellschaftlicher Wandel: für Norbert Lohfink SJ*, ed. Georg Braulik et al. (Freiburg: Herder, 1993), 260–78. Although Levinson treats the block of Deuteronomy 12–26 as a legal corpus, he does not discuss the family-oriented laws in detail but instead focuses on those units that either mandate centralization or reflect responses to it: Deuteronomy 12, 16:1–17, and 16:18–17:13. Similarly, the only "family law" on Lohfink's chart is Deut 21:18–21 (174). Otto likewise includes the "family laws" in his reconstruction of the earliest literary phase of Deuteronomy, but does not draw direct connections between most of these units and units in the CC. To his mind, the family laws reflect a supplementation to the CC on the part of Deuteronomy's composers, given the lack of such laws in the CC. He discusses this point and related ones in countless publications; for a brief sketch, see, e.g., Otto, "Vom Bundesbuch zum Deuteronomium," 272–75. For a helpful chart regarding Otto's understanding of the relationship between the units in CC and Deuteronomy, see William Morrow, "The Arrangement of the Original Version of Deuteronomy According to Eckart Otto," *ZAR* 25 (2019): 196–97.

a once-independent collection of "family law," a work akin to Tablet A of the Middle Assyrian Laws (MAL), a collection of over sixty laws pertaining almost entirely to women.[5]

One problem with the "family law collection" theory, however, is that stylistically, these laws do not constitute a homogenous group. A subset of them—Deut 21:18–21, 22:20–21, 22:22, and 22:23–24—conclude with an identical second-person formulaic statement: וּבִעַרְתָּ הָרָע מִקִּרְבֶּךָ ("And you shall exterminate the evil from your midst"). This statement is also used in Deut 13:2–5 and 17:2–7, two parallel units that prescribe the death penalty for non-Yahwistic worship. Scholars have naturally recognized the recurrence of the "*biʿartā*-formula," and some surmise that it was systematically added to laws within the collection.[6] Yet the *biʿartā*-formula cannot simply be extricated on its own. In each case, it is bound to a death sentence for the guilty party; and moreover, in Deut 21:18–21, 22:20–21, and 22:23–24, the guilty party is to be hauled out in public and pelted with

5. For Eckart Otto, the "Familienrechtsammlung" includes Deut 21:15–21aα; 22:13–21a, 22a, 22:23, 22:24a, 22:25, 22:27, 22:28–29, 24:1–4aα, 5; and 25:5–10 (*Das Deuteronomium: Politische Theologie und Rechtsreform in Juda und Assyrien*, BZAW 284 [Berlin: De Gruyter, 1999], 216); and with slight variation, Otto, "False Weights in the Scales of Biblical Justice? Different Views of Women from Patriarchal Hierarchy of Religious Equality in the Book of Deuteronomy," in *Gender and Law*, 133. Along with the usual set, Pressler includes the law pertaining to the captive bride in Deut 21:10–14 (*View of Women*, 4, 9–10). Alexander Rofé specifies that the laws "originated in a common source, a single written document." He does not limit the old collection to laws in Deuteronomy but also includes MT Exod 22:15–16 and Exod 21:22–25 ("Family and Sex Laws in Deuteronomy and the Book of Covenant," *Hen* 9 [1987]: 131–32). For Rofé, sections were "transferred" to both the CC and Deuteronomy by "D_2," his designation for the author who was responsible for incorporating the family laws into Exodus and Deuteronomy and for introducing some additions ("Family and Sex Laws," 135). Both Otto and Rofé draw parallels between the biblical set of laws and MAL Tablet A (Otto, *Das Deuteronomium: Politische Theologie*, 216–17; Alexander Rofé, *Deuteronomy: Issues and Interpretation*, OTS [London: T&T Clark, 2002], 172); see also Wright, *Inventing God's Law*, 112–13. Westbrook does not specify the laws but notes that "an independent legal source can be discerned" in Deuteronomy 21–25, even if it has been heavily redacted and interspersed with additional material ("Biblical and Cuneiform Law Codes," 4).

6. See, e.g., Otto, "False Weights," 141.

stones by the men of the city.[7] The parallels (signaled below in bold) are striking, particularly when compared to the protocol required for apostates in Deut 17:2–7:

Deut 17:5

וְהוֹצֵאתָ אֶת־הָאִישׁ הַהוּא אוֹ אֶת־הָאִשָּׁה הַהִוא אֲשֶׁר עָשׂוּ אֶת־הַדָּבָר הָרָע
הַזֶּה אֶל־שְׁעָרֶיךָ . . . וּסְקַלְתָּם בָּאֲבָנִים וָמֵתוּ

And you (2MS) shall take this man or this woman who did this evil thing to your gates . . . and you shall pelt them (2MP) to death with stones.

Deut 21:19–21

וְהוֹצִיאוּ אֹתוֹ אֶל־זִקְנֵי עִירוֹ וְאֶל־שַׁעַר מְקֹמוֹ. . . וּרְגָמֻהוּ כָּל־אַנְשֵׁי עִירוֹ
בָאֲבָנִים וָמֵת

And [the disobedient son's parents] shall take [their son] to the elders of his city, and to the gate of his place . . . and all the men of his city shall stone him to death with stones.

Deut 22:21

וְהוֹצִיאוּ אֶת־הַנַּעֲרָ אֶל־פֶּתַח בֵּית־אָבִיהָ וּסְקָלוּהָ אַנְשֵׁי עִירָהּ בָּאֲבָנִים וָמֵתָה

And they shall take the young woman to the entrance of her father's house and the men of her city shall pelt her to death with stones.

Deut 22:24

וְהוֹצֵאתֶם אֶת־שְׁנֵיהֶם אֶל־שַׁעַר ׀ הָעִיר הַהִוא וּסְקַלְתֶּם אֹתָם בָּאֲבָנִים וָמֵתוּ
אֶת־הַנַּעֲרָ . . . וְאֶת־הָאִישׁ עַל־דְּבַר אֲשֶׁר־עִנָּה אֶת־אֵשֶׁת רֵעֵהוּ

7. Rofé attributes Deut 22:20–21 and 21:18–21 to his later redactor "D_2" (see n. 5 above), though he apparently understands Deut 22:22 and 23–27 as originating in the family law collection (with subsequent additions by D_2) ("Family and Sex Laws," 148–51).

> And you (2MP) shall take the two of them to the gate of that city and pelt them to death with stones—the young woman . . . and the man because he debased the wife of his fellow man.[8]

It is not only that these texts all prescribe the death penalty, but also that they stipulate public participation for carrying out the punishment.[9] This public involvement is intimately bound to the *bi'artā*-formula, in that the crime pollutes the land with "evil," while the death penalty brings about the elimination of this pollutant. The combination of the death penalty, public participation, and the second-person *bi'artā*-formula in this set of laws contrasts with Deut 21:15–17, 22:13–19, 22:28–29, 24:1–4, and 25:5–10, none of which includes these elements. On the contrary, even in the cases of assault (22:28–29) and false accusation (22:13–19), the texts in this other group consistently feature *pecuniary* penalties. In addition, it is notable that in comparison with Deut 21:15–17, 22:13–19, 24:1–4, and 25:5–10, the units of Deut 22:20–21, 22:22, and 22:23–24 in particular are marked by brevity, a lack of literary flourishes, and an absence of perplexing points of law. Rather, Deut 22:20–21, 22, and 23–24 simply outline the crime—adultery and/or assault—and the punishment.

A second problem with the "family law collection" theory is that by definition it must exclude Deut 19:4–13, another pair of casuistic laws in Deuteronomy that is devoted to interpersonal affairs yet does not deal with family or women. The first case is an account of innocent manslaughter

8. Although Deut 22:22 and 22:25–27 do not prescribe stoning to death, both issue the death penalty, and Deut 22:22 in particular echoes the command to kill "the two of them" in Deut 22:23–24: וּמֵ֙תוּ֙ גַּם־שְׁנֵיהֶ֔ם הָאִ֛ישׁ הַשֹּׁכֵ֥ב עִם־הָאִשָּׁ֖ה וְהָאִשָּׁ֑ה ("Both of them shall die, the man who lay with the woman and the woman") as well as the passive opening of Deut 17:2: כִּי־יִמָּצֵא אִישׁ (in Deut 22:22, "If a man is caught . . ."). The verb ענה is treated in a careful and illuminating study by Ellen Van Wolde in "Does *'innâ* Denote Rape? A Semantic Analysis of a Controversial Word," *VT* 52.4 (2002): 528–44. Van Wolde concludes that the term in its Deuteronomic contexts denotes debasement of the social status of the woman, which in turn has an impact on the social status of the men who are associated with her (537).

9. Rofé likewise emphasizes the shift from private to public in his discussion of the adultery laws: to his mind, D_2 brought adultery into the domain of criminal law ("Family and Sex Laws," 148).

involving a man who slays his companion when his axe-head slips off of its handle. The man is not to be given the death penalty because he was not his victim's enemy. The second then considers an actual case of murder, prescribes death for the perpetrator, and closes with a variation on the *bi'artā*-formula: וּבִעַרְתָּ֛ דַֽם־הַנָּקִ֖י מִיִּשְׂרָאֵ֑ל וְט֖וֹב לָֽךְ׃ ("And you shall exterminate the innocent blood from Israel and it shall go well for you"). In contrast to the first case, this counter-case lacks colorful detail and simply outlines the crime and punishment. In this way, it shares certain elements with the other *bi'artā*-units.

In this light, a basic division in style, content, and protocol among these laws emerges:

Non-death penalty / private cases	**Death penalty / public cases / *bi'artā*-formula**
Deut 19:4–6 (accidental manslayer) Deut 21:15–17 (man with two wives) Deut 22:13–19 (slandered bride) Deut 22:28–29 (assaulted virgin) Deut 24:1–4 (two-time divorcee) Deut 25:5–10 (widowed woman and *levir*)	Deut 13:2–19 (non-Yahwistic worshipers) Deut 17:2–7 (non-Yahwistic worshipers) Deut 19:11–13 (intentional murderer) Deut 21:18–21 (disobedient son) Deut 22:20–21 (adulterous bride) Deut 22:22 (adulterers) Deut 22:23–24 (illicit intercourse in the city) Deut 22:25–27 (assault in the field)

This division yields three initial observations. First, half of the cases on the left (Deut 21:15–17, 24:1–4, and 25:5–10) are standalone cases; that is, each one lacks related units in which a factor has been changed so as to yield an alternative outcome. Second, in each of the three interpersonal clusters of law (i.e., Deut 19:4–6 and 11–13; 22:13–19 and 20–21; and Deut 22:23–24, 25–27, and 28–29), an independent *private* case is paired with laws that instead center on guilty parties and harsh *public* penalties.[10] Third, the six laws on the right that pertain to homicide, disobedience, adultery, and assault follow the same protocol as the units dealing with apostates in Deuteronomy 13 and 17. It is thus apparent that the laws in the right-hand column reflect a shared agenda that extends beyond the legal sphere. I propose that at an earlier phase, the "private cases" circulated as independent texts. The clusters of law were then generated by later scribes who modified one or more of the factors in these cases—that is, the same method of composition that is attested in ancient Near Eastern law collections, as well as in medical collections, omen collections, and other "scientific" corpora.[11] This likeness, however, was in form, not function. As I intend to show, the interest in generating these clusters and the other units was radically different from that which drove the Near Eastern law collections, to the extent that it calls into question the very category of "biblical law."

THE APPARENT CLUSTERS OF LAW IN DEUTERONOMY

It is well known that ancient Near Eastern collections are marked by sequences of related laws. In order to generate a series of laws on a

10. As Moshe Greenberg notes, biblical law uniquely brings certain private offenses, such as adultery, into the criminal sphere ("Some Postulates of Biblical Criminal Law," in *A Song of Power and the Power of Song*, 283–300). Greenberg does not, however, treat this pattern in diachronic terms.

11. This pattern of Mesopotamian scientific thought is explicated eloquently by Bottéro ("'Code' of Ḫammurabi"). Rather than develop principles or abstractions, Bottéro explains that the Mesopotamians generated "indefinite litanies of cases" (177). On the correlation between LH and omen collections, see Westbrook, "Biblical and Cuneiform Law Codes." In Westbrook's estimation, the similarity between the two was beyond method, in that both constituted reference works for professionals, whether judges or diviners (10–11). For an exhaustive treatment of the methods at work in producing the omen collections, see Abraham Winitzer, *Early Mesopotamian Divination Literature: Its Organizational Framework and Generative and Paradigmatic Characteristics*, AMD 12 (Boston: Brill, 2017). Winitzer uses the term "generative" to characterize the efforts by diviners to generate new omens from extant ones through various "hermeneutic and organizational principles" (15).

particular topic, the lawmakers would take a legal situation and then alter it by changing the status of the perpetrator or the victim, the nature of the injury or damage, the *mens rea* of the defendant, or some other factor. In certain cases, the lawmakers would modify a feature in the protasis, while in some cases, they would alter the apodosis, producing sub-laws.[12] A paradigmatic example from LH suffices to illustrate this pattern:[13]

§22 *šumma awīlum ḫubtam iḫbutma ittaṣbat awīlum šū iddâk*	§22 If a man executes a robbery and is seized, that man shall be killed.
§23 *šumma ḫabbātum la ittaṣbat awīlum ḫabtum mimmâšu ḫalqam maḫar ilim ubârma ālum u rabiānum ša ina erṣetišunu u paṭṭišunu ḫubtum iḫḫabtu mimmâšu ḫalqam iriabbušum*	§23 If the robber *is not seized*, the robbed man shall declare whatever of his is missing before the god; the city and the mayor in whose territory and district the robbery was executed shall restore to him all of his missing [possessions].
§24 *šumma napištum ālum u rabiānum 1 mana kaspam ana nišīšu išaqqalu*	§24 *If a life* [is taken during the robbery], the city and the mayor shall pay one mina of silver to his people.

In this cluster, the first scenario of robbery in flagrante is followed by two additional laws that modify different elements in the protasis: if the robber is not seized, then the man must report his losses and the city and the mayor will cover the damages. In the third scenario, the victim is killed

12. Similar methods of composition are attested in the omen collections. The most basic mode of generating new omens was to contrast the situation outlined in the initial omen with its opposite; see Winitzer, *Early Mesopotamian Divination Literature*, 172–88. In other cases, a single variable was altered (232). The modification of the injury in the laws is paralleled in the omen collections in what Winitzer labels "the expression of intensity." Thus, e.g., one omen considers the ramifications "if the right kidney was punctured," while another considers the ramifications "if the kidney on the right was extensively punctured" (400).

13. The transliterations derive from Roth, *Law Collections from Mesopotamia*, 85; the translations are my own.

in the course of the robbery. This element, too, changes the outcome: in that case, the man's family is to be compensated with a fixed amount. It is worth adding that the unit is governed by a logical sequence: it starts with the most basic scenario—a robber caught in the act—and then moves to more exceptional circumstances.

Although not every law within LH belongs to a cluster, this is a defining feature of LH and other collections, and so it is striking that a number of the laws in what scholars identify as the so-called family law collection are standalone units (Deut 21:15–17, 21:18–21, 22:22, 24:1–4, 25:5–10, and 25:11–12). In certain cases, moreover, these laws are preceded and/or followed by unrelated content.[14] In turn, it is worth emphasizing that the laws in question are not presented in an uninterrupted sequence. There are, however, two clusters of law that appear comparable to the types of clusters that appear in the Near Eastern collections. These include the case and counter-case of the slandered bride in Deut 22:13–21 and the three laws regarding illicit intercourse in Deut 22:23–29; to these two we can add the case and counter-case of manslaughter in Deut 19:4–13. Upon closer examination, however, it becomes apparent that each cluster is rooted in a once-independent unit that has been supplemented with "laws" of an entirely different nature. It is now worth addressing these three clusters in greater detail so as to make evident their complex literary histories.

The "Slandered Bride Cluster" in Deuteronomy 22:13–21

Deuteronomy 22:13–19 deals with a rather specific situation. A man marries a woman, sleeps with her, and then makes an incendiary claim against

14. Thus, e.g., Deut 24:1–4 and 25:5–10 are preceded by completely unrelated laws, both of which are delivered in the second person. Deuteronomy 24:1–4 follows a second-person apodictic stipulation that one may gather grapes and grain from his neighbor but not excessively, and Deut 25:5–10 follows a second-person admonishment not to muzzle an ox when it is threshing. Although Deut 25:11–12 also features a married woman, the focus is not on the marriage but instead on the injury that she inflicts on her husband's combatant, and the harsh verdict is delivered in the second person. In no way does it constitute a related law.

her, saying that he did not find "proof of virginity" (בְּתוּלִים) within her.[15] Implicit is the fact that a man would do this for financial reasons, possibly to get a refund on his bride-price and to keep the dowry.[16] In such a case, the woman's parents are to bring hard evidence of their daughter's virginity before the elders and the father is to make a statement attesting to its validity. Subsequently, the husband is to be fined one hundred shekels, and he loses his rights to divorce. In terms of style, the unit is highly detailed, with the repetition of entire statements, the use of direct speech, and the involvement of multiple parties.[17] Although it technically follows the format of a casuistic law, it reads more like a legal narrative, with a dramatic plotline that is justly resolved in the woman's favor. The case deals with a challenging dilemma: what happens if a man brings false charges against his wife? Such a problem is compounded by the lack of access to witness testimony. In such a case, how would a father protect his daughter's innocent reputation?

15. The standard interpretation is that the "evidence" is the couple's bloodstained sheets on the night of consummation, the lack of which would indicate that the woman had previously had intercourse. In a different take, however, Gordon J. Wenham argues that the "evidence" (בְּתוּלִים) refers to a piece of the woman's clothing that is stained by menstrual blood. In other words, the man claims that after the wedding, his wife failed to menstruate, indicating that she entered the marriage already pregnant. His argument relies on a definition of the related term בתולה not as "virgin" but as "a girl of marriageable age," which he maintains on the basis of Akkadian and Ugaritic cognates ("*Bᵉtûlāh*: A Girl of Marriageable Age," *VT* 22.3 [1972]: 326–48). The argument is clever but a bit of a stretch with respect to the evidence that the parents unveil before the elders. If we compare the use of the plural noun in the story of Jephthah's daughter in Judg 11:34–40, it seems that the notion of "virginity" is more apropos. After Jephthah's daughter laments her בְּתוּלִים in the hills, the narrator states, וְהִיא לֹא־יָדְעָה אִישׁ ("She had not known a man"). See also Pressler for a thorough critique (*View of Women*, 26–28). In any case, as Bruce Wells points out, the issue is evidently the woman's sexual purity upon entering the marriage ("Sex, Lies, and Virginal Rape: The Slandered Bride and False Accusation in Deuteronomy," *JBL* 124.1 [2005]: 42).

16. Near Eastern law differentiated between justified and unjustified acts of divorce; the former freed the husband of financial obligations, while the latter resulted in financial compensation delivered to the wife. Cf., e.g., the apodoses regarding unjustified divorce in LH §§138–40 and justified divorce in §141. For further discussion, see Wells, "Sex, Lies, and Virginal Rape," 59–61.

17. Locher notes that the elements of direct speech and the repetition of statements were deemed as extraneous to typical casuistic law and were thus eliminated by some scholars in their reconstructions of the unit's earlier form ("Deuteronomium 22, 13–21," 301–2).

In the counter-case in vv. 20–21, however, the claim proves true—no evidence of the woman's virginity is available—and she is promptly stoned to death by the men of the city. There are a number of indicators that this case is secondary. First, it is far shorter, with none of the literary flourishes of the first case. There is no direct speech. The elders vanish. In addition, as Rofé notes, the counter-case does not modify the terms of the protasis ("If a man takes a wife, has intercourse with her, and hates her; and he makes an incendiary claim against her . . .") but is incompatible with it.[18] Moreover, the sequence of the two cases is illogical. In a typical cluster, the first law outlines the basic scenario while the subsequent laws consider exceptional circumstances. This sequence, however, *starts* with the exceptional situation (a husband invents false charges) and then proceeds to the less complicated scenario (a husband justifiably accuses his wife of adultery).[19] Also, unlike the first case, the counter-case is replete with the language and themes in Deut 13:2–19 and 17:2–7.[20] It reads: וְאִם־אֱמֶת הָיָה הַדָּבָר הַזֶּה . . . וְהוֹצִיאוּ אֶת־הַנַּעֲרָ אֶל־פֶּתַח בֵּית־אָבִיהָ וּסְקָלוּהָ אַנְשֵׁי עִירָהּ בָּאֲבָנִים וָמֵתָה ("But if this claim was true . . . they shall take the young woman to the entrance of her father's house, and the men of her city shall pelt her to death with stones"). Specifically, the protocol is nearly identical to that prescribed in Deut 17:4–6, down to the verification of the claim: וְהִנֵּה אֱמֶת נָכוֹן הַדָּבָר נֶעֶשְׂתָה הַתּוֹעֵבָה הַזֹּאת בְּיִשְׂרָאֵל׃ וְהוֹצֵאתָ אֶת־הָאִישׁ הַהוּא אוֹ אֶת־הָאִשָּׁה הַהִוא אֲשֶׁר עָשׂוּ אֶת־הַדָּבָר הָרָע הַזֶּה אֶל־שְׁעָרֶיךָ אֶת־הָאִישׁ אוֹ אֶת־הָאִשָּׁה וּסְקַלְתָּם בָּאֲבָנִים וָמֵתוּ ("If it is true, the claim is established, this abomination occurred in Israel, you shall take this man or this woman who did this evil thing to your gates and you shall pelt them to death with stones"). As noted earlier, both units likewise conclude with the *biʿartā* refrain.

18. Rofé, "Family and Sex Laws," 136.

19. Fittingly, the Temple Scroll reverses the sequence in its rendition (see already Rofé, who compares the order to that found in Num 5:27–28 ["Family and Sex Laws," 157]).

20. This likeness has been noted by scholars; see, e.g., Cynthia Edenburg, "Ideology and Social Context of the Deuteronomic Women's Sex Laws (Deut 22:13–29)," *JBL* 128.1 (2009): 57–58.

Although a number of scholars have identified vv. 20–21 as secondary, and some have likewise emphasized the overlap with Deut 17:2–7, the implications of these observations have not been fully realized.[21] This addition resulted in the *illusion* of a cluster of law. While the scribe responsible for it employed the standard technique of law composition—that is, modifying the factor of the woman's innocence so as to yield an alternative outcome—his aim was not strictly "legal" in the Near Eastern sense of the term.[22] Rather, he repurposed an old "private" case concerning false accusations for use in a cluster of law that recast adultery as a public offense. Whether this case was modeled on Deut 17:2–7 or the reverse, the two units reflect a shared sensibility, as Cynthia Edenburg highlights: a lack of loyalty, whether to Yahweh or one's husband, threatens the stability of the community at large.[23]

The "Manslaughter Cluster" in Deuteronomy 19:4–13

The next cluster to consider is Deut 19:4–13. In the first scenario, a man goes into the thicket to chop wood with a fellow man, swings his axe to cut the tree, and the axe-head slips from its handle and accidentally kills his companion. The text confirms that the two were not enemies in the

21. On the secondary nature of the unit, see Otto, "False Weights," 134; Georg Braulik, *Das Deuteronomium*, ÖBS 23 (Bern: Peter Lang, 2003), 164; Pressler, *View of Women*, 22, 29–30; Rofé, "Family and Sex Laws," 135–43; Edenburg, "Ideology and Social Context," 50 n. 21. I concur with Rofé, who attributes the unit to the same author whom he deems responsible for Deut 13:2–19 and 17:2–7 ("Family and Sex Laws," 135–43). Not all, however, take the second case to be secondary; see, e.g., Wells, whose treatment of Deut 22:13–21 as a unity is tied to a larger argument regarding its complete compatibility with the laws governing false accusation in Deuteronomy 19 ("Sex, Lies, and Virginal Rape," 56–72).

22. While Rofé does not treat the combination of Deut 22:13–19 and 20–21 as an "illusion," he does identify Deut 22:20–21 as "more like a moralistic amplification than a piece of legislation," labeling the author "more preacher than jurist" ("Family and Sex Laws," 142).

23. Specifically, Edenburg states that the concentration of the *bi'artā* formula in the wider set of "sex laws" (Deut 22:13–29) implies that "maintaining the proper relations between the sexes . . . is as critical to preserving the proper social order as maintaining exclusive fidelity to YHWH" ("Ideology and Social Context," 57).

past. The counter-case deals with cold-blooded murder: a man who *is* the enemy of another lies in wait for him and fatally strikes him. The man then flees to one of the cities of refuge, but the elders retrieve him and turn him over to the blood avenger. The addressee of the unit is advised "not to look with compassion" on the murderer but rather to exterminate the innocent blood from Israel. While commentators acknowledge the complex literary history of this section, most regard both cases as belonging to the core layer.[24]

Although both cases are now embedded in a discussion of the cities of refuge, however, the first case can be detached from that context. This is suggested first by the doubling of the relative clause in v. 4: אֲשֶׁר־יָנוּס שָׁמָּה וָחָי אֲשֶׁר יַכֶּה אֶת־רֵעֵהוּ בִּבְלִי־דַעַת ("*who* escapes there and lives, *who* strikes his fellow unintentionally"). Second, the unit features two apodoses with competing concerns, each of which corresponds respectively to the first and second relative clauses. The first involves the institutions of refuge and the blood avenger: "[the manslayer] may flee to one of these cities and live, lest the blood avenger pursue the manslayer in the heat of anger and overtake him"). The second, however, is delivered in the form of a court ruling: "There is no death penalty for him, for he was not an enemy of his in the past." Third, a Wiederaufnahme in v. 7 reiterates the command in vv. 1–3 to "set apart three cities for yourself" (in v. 2, שָׁלוֹשׁ עָרִים תַּבְדִּיל לָךְ; in v. 7, שָׁלֹשׁ עָרִים תַּבְדִּיל לָךְ). This suggests that vv. 4–6*

24. The one exception is Rosario P. Merendino, though he ties the first case already to the separation of cities of refuge, while I deem this a secondary association (*Das deuteronomische Gesetz: Eine literarkritische, gattungs- und überlieferungsgeschichtliche Untersuchung zu Dt 12-26*, BBB 31 [Bonn: Hanstein, 1969], 201–14). For an overview of the various diachronic analyses of Deut 19:1–13, see Eckart Otto, *Deuteronomium 12–34: Erster Teilband 12,1–23,15*, HThKAT (Freiburg: Herder, 2016), 1518–19 (henceforth, *Deuteronomium 12–34*); and Bruce Wells, "Is It Law or Religion? Legal Motivations in Deuteronomic and Neo-Babylonian Texts," in *Law and Religion in the Eastern Mediterranean: From Antiquity to Early Islam*, ed. Anselm C. Hagedorn and Reinhard G. Kratz (Oxford: Oxford University Press, 2013), 294 n. 4. See also the detailed discussion of the unit by Jan Christian Gertz, who regards vv. 2a, 3b, 4, 5b, 6, and 11–12 as belonging to the oldest layer of the unit (*Die Gerichtsorganisation Israels im deuteronomischen Gesetz*, FRLANT 165 [Göttingen: Vandenhoeck & Ruprecht, 1994], 117–57, with brief overview on pp. 156–57).

are an insertion that has been tied only secondarily to the refuge context.[25] The first unit, moreover, is presented not as a law per se, but rather as a single paradigmatic case that highlights the importance of intent with respect to manslaughter: "*This* is the case of the manslayer who strikes his fellow unintentionally, and was not an enemy of his in the past." As noted by Zipora Talshir, the clause וְזֶה֙ דְּבַ֣ר ("And this is the case . . .") is paralleled in the Siloam Tunnel Inscription, where the account of the two sets of diggers finally meeting one another—intriguingly, also with axes—is memorialized: וזה·היה·הדבר·הנקבה, "This was the account of [how] the tunnel. . . ."[26] There is, then, material evidence of the phrase וזה (ה)דבר being used to introduce a single important event.

The counter-case, however, is once again of a different nature. First, the unit opens not with the classic introductory term for sub-laws (וְאִם, "But if . . .") but rather with a כִּי clause: "And if there is a man (אִ֗ישׁ, not רֹצֵחַ, "manslayer," as in the first case) who is the enemy of his fellow man and lies in wait for him, rises up against him and fatally strikes him. . . ." Second, while the use of the term "fellow man/friend" (רע) suits the first case, which emphasizes the manslayer's lack of intent to harm, it is out of place here, where the killer is identified as the victim's enemy. Third, in comparison with the vivid wood-chopping scene, the counter-case is lacking in literary flourishes. Finally, unlike the first case, this counter-case cannot be detached from the context of the cities of refuge. For as soon as the murderer does the deed, he flees to one of these cities, prompting the elders to take him from there and deliver him to the blood-avenger. This case, then, is not actually about establishing *intent*, as with the first case: rather, it is concerned with a real murderer who tries to exploit a system that is designed to protect innocent manslayers.

25. Based on the preceding discussion, I thus omit the phrases tied to the cities of refuge context from the original case; for my reconstruction, see the appendix.

26. Zipora Talshir, "The Detailing Formula 'וזה (ה)דבר,'" *Tarbiz* 41 (1981–82): 23–36 (Heb.). The phrase occurs in several other biblical texts: Exod 29:1, Deut 15:1–2, Josh 5:3–7, and 1 Kgs 9:15–22 and 11:26–28. The use of the phrase in Deut 19:4 may be linked to its secondary attachment to the cities-of-refuge context, a shift that appears to have preceded the development of the counter-case. It is worth noting that Deut 4:41–42 only acknowledges the first case.

Moreover, unlike the first case, the counter-case manifests overlap with Deut 13:2–19 and 17:2–7. First, it concludes with the same harsh second-person statement that occurs in Deut 13:9 (וְלֹא־תָחוֹס עֵינְךָ עָלָיו): "You shall not look with compassion on him." Second, in each of these instances, the punishment is the death penalty. And like these other cases, the death penalty is expiatory: it "exterminates" the innocent blood from Israel. In addition, as in Deut 13:2–19 and 17:2–7, the apodosis is procedural and judgmental, detailing the involvement of the elders in seizing the guilty party and tying the crime to Israel's purity. Finally, it is worth emphasizing that the two cases (vv. 4–6* and 11–13) are not presented back-to-back but instead are separated by additional material about the cities of refuge. In this instance, it thus appears that a scribe took up the old "case of the accidental manslayer," incorporated it into a unit on the establishment of the cities of refuge, and supplemented it with a "counter-case" in which a real murderer tries to game the system. This compositional process again resulted in an illogical sequence by Near Eastern legal standards: dealing with the exceptional case (accidental manslaughter) before the more straightforward scenario (homicide).[27]

27. A similar sequence of accidental manslaughter followed by homicide occurs in Exod 21:13–14. After a general apodictic statement regarding homicide in v. 12, two scenarios follow. The first pertains to a man who does not intentionally kill another; in that case, God states, "I will appoint you a place where he can flee." The second scenario deals with intentional homicide; in that case, God states, "You shall take him from my altar to be put to death (lit., to die)." The traditional view, promulgated by Julius Wellhausen and generally upheld today, is that Deut 19:1–13 is a revision of Exod 21:13–14 in the light of centralization. According to this logic, due to the abolishment of local altars, which originally would have provided a safe haven for manslayers, cities of refuge had to be set up as a compensatory measure (see discussion in Pamela Barmash, *Homicide in the Biblical World* [Cambridge: Cambridge University Press, 2005], 71–93; see also Otto, *Deuteronomium 12–34*, 1529–30). Barmash observes, however, that there is little evidence for altar asylum for manslayers in earlier periods; and that moreover, there is no indication that the "place" in v. 13 is meant to anticipate the altar in the next verse (73–78; but cf. the thorough critique by Jeffrey Stackert, *Rewriting the Torah: Literary Revision in Deuteronomy and the Holiness Legislation*, FAT 52 [Tübingen: Mohr Siebeck, 2007], 33–57).

Before evaluating the question of the relationship between the two sets of manslaughter laws, it is first important to note that Exod 21:13–14 interrupts the sequence of מוֹת יוּמָת ("he shall

The "Illicit Intercourse Cluster" in Deuteronomy 22:23–29

Much discussion has been devoted to the internal logic of Deut 22:23–29, three laws regarding illicit intercourse between a man and a young woman.[28] At first glance, the unit indeed appears to reflect typical Near Eastern legal reasoning, in that a core scenario is followed by two cases that substitute different factors in order to yield different outcomes. First, a man lies with an engaged young woman in the city and she does not cry out; both are killed as a result (Deut 22:23–24). Second, she is situated in the field, where she is definitively raped and does cry out; in this case, only the man is killed and the woman is spared (Deut 22:25–27). In the third instance, an unengaged woman is assaulted, with no location provided; the offender must pay her father fifty shekels and loses his right to divorce his victim (Deut 22:28–29). Other Near Eastern collections likewise

surely die") laws in 21:12 and 21:15ff. Verses 12 and 15 are nearly identical in construction and plausibly followed one another at an earlier point ("He who strikes a man so that he dies shall surely be put to death. He who strikes his father or his mother shall surely be put to death"). These laws are followed by two additional apodictic prescriptions to put to death a kidnapper (v. 17) and one who curses his father or mother (v. 18). Verses 13 and 14 stand out not only because they depart from this repeated construction but also because both employ the first-person voice ("I shall appoint . . . my altar"). It thus appears likely that vv. 13–14 constitute a secondary addition within vv. 12–18. As for the relationship between Exod 21:12–14 and Deut 19:4–13, it is first important to acknowledge that the two both share terminology and diverge from one another. As Stackert (*Rewriting the Torah*, 41–47) notes, both units include the terms or phrases אֲשֶׁר־יָנוּס שָׁמָּה ("who flees there / where he can flee"), יד ("hand"), and רע ("fellow"), but as Barmash points out, the terminology regarding the two acts of manslaughter in Exod 21:13–14 is unique to this unit ("[as for the one] who does not lie in wait but the gods let him fall into his hand . . . but if a man surreptitiously plots to kill his fellow") (*Homicide in the Biblical World*, 80). If the two passages are indeed related, it is plausible that Exod 21:13–14 constitutes an addition that was inspired by Deut 19:4–13, given the shared illogical sequence and the vague reference to Yahweh appointing "a place to which [the killer] can flee." Bernard Jackson likewise views Exod 21:13–14 as a secondary derivation from Deut 19:4–13 (*Wisdom Laws: A Study of the Mishpatim of Exodus 21:1–22:16* [Oxford: Oxford University Press, 2006], 127–28).

28. See, e.g., Eckart Otto, *Kontinuum und Proprium: Studien zur Sozial- und Rechtsgeschichte des Alten Orients und des Alten Testaments*, OBC 8 (Wiesbaden: Harrassowitz, 1996), 15–38; Otto, *Das Deuteronomium: Politische Theologie*, 203–21; Edenburg, "Ideology and Social Context"; Robert S. Kawashima, "Could a Woman Say 'No' in Biblical Israel? On the Genealogy of Legal Status in Biblical Law and Literature," *AJSR* 35.1 (2011): 1–22; and Pressler, *View of Women*, 21–43.

outline sequences of different scenarios involving assault.[29] The biblical block displays a set of linguistic and structural links to Deut 22:13–22. It is thus not surprising that a number of studies emphasize either the interconnectedness of Deut 22:23–29 or that of Deut 22:13–29 as a whole.[30]

As noted earlier, however, the language and procedure in the first case closely parallel those in Deut 13:2–19, 17:2–7, and 22:20–21: וְהוֹצֵאתֶם אֶת־שְׁנֵיהֶם אֶל־שַׁעַר ׀ הָעִיר הַהִוא וּסְקַלְתֶּם אֹתָם בָּאֲבָנִים וָמֵתוּ ("You shall take the two of them to the gate of that city and pelt them to death with stones"), an act that will enable the people to "exterminate the evil" from their midst. The second unit, Deut 22:25–27, is also marked by the second-person voice: וְלַנַּעֲרָ לֹא־תַעֲשֶׂה דָבָר ("As for the young woman, you shall not do a thing"), and the crime likewise results in the death penalty for the perpetrator. Moreover, the second unit compares the crime of assault in the field to the secondary counter-case in Deut 19:11–13: כִּי כַּאֲשֶׁר יָקוּם אִישׁ עַל־רֵעֵהוּ וּרְצָחוֹ נֶפֶשׁ כֵּן הַדָּבָר הַזֶּה ("For this is like a man who rises up against his fellow man and murders him; so is this case"). While the second case lacks the formulaic language that marks the first case, its structure binds it to

29. The Hittite Laws (HL) are the only Near Eastern collection that likewise ties location to the penalty for the woman (§§197–98), though in this case, the woman is married, the two locations are in the mountains or in the woman's house, and the husband is given impunity to kill them if he catches them in the act. The Laws of Ur-Namma (LU) §6, the Laws of Eshnunna (LE) §26, and the Laws of Hammurabi (LH) §130 all deal with the assault of an engaged virgin, and MAL A §55 treats the assault of an unengaged virgin. Although MAL A §55 refers to various locations of the crime, the factor of location is ultimately deemed irrelevant. The harsh punishment for the engaged virgin in Deut 22:23–24 is unparalleled in the Near Eastern collections (Edenburg, "Ideology and Social Context," 53).

30. Gordon J. Wenham and J. G. McConville see Deut 22:13–29 as reflecting an "essential unity" and draw attention to the logical order of the cases, the chiastic order of the punishments, and the triadic division of the entire section ("Drafting Techniques in Some Deuteronomic Laws," *VT* 30.2 [1980]: 248–49). For Rofé, Deut 22:22–29 and Exod 22:15–16 reflect the application of "systematic legal thinking . . . with both an attention to detail and an awareness of the larger picture" ("Family and Sex Laws," 150). Kawashima identifies a chiastic arrangement in Deut 22:22–29 with regard to "various combinations of two features: +/– virginity and +/– married" ("Could a Woman Say No," 15). Edenburg deems the larger unit of Deut 22:13–29 "a carefully drafted, self-contained collection of laws," unlike the "haphazard" rulings that precede and follow it ("Ideology and Social Context," 44). She determines that while Deut 22:13–29 may have derived from multiple sources, this section of laws "was conceived and composed as a whole" (48). Pressler finally points to the unification of Deut 22:13–29 at "a redactional level" in terms of content, form, and wording (*View of Women*, 21).

the first: "*But if* the man comes upon the engaged young woman *in the field*. . . ." It thus appears that vv. 23–24 and 25–27 belong to the same hand.

The third unit, however, is substantially different from the other two. First, it lacks all formulaic language and uses only the third person. Second, despite the severity of the crime, it results only in a financial penalty. Third, it uniquely features the young woman's father as a victim to be compensated. Fourth, it is concerned neither with location nor with the woman's reaction. All of these features are mirrored in MT Exod 22:15–16 (LXX 22:16–17), a parallel unit that likewise deals with a man who has illicit intercourse with an unengaged virgin. It is notable that MT Exod 22:15–16, which likewise involves a man who has intercourse with an unengaged virgin and results in a payment to the father, is a standalone unit in its larger context. It thus appears—as both Eckart Otto and Rosario Merendino likewise surmise—that Deut 22:28–29 has been supplemented at the front with a pair of cases that recast illicit intercourse as a public offense.[31] In this sense, the motivation for this redaction is similar to that for Deut 22:20–21. By rendering the young woman engaged, Deut 22:23–27 introduces a new victim, her fiancé, and in turn, a new incentive for the death penalty.

* * *

What emerges from this survey is that all of the ostensible clusters of law in Deuteronomy 19–25 are the products of later scribes who took up standalone cases featuring *innocent* parties—the innocent slandered bride, the innocent manslayer, and the innocent unengaged virgin—and used them as fodder for creating a radically different kind of "law collection," one that introduced the notion of crime as a public toxin that had to be expunged for the sake of Israel at large. If we consider the possibility that Deut 22:13–19, 19:4–6*, and 22:28–29 had independent origins, however,

31. Otto treats v. 22a and vv. 28–29 as the "literary and legal historical core" of Deut 22:22–29 with vv. 23–27* reflecting a scholarly expansion ("False Weights," 132–34); see also Otto, *Kontinuum und Proprium*, 129. Merendino likewise views vv. 23–24 and vv. 25–27 as secondary to v. 22 and vv. 28f, and outlines a similar theory (*Das deuteronomische Gesetz*, 262). I depart here from my earlier supposition that vv. 25–27 constituted the kernel of the unit (Sara Milstein, "Separating the Wheat from the Chaff: The Independent Logic of Deuteronomy 22:25–27," *JBL* 137.3 [2018]: 625–43).

this raises the question as to the original function of these units. Why were they composed and toward what ends? The same question can be asked of the standalone units Deut 21:15–17, 24:1–4, and 25:5–10. If they, too, did not belong to an old "law collection," in what context did they originate and circulate? Before tackling these questions, it is necessary to examine this subset of texts in more detail. In order to (a) distinguish these units from the concept of a law collection, (b) highlight their unique combination of legal and literary qualities, and (c) identify them as a native but analogous group to the Mesopotamian fictional cases, I shall refer to them as "Hebrew Legal Fictions" (HLFs).[32] Given the high degree of overlap between Deut 22:28–29 and Exod 22:15–16, as well as the stylistic parallels between Exod 21:7–11 and the HLFs, I also include these two texts within this subset.[33]

SHARED FEATURES AMONG THE HEBREW LEGAL FICTIONS

Once Exod 22:15–16 and 21:7–11 and Deut 19:4–6*, 21:15–17, 22:13–19, 22:28–29, 24:1–4, and 25:5–10 are demarcated as a group, it is easier to recognize the quantity and quality of their overlapping characteristics. In addition to the recurring themes of marriage, divorce, and inheritance, these include colorful features and unusual legal situations, resonance with contracts, overlapping terminology, abundant reference to social roles, variations on roots within units, and exchanges of currency/pecuniary penalties. These features both overlap with some of the characteristics in

32. This argument is in line with Locher's observation regarding the parallels between Deut 22:13–19 and the Sumerian fictional case of the raped slave-girl ("Deuteronomium 22, 13–21," 301–3). Both include direct speech, feature a threefold repetition of the facts, anticipate the verdict at the beginning of the text, and provide an explanation for the judgment. For Locher, these similarities point to the origins of the biblical law in an Israelite document that was comparable to the Sumerian "Prozessprotokoll" (302).

33. Rofé likewise includes two laws from Exodus (22:15–16 and 21:22–25) in his reconstruction of the old "family law collection" ("Family and Sex Laws").

the Mesopotamian fictional cases and point to the pedagogical origins of the biblical units.

Colorful Features and Unusual Legal Situations

Like the Sumerian fictional cases, the HLFs are marked by a combination of colorful features and unusual and/or specific legal situations. This applies especially to Deut 22:13–19 and 25:5–10. As Rofé observed, these units "almost read like transcripts of trials later rewritten as laws."[34] First of all, both involve highly particular situations with multiple speech acts.[35] As detailed above, Deut 22:13–19 deals with the specific scenario of a man who marries a woman, "hates" her, and invents false charges against her. In Deut 25:5–10, adult brothers live together and one of them dies without a son, leaving the widowed woman in need of protection and the dead man in need of an heir. Both cases then detail legal proceedings involving a body of elders, with statements issued first by each of the vulnerable parties. Like Deut 22:13–19, the woman in Deut 25:5–10 proclaims her designated guardian's negligence before the elders. The elders then summon the designate, who confirms that he refuses to support his sister-in-law. In Deut 22:13–19, these proceedings result in a compound penalty: the elders prescribe a fine, flogging, and issue a no-divorce clause. In Deut 25:5–10, the rejected woman removes the negligent man's sandal, spits in his face, and curses him; this results in shame brought on his "name"—the very commodity that he failed to maintain for his brother. This physical and public humiliation echoes the humiliation of the adulterous woman in Greengus's fictional case: "[The assembly] decided . . . her pudendum they

34. Rofé, *Deuteronomy*, 184; for a similar suggestion, see Otto, "False Weights," 134; and (with respect to Deut 22:13–19) Braulik, *Das Deuteronomium*, 164.

35. See Assnat Bartor's thoughtful discussion of the speech used in these units (*Reading Laws as Narrative: A Study in the Casuistic Laws of the Pentateuch*, AIL 5 [Atlanta: SBL Press / Leiden: Brill, 2010], 101–10).

shaved; they bored her nose with an arrow and to be led around the city, the king gave her over."[36]

While these two units are the most detailed, the other HLFs have no shortage of colorful details and unusual legal situations. In Deut 19:4–6*, a man goes to the thicket with his friend to chop wood and inadvertently kills him when the axe-head flies off the wooden handle. Not only is this case vivid, but it also deals with an interesting point of law: under what circumstances might a manslayer be considered innocent, especially if there are no available witnesses?[37] The example used to illustrate this conundrum introduces two crucial factors for adjudication: the prior relationship between the individuals and the accidental nature of the incident, both of which could be proven with recourse to testimony and hard evidence.[38]

Deuteronomy 21:15–17 deals with another highly specific case. A man has two wives, one "loved" and the other "hated"; both bear sons; and he wishes to render as firstborn the second-born son of the loved wife.[39] What may be implied but not stated is that the man's first wife was infertile, which prompted him to take another wife, and yet after this second marriage and the birth of his son by the second wife, the first wife was able to conceive.[40] Presumably, then, this situation falls outside the norm.

36. Greengus, "Textbook Case of Adultery," 35.

37. Intriguingly, the Nippur Homicide Trial approaches the question from the opposite angle: under what circumstances might an accessory to murder be considered guilty, again if there are no witnesses?

38. I.e., witnesses could attest to the relationship between the two men, and the axe handle could be brought in for evidence of damage. Wood shrinks and swells due to changes in moisture content and temperature. When the air is dry, wood loses its moisture and shrinks.

39. As Braulik notes, these are technical terms of marriage law (*Das Deuteronomium*, 156). In a nuanced argument, Bruce Wells asserts that the reference to the wife as "hated" indicates that she was arbitrarily demoted without grounds; as such, her son—the biologically firstborn son of the husband—cannot also be demoted arbitrarily ("The Hated Wife in Deuteronomic Law," *VT* 60.1 [2010]: 131–46). For further discussion of the term, see n. 49 below.

40. Cf. Braulik, who presumes that the loved wife is the younger and later married (*Das Deuteronomium*, 157).

Moreover, this case deals with another curious point of law: in such a case, can a man choose to promote the (second-born) son of his primary wife?

Deuteronomy 24:1–4* also deals with a complex "triangular" situation, though in this case involving one woman and two husbands as opposed to one man and two wives. In this case, a woman is issued a divorce contract by her first husband and then remarries another who divorces her (or dies). The unit states that she cannot remarry her first husband after the second marriage.[41] It is the only law in the Hebrew Bible that is devoted to the topic of divorce. Traditionally the prohibition was interpreted in the context of adultery, most likely due to its reverberations in the New Testament.[42] Raymond Westbrook, however, cleverly suggested that this prohibition was designed to prevent a husband from making a profit twice over: first, by keeping his wife's dowry, and then by taking her back when she is a wealthier widow or divorcee. He bases this argument on the fact that the term שנא ("to hate") is only used in the case of the second husband. The legal usage of the term denotes rejection or demotion without grounds. In the context of divorce, if a man "hates" his wife, it would thus result in her favor, in that his action was unjustified.[43] In the first case, the man is not said to "hate" his wife but instead finds something "repulsive" about her. Accordingly, his decision to divorce her is justified and he owes the woman nothing. In the second case, however, the second husband "hates" the woman, implying that his act of divorce is unjustified. In that case, he would be obligated to provide her with financial compensation, and the

41. I surmise that the original HLF simply closed with the prohibition of remarriage to the first husband (לֹא־יוּכַל בַּעְלָהּ הָרִאשׁוֹן אֲשֶׁר־שִׁלְּחָהּ לָשׁוּב לְקַחְתָּהּ לִהְיוֹת לוֹ לְאִשָּׁה), with no reference to the woman being defiled or the act being considered an "abomination" (כִּי־תוֹעֵבָה הִוא). See also Otto, "False Weights," 131.

42. On this interpretation, see, e.g., Samuel Rolles Driver, *A Critical and Exegetical Commentary on Deuteronomy*, International Critical Commentary on the Holy Scriptures of the Old and New Testaments 3 (New York: Charles Scribner's Sons, 1895), 272. Matthew 5:32 takes the prohibition further by stating that "anyone who divorces his wife, except on the ground of unchastity, causes her to commit adultery; and whoever marries a divorced woman commits adultery" (NRSV); see also Mark 10:2–12. It is notable that the New Testament references have no interest in the specificity of the situation in Deuteronomy, but only in what can be gleaned indirectly from it, namely, that "Moses" permitted men to divorce their wives.

43. See Wells, "Hated Wife," 131–46.

first husband could thus stand to benefit if he remarries his wife. The same would be true if she is provided with compensation as a widowed woman.[44]

Resonance with Contracts

Again, like the Sumerian fictional cases, several of the HLFs include standard contract clauses and themes. Exodus 21:7–11, Deut 21:15–17, and Deut 25:5–10 all deal with an explicit agreement between two or more parties (the father and another man in Exod 21:7–11; the man and his two wives/sons in Deut 21:15–17; the widowed woman and her appointed designate in Deut 25:5–10) and then with the potential breach of that agreement. Regarding Exod 21:7–11, we can note that a similar phenomenon of fathers selling their daughters is also attested in a subset of Nuzi marriage documents known as "daughterhood" and/ or "daughter- in- lawhood" contracts. As I discuss in Chapter 3, the text is formulated similarly to contracts, with an agreement followed by various conditional clauses. Deuteronomy 21:15–17 is not focused on consequences for a breach but rather is concerned with preventing one in the first place. Stipulations regarding marriage and inheritance, including references to a double portion for firstborn sons and provisions for the woman's status, are likewise attested in a range of Near Eastern contracts.[45] Deuteronomy 25:5–10 finally includes a stipulation that overlaps closely with stipulations that appear in wills from Emar: the woman is not permitted to marry a "stranger" outside the family. In addition, Deut 25:5–10 specifies consequences for a designate who fails to fulfill his familial obligations. This detail again parallels the Emarite wills, which stipulate harsh consequences for family members who fail to abide by the terms outlined by the testators. Finally,

44. Raymond Westbrook, "The Prohibition on Restoration of Marriage in Deuteronomy 24:1–4," in *LTT* 2:400–3. To this scenario one could imagine another one of collusion: a husband could divorce his wife with the *intention* that she remarry another, get divorced, and return to him, in turn earning him/them a profit. I differ from Westbrook, however, in that I do not take the latter half of Deut 24:4 to belong to the original unit.

45. See Braulik, *Das Deuteronomium*, 156, and also Wells, "Hated Wife."

Deut 24:1–4 makes reference to a “divorce contract,” literally, a severance document (סֵפֶר כְּרִיתֻת).[46]

Overlapping Terminology

The quantity of overlapping terminology in the HLFs is high, as indicated in the appendix. The phrase כִּי־יִקַּח אִישׁ אִשָּׁה (“If a man takes a wife . . .”) appears with variation in Deut 22:13, 24:1, and 25:5. Both Deut 22:13 and SP Deut 24:1 extend this clause with another identical phrase: כִּי־יִקַּח אִישׁ אִשָּׁה וּבָא אֵלֶיהָ (“If a man takes a wife and has intercourse with her . . .”).[47] Deuteronomy 22:19 and 22:29 also issue nearly identical penalties for the man; in both cases, he must pay a specific fine (fifty shekels in the former; one hundred shekels in the latter) and לֹא־יוּכַל לְשַׁלְּחָהּ כָּל־יָמָיו (“he is not allowed to divorce her during his lifetime”). Notably the phrase לֹא־יוּכַל (“he cannot/is not allowed”) is present in four of the HLFs: in addition to Deut 22:19 and 22:29, it also occurs in Deut 21:16 and 24:4.[48] In terms of verdicts, the combination of מִשְׁפָּט (“the right/entitlement/law/custom/sentence”) and another noun is used in Exod 21:9 (כְּמִשְׁפַּט הַבָּנוֹת, “the right/entitlement of daughters”), Deut 21:17 (לוֹ מִשְׁפַּט הַבְּכֹרָה, “to him belongs the right of the firstborn”), and Deut 19:6 (וְלוֹ אֵין מִשְׁפַּט־מָוֶת, “there is no death penalty for him”). A construction similar to Exod 21:9 and Deut 21:17 is used in Exod 22:16 (כְּמֹהַר הַבְּתוּלֹת, or “according to the bride-price of virgins”). Finally, the root שנא (“to hate,” with legal valence)

46. The term is also attested in Isa 50:1 and Jer 3:8. Braulik claims that the document insures the woman against accusations of adultery (*Das Deuteronomium*, 176).

47. In this case, SP Deut 24:1 may provide the original reading, given that the MT sequence כִּי־יִקַּח אִישׁ אִשָּׁה וּבְעָלָהּ (“If a man takes a wife and marries her . . .”) is redundant. The redundancy may be explained in several ways: (a) the extra verb might have been inserted accidentally; (b) the scribe might have been practicing a sequence of synonymous clauses; or most attractively, (c) the scribe made a homophonous error, writing וּבְעָלָהּ (“and marries her”) for ובא אליה (“and he has intercourse with her”).

48. Rofé, “Family and Sex Laws,” 133. Although Exod 21:7–11 does not use the phrase לֹא־יוּכַל, it preserves a similar type of construction in v. 8 (“He does not have the jurisdiction to sell her to an outsider, for he has breached [his contract with] her”).

is used in Deut 21:15–17, 22:13, 24:3, and 19:4–6; and as Carolyn Pressler notes, the use of the verb בעל ("to marry") and the *piel* of שלח ("to divorce") are featured in both Deut 22:13–29 and 24:1–4.[49]

Abundant Reference to Social Roles

The HLFs are replete with societal roles. Thus, MT Exod 22:15–16 mentions "a man," "an unengaged virgin," "his wife," "her father," and "virgins." Exodus 21:7–11 refers to "a man," his daughter," "as a slave-woman," "an outsider," "his son," "daughters," and "another [woman]." Deuteronomy 19:4–6* refers to "the manslayer," "his fellow," and "an enemy." Deuteronomy 21:15–17 mentions "a man," "two wives," "the loved one," "the hated one," "sons," "the firstborn," "his sons," "the son of the loved one," and "the son of the hated one." Deuteronomy 22:13–19 considers "a man," "a wife," "this woman," "the father of the young woman," "her mother," "the elders," "my daughter," "this man," "for a wife," "your daughter," "before the elders of the city," "the elders of that city," and "virgin of Israel." Deuteronomy 22:28–29 includes "a man," "a young woman," "an unengaged virgin," "the man," "the father of the young woman," and "his wife." Deuteronomy 24:1–4* refers to "a man," "a wife," "another man," "the subsequent man," "for himself as a wife," and "the first husband." Finally, Deut 25:5–10 considers "brothers," "one of them," "son,"[50] "the wife of the dead man," "a stranger,"

49. Pressler, *View of Women*, 4. Zvi Henri Szubin and Bezalel Porten have demonstrated that in ancient Near Eastern legal texts, the verb "to hate" (שנא in Hebrew; *zêru* in Akkadian) signifies "repudiation or rejection" and is tied to "the demotion of status within an existing relationship" ("The Status of a Repudiated Spouse: A New Interpretation of Kraeling 7 [*TAD* B3.8]," *ILR* 35.1 [2001]: 46–78). Westbrook has argued that in legal contexts the term is associated with an unjustified motivation for the divorce ("Prohibition on Restoration," 401–4; see also the discussion in Wells, "Sex, Lies, and Virginal Rape," 59 n. 58 and Wells, "Hated Wife," 136–37). Otto notes that the use of the term לֹא־שֹׂנֵא ("he is not an enemy") in Deut 19:4–6 also has legal connotations (*Deuteronomium 12–34*, 1531).

50. Cf. LXX Deut 25:5, which instead reads σπέρμα ("seed"). The term σπέρμα usually translates זֶרַע ("seed") in the MT (Deut 4:37, 10:15, 22:9, 28:38, 30:19), while the term בֵּן ("son") is instead usually translated in the LXX with υἱός (98 out of 117 times in Deuteronomy). Nowhere else does LXX Deuteronomy read σπέρμα for בֵּן in the MT. This datum may suggest that LXX Deut

"her husband's designate," "as a wife," "the firstborn,"[51] "the name of his dead brother," "the man," "his sister-in-law," "the elders," "my husband's designate," "for his brother," "the elders of his city," "before the elders," "to the man," and "his brother's house." To put this abundance in perspective, 41% of the words in Deut 21:15–17 and 29% of the words in Deut 25:5–10 are devoted to societal roles.

Two patterns are worth noting. First, there is considerable overlap across units: in addition to the common nouns "man" and "wife," the terms "unengaged virgin" and/or "virgins" are used in Exod 22:15–16, Deut 22:13–19, and Deut 22:28–29; "a young woman" is featured in Deut 21:13–19 and 22:28–29; "firstborn [son]" occurs in Deut 21:15–17 and 25:5–10; a woman's father appears in Exod 21:7–11, Exod 22:15–16, Deut 22:13–19, and Deut 22:28–29; and "the elders" adjudicate in Deut 22:13–19 and 25:5–10. Finally, the use of שנא ("to hate") in conjunction with a status occurs in Deut 19:4–6* (שֹׂנֵא, "enemy") and 21:15–17 (וְהַשְּׂנוּאָה, "the hated [wife]"). Second, several of the units are marked by the reiteration of certain roles in different grammatical forms. Thus, for example, Deut 21:15–17 refers to "two wives / the loved one / the hated one" and "sons / the firstborn son/ his sons / the son of the loved one / the son of the hated one, the firstborn." Deuteronomy 24:1–4 refers to "a man / another man / the subsequent man." Deuteronomy 22:13–19 refers to "the elders / the elders of the city / the elders of that city"; also in this unit, we find "virgin / virgin of Israel" and "my daughter / your daughter." Deuteronomy 25:5–10 finally includes such variations as "her husband's designate / my husband's designate," "brothers / the name of his dead brother / his brother's house / for his brother," and "the elders / the elders of his city / before the elders."

25:5 had a different Hebrew Vorlage that read זֶרַע. I thank Ville Mäkipelto for his assistance on this note and on the following footnote.

51. Cf. LXX Deut 25:5, which instead uses παιδίον ("child") for בְּכוֹר ("firstborn"). In all other instances in Deuteronomy (ten in all), however, LXX consistently uses the term πρωτοτόκος ("firstborn") for the MT בְּכוֹר. Once again, then, LXX Deut 25:5 may reflect a different Hebrew Vorlage that featured either יֶלֶד ("child") or בֵּן ("son"). Although a few Greek manuscripts read πρωτοτοκον, these attestations may reflect a secondary change that attempted to conform the text to the MT. Notably, the SP has a conflate reading הבן הבכור ("the son, the firstborn").

As we shall see, these patterns may point to the pedagogical origins of these texts.

Variations on Roots

A related phenomenon is variation on the same root within a single unit. In all cases, this repetition includes rare or elsewhere unattested words or forms. This phenomenon is represented most overtly in Exod 22:15–16 and Deut 25:5–10. I begin with the root מהר in Exod 22:15–16. The unit states that if a man lures an unengaged virgin into sex, מָהֹר יִמְהָרֶנָּה ("he must surely acquire her by means of a bride-price") and make her his wife. The end of the unit states that even if the father refuses to hand over his daughter, the assailant must still pay כְּמֹהַר הַבְּתוּלֹת ("according to the bride-price of virgins"). Though not particularly common, the noun מֹהַר ("bride-price") is attested elsewhere in the Bible. The denominative verb "to acquire by means of a bride-price," however, is arguably attested only here.[52] The use of the infinitive absolute in this phrase is also unusual: although one would expect the assailant to pay the bride-price, the reason for the emphasis is unclear.[53] The same applies to the next phrase, which considers the ramifications if the father "flat-out refuses" (אִם־מָאֵן יְמָאֵן). The root מאן ("to refuse") is only represented in the infinitive absolute in this instance. This unit finally represents the term "virgin" in both singular (בְּתוּלָה) and plural form (כְּמֹהַר הַבְּתוּלֹת). The latter phrase, which

52. Although *BDB* cites Ps 16:4 as a possible instance of the use of the denominative verb, it is not at all clear that "to acquire by means of a bride-price" is the meaning of the verb in its context: יִרְבּוּ עַצְּבוֹתָם אַחֵר מָהָרוּ ("The sorrows of those who מָהָרוּ another shall multiply"). Even if the verb is extended to mean "to marry / take as a wife," this definition seems ill-fitting, especially as Israel is consistently depicted as the female in metaphorical marital relationships to deities. The more common meaning of מהר, "to hurry, hasten," though also imperfect, seems more suitable.

53. It may simply be a reflex of rendering apodoses in the infinitive absolute, as is the case throughout Exod 21:37–22:16.

implies a standard price for virgins, is unattested outside of this unit. Deuteronomy 25:5–10 likewise includes multiple forms of a rarely attested root, in this case, יבם: "husband's designate" (יבם), "sister-in-law" (יבמה), and "to support" (יבם). While the latter two terms are attested elsewhere, the male noun יבם is featured only here.[54]

Exchanges of Money and Pecuniary Penalties

As a general rule, the HLFs are marked by pecuniary penalties and/or the absence of the death penalty. Notably, Deut 19:4–6* even stipulates that the accidental manslayer does *not* merit the death penalty (וְלוֹ אֵין מִשְׁפַּט־מָוֶת) for he was not the victim's sworn enemy. The other cases then frequently reference either specific or general payments, whether as a punishment or as an expectation tied to the agreement. Deuteronomy 21:15–17, for example, refers to the "double portion" assigned to the firstborn son; and the compound noun in Exod 22:16, כְּמֹהַר הַבְּתוּלֹת ("according to the bride-price of virgins") likewise corresponds to a payment. As discussed previously, the man's obligation in Exod 22:16 to "acquire her by means of a bride-price" (מָהֹר יִמְהָרֶנָּה) is also stipulated. It is notable that Exod 21:7–11 is preoccupied entirely with tangible obligations to the daughter and with restrictions on her resale. Reference to "silver" (כסף) occurs in Exod 21:11, Deut 22:19, and Deut 22:29. Finally, money matters also appear to be at the root of the verdicts in Deut 24:1–4 and Deut 25:5–10.[55]

54. The term "sister-in-law" is used in Ruth 1:15, and the corresponding verb occurs in Gen 38:7, likewise with the woman as the object. An Akkadian cognate of the male noun (*yabamum/ yabāmum*) does appear in a letter written on behalf of a woman who is seeking protection outside of her marriage. See Chapter 3 for discussion.

55. Regarding the latter, Otto suggests that the symbolic act of removing the sandal would have indicated the guardian's loss of title to his brother's property ("False Weights," 139).

PEDAGOGICAL INDICATORS IN THE HEBREW LEGAL FICTIONS

Collectively, these characteristics suggest pedagogical origins for the HLFs. First, it is significant that some of these elements overlap with elements in the Mesopotamian fictional cases that were discussed in Chapter 1. Both groups deal with homicide, adultery, assault, slave-women, and inheritance squabbles. Both groups are also marked by colorful features, and several of the Mesopotamian cases likewise appear to deal with interesting points of law, such as the culpability of an alleged accessory to murder in NHT or the "statute of limitations" in an inheritance case.[56] While the Mesopotamian fictional cases do not follow the format of contracts per se, several of them are concerned with inheritance disputes and six of them feature clauses that are known from contracts. As discussed in Chapter 1, the use of contractual clauses in the Mesopotamian fictional cases appears to reflect a pedagogical aim. Several of the HLFs (Exod 21:7–11, Deut 21:15–17, and Deut 25:5–10) appear to reflect a similar phenomenon.

It is also possible that the repetition of social roles in different forms in the HLFs can be explained in the light of other Mesopotamian legal-pedagogical texts. As discussed in Chapter 1, Mesopotamian scribes developed phrasebooks that played a long-standing role in scribal education and had practical value, both within Babylonia and beyond, with fragments attested at Emar, Ugarit, and Hazor.[57] The phrasebooks feature series of words or phrases that are associated with contracts and other legal documents. Several sequences are worth highlighting in the context of the HLFs. Middle Babylonian (MB) Ḫḫ I includes a series of familial roles with different descriptors and possessives: "his daughter, brother, younger brother, his sister, family, my family."[58] It also features the longer phrase

56. Jacobsen, "Ancient Mesopotamian Trial," 196; Hallo, "Model Court Case," 151.

57. The Hazor fragment reads "high price, small price, strong price, good price, bad price, [. . . pri]ce," and corresponds to Ḫḫ II 130–35 (Horowitz and Oshima, *Cuneiform in Canaan*, 73–74).

58. All translations of excerpts from Ḫḫ are from http://oracc.museum.upenn.edu/dcclt/pager.

"he took her as his wife," a phrase that is represented in three of the HLFs. In addition, MB Ḫḫ II includes the series "elder, elders of the city, elders of the king . . . before the elders of the city." Here the resonance with the HLFs is even more striking, given that Deut 22:13–19 and 25:5–10 feature "elders / the elders of the city / the elders of that city / before the elders / before the elders of the city."

The resonance of phrases in the HLFs with those in the legal phrasebooks is not limited to social roles. MB Ḫḫ I includes the phrases "a piece of silver, bridewealth," terms that are used in Exod 22:15–16, Deut 22:13–19, and Deut 22:28–29. MB Ḫḫ II also features the series "estate," "his estate," "his name," "their name," terms that resonate with the six references to the dead man's "name" and "house" in Deut 25:5–10. MB Ḫḫ II includes the phrase "for the lifetime of," a phrase that occurs in both Deut 22:19 and 22:29 (כָּל־יָמָיו). In a related vein, the pedagogical prism SLHF features the sequence of clauses "he deflowered her, he disliked her," a sequence that is represented exactly in Deut 22:13 ("If a man . . . has intercourse with [a woman] and hates her . . .").[59] Deuteronomy 25:5–10 also features a set of verbs that are tied specifically to legal action and protocol: "to take her for himself as a wife," "to support," "to go up [to the elders]," "to state," "to refuse," "to summon," "to take a stand," "to approach," and "to testify." Similar sequences are likewise attested in Ḫḫ.[60]

While I would not claim that the Israelite/Judahite scribes responsible for the HLFs had access to Ḫḫ I–II per se, it is likely that they had analogous lists of common legal clauses. Given the presence at Hazor of at least one fragment of Ḫḫ, it is possible that such lists were based on Mesopotamian antecedents.[61] Just as teachers or advanced Mesopotamian students drew on these phrasebooks to produce model contracts and fictional cases, it is

59. The translation of this phrase from SLHF derives from Roth, *Law Collections from Mesopotamia*, 50.

60. E.g., in MB Ḫḫ I: "He took, he did not take, he took her as his wife, she will eat his food, she will wear his clothing . . . when he dies (or flees), or escapes, when he stops working."

61. Schniedewind draws upon Hebrew inscriptions to make a case for the use of Mesopotamian-inspired lexical lists in Israelite scribal education. Specifically, he reclassifies the Gezer Calendar as a "local alphabetic adaptation of the Mesopotamian lexical tradition" and draws parallels to Ḫḫ I and II, which likewise feature a sequence of agricultural terms (lines 148–75) and a sequence of units of time (lines 176–234) (*Finger of the Scribe*, 82). He also identifies inscriptions

plausible that advanced Israelite/Judahite scribes or teachers generated the HLFs using comparable lists of phrases as building blocks for their compositions.[62] The existence of Israelite/Judahite phrasebooks or legal lists would help explain the preponderance of these terms within the units, the degree of overlap across units, and the abundant variation among the phrases. This proposal may also account for some of the redundancies in expression, which could reflect scribal practice with like clauses (e.g., in Deut 22:28–29, "a young woman, an unengaged virgin," and in Deut 21:15–17, "the firstborn, the son of the hated one"). As Andrew George playfully notes with respect to an Akkadian school letter that closes with four standard concluding clauses, it "might be considered a case of overegging the pudding by a student keen to exhibit all his learning at once."[63]

Finally, the variations in roots may also point to the HLFs' pedagogical origins. Although scribes can certainly play on roots within a text for nonpedagogical purposes, it is worth considering that the repetition of roots in Exod 22:15–16 and 25:5–10 was tied to the original use of these texts in scribal education. As William Schniedewind highlights with respect to the Kuntillet ʿAjrud inscriptions, scribes apparently played with roots in the production of scribal exercises as a way of practicing Hebrew morphology.[64] A similar phenomenon is paralleled in the legal phrasebooks

from Kuntillet ʿAjrud and Khirbet Qeiyafa as including lexical material in the forms of lists of names and geographical locations. Outside of inscriptions, lists are also a common feature of biblical literature, a literary phenomenon that again could support the notion that they played a role in scribal education (ibid., 88–94). For Schniedewind, the Israelites did in fact have access to traditional "cuneiform lexical curricula," given that a handful of Late Bronze Age Canaanite sites have yielded fragments of lexical lists (89).

62. Schniedewind proposes a similar argument for Prov 30:24–28, a text that refers to ants, badgers, locusts, and lizards in succession. Given the zoological theme, he posits that the unit may reflect the adaptation of a thematic lexical list of animals (ibid., 135).

63. George, "Old Babylonian School Letters," 28.

64. In particular, he draws attention to the puns on the root *ʾmr* in Inscription 3.6, a text that he suggests is best understood as a "model letter." Literally, the line reads (in Schniedewind's rendering), "An *ʾōmer* [i.e., "speech"] of *ʾAmaryaw* [i.e., "The-Speaker-of-Yahweh"]: *ʾemōr* [i.e., "Speak"] to my lord" (*ʾmr ʾmryw ʾmr l. ʾdny*). In this reading, *ʾAmaryaw* is "probably not a real person but rather a scribal invention." Schniedewind understands this example of punning as "an effective teaching tool" for understanding "the role of etymological roots in the Hebrew alphabetic writing system" (*Finger of the Scribe*, 36–37).

and SLHF, both of which include verbal paradigms (e.g., "he gave," "he did not give," "he has given," "he has not given" or "he seized," "they will seize"). Moreover, while it is possible that the scribes drew solely on actual terms for their compositions, it is also worth considering that the denominative verb for מהר ("to acquire by means of a bride-price") was generated for this particular context.[65] In any case, the repetition of these roots, combined with the rare usages of the infinitive absolute in Exod 22:15–16, is suggestive of scribal play in the production of legal exercises. A pedagogical context could also account for the existence of both Exod 22:15–16 and Deut 22:28–29. The two outline the same basic scenario yet differ in ways that cannot easily be explained in terms of revision (e.g., "lures . . . and lies with her" versus "comes upon . . . seizes her and lies with her"). It is possible that the two instead reflect variant exercises on the theme of assault that were both preserved.

FROM VICTIM TO PERPETRATOR: THE DEVELOPMENT OF DEUTERONOMY

The scribes who invented the HLFs may simply have been teaching or practicing legal terminology, but it seems hardly coincidental that these texts customarily feature innocent victims who are at risk of unfair punishment or a loss of rights: the assaulted virgin and her father, the rejected slave-woman, the unintentional manslayer, the snubbed firstborn son, the slandered bride, the exploited second husband, and the spurned widow. Both Deut 22:13–19 and 25:5–10, for example, involve a man putting the woman under his jurisdiction in a vulnerable position.[66] In the former, the

65. The noun מֹהַר is a *qutl* noun, a form that is commonly used for isolated nouns and nouns of action, especially for intransitive verbs. There are no (other) *qutl* nouns for transaction or transfer. In an apparent effort to make sense of the verb, the Peshitta translates it with *nsb*, "to take." I thank Aren Wilson-Wright and Daniel Fleming for their insights on this matter.

66. Although I do not take these texts to reflect an old collection, this estimation resonates with Otto's sense that the old family law collection "ist ein Reformprogramm, das dem rechtlichen Schutz der jeweils Schwächeren in der Familie dient" (is a reform program that provides legal

husband brings false charges of adultery against his bride, an accusation that could result in serious punishment, if not execution. In the latter, a woman's guardian refuses to provide for her, a stance that leaves her in a vulnerable state. In a number of cases, moreover, the innocent/vulnerable party is protected: the innocent manslayer is not given the death penalty, the firstborn son receives his double portion, the offended father receives a bride-price, and the slandered bride and assaulted virgin(s) can never be divorced. This apparent interest in vulnerable individuals helps explain the preponderance of women and children in these texts. The theme that emerges from the HLFs is that a conspirator cannot so easily exploit the system—be it divorce proceedings, marriage arrangements, or inheritance provisions.

With the heavy-handed slant of the scribe(s) who incorporated these texts into what would become Deuteronomy, however, the HLFs' original focus on justice was eclipsed by the violent crimes and harsh penalties that became their counterparts. For Deut 19:4–6*, 22:13–19, and 22:28–29 in particular, related "laws" were produced that featured serious perpetrators who were to be executed by the community. This redaction also involved the composition of completely new laws: the case of the disobedient son in Deut 21:18–21, the case of the adulterers in Deut 22:22, and the units on apostates in Deut 13:2–19 and 17:2–7.[67] The first case is striking in that it closely mirrors the HLFs. Unlike Deut 19:11–13, 22:20–21, 22:22, 22:23–24, and 22:25–27, the case of the disobedient son in Deut 21:18–21 is detailed, features direct speech, involves legal protocol, and includes repetitive statements—all classic characteristics of the HLFs. Moreover, it includes a handful of more specific terms that appear in the other HLFs.[68] It is no wonder, then, that commentators regularly assign it to

protection for the weak ones in the family) (*Deuteronomium 12–34*, 1690); see also Pressler, *View of Women*, 64.

67. Cf. Otto, who sees in Deut 22:22 an old core of a legal sentence against adultery (*Deuteronomium 12–34*, 1692).

68. The phrase "they discipline him" (וְיִסְּרוּ אֹתוֹ) also occurs in Deut 22:18, the verb "to seize" (וְתָפְשׂוּ בוֹ) is in Deut 22:28, and the combination of "the elders of the city" and the "gate" occurs in both Deut 22:13–19 and Deut 25:5–10.

a pre-Deuteronomic collection of family laws.[69] In contrast to the HLFs, however, this case involves no curious "point of law": the parents simply have a "rebellious and disobedient" (סוֹרֵר וּמוֹרֶה) son who must be punished. As some have noted, elsewhere these descriptors are almost exclusively associated with rebellion against God.[70] Moreover, the protocol for punishment precisely parallels that in Deut 17:2–7, 22:20–21, and 22:23–24: the son is to be brought out and all the men of his city are to stone him to death, an action that will "exterminate" the evil from the people's midst. Thus, while it draws on the template of the HLFs, it nonetheless reflects the agenda of the later scribes. Notably, most of these additional laws (Deut 13:2–19, 17:2–7, 21:18–21, 22:22, and 22:23–24) deal with the violation of loyalty—whether to parents, one's husband, or Yahweh himself. It is surely not coincidental that "father" and "husband" are two metaphors that are used for Yahweh with respect to Israel.[71]

It appears that the very incorporation of the HLFs into Deuteronomy is what prompted the production of these new units.[72] On the surface, these supplementary laws appear to be similar to the HLFs: they deal (mainly) with interpersonal affairs, they are delivered in casuistic format, and they treat some of the same issues that are featured in the law collections. It is thus not surprising that they have been treated as original components of an alleged old "law collection," albeit with additions by a later hand. Rather than detail unusual quandaries or curious points of law, however,

69. See overview in Otto, *Deuteronomium 12–34*, 1636–37. An exception to the rule, however, is Rofé, who likewise recognizes the parallels between Deut 21:18–21 and 22:20–21 and deems it a secondary addition ("Family and Sex Laws," 144–46).

70. Pressler, *View of Women*, 18; Braulik, *Das Deuteronomium*, 157.

71. Edenburg indeed emphasizes the analogy between marital fidelity and fidelity to Yahweh and rightly notes that both relationships demand fidelity, "even in the face of coercion" ("Ideology and Social Context," 60).

72. Here my conclusions are in line with those of Rofé, even though I do not contend that we are dealing with an old law collection. Nonetheless, Rofé contends that the writer "D_2" was both responsible for the integration of the collection of the family laws into Deuteronomy and for the composition of Deut 13:2–19, 17:2–7, 21:18–21, and 22:20–21 ("Family and Sex Laws," 143 and *passim*).

they are more preoccupied with punishment. For these scribes, it was the apodosis, not the protasis, that occupied their attention.

The close parallels between these additional texts and Deut 13:2–19 and 17:2–7, moreover, reflect an interest beyond the scope of legislative concerns. By prescribing the same penalty for a disobedient son, an adulterous woman, or a worshiper of celestial bodies, these later scribes innovatively imported the concept of law into the religious sphere. In this new imagined context, all "crime"—be it directed toward individuals or Yahweh himself—was seen to threaten the stability of Israel and had to be dealt with accordingly. As such, these scribes supplemented the cultic regulations in "core" Deuteronomy with texts that promoted an exclusive brand of Yahwistic worship, the departure from which warranted the death penalty. In addition, by casting this content in the guise of law with the use of casuistic format and depictions of legal protocol, they imbued their platform with legal authority. A comparable logic lies behind Lev 24:10–23 and Num 15:32–26, two pseudo-legal narratives that detail "cultic crimes" with consequences identical to those in Deut 13:2–5 and 17:2–7. In the former, a man curses Yahweh; in the latter, a man gathers wood on the Sabbath. Moses brings both "cases" before Yahweh, and in both instances, Yahweh issues a verdict ordering the entire congregation to stone the guilty party to death (in Num 15:35, רָג֨וֹם אֹת֤וֹ בָֽאֲבָנִים֙ כָּל־הָ֣עֵדָ֔ה and in Lev 24:14, וְרָגְמ֥וּ אֹת֖וֹ כָּל־הָעֵדָֽה). By this point, the lines between cult and law are blurred beyond the point of disentanglement, with Yahweh now occupying the sole seat of "judge." In Deuteronomy 19–25, however, these lines remain visible, in part because the redactors chose to supplement the old HLFs rather than rewrite them entirely.

The "discovery" of the HLFs reveals that the casuistic laws in Deuteronomy 19–25 do not constitute fragments of an old law collection, akin to those produced by their Mesopotamian neighbors. What we have instead is the *illusion* of a law collection, facilitated by the later scribes' employment of the same methods of composition and format that are present in the collections. This need not mean that they had direct exposure to Near Eastern law collections, however. Most likely, they simply adapted this format from Exod 21:18–22:16. Rather than use the "cluster" method to cover as much legal ground as possible, however, they used it to re-present old quandaries as new threats to the cultic order. In their hands, law was no longer an end in and of itself but instead a method of composition that could be put to new ends.[73] This process was similar—if not directly related—to the reuse of Near Eastern treaty language for theological purposes in Deuteronomy 13 and 28.[74] At the same time, even if the Israelites/Judahites were not inclined to produce their own law collections, the HLFs indicate that they were prone to contemplate tough legal-ethical dilemmas and to produce "native" texts that illustrated these quandaries. In particular, they were especially attracted to the problem of broken agreements. In the next chapter, I address in more detail the presence of contract terminology in the HLFs.

73. One could argue, as Finkelstein has, that the primary purpose of the Near Eastern "law collections" was also not legislation but instead to champion the king; as such, he classifies them in the genre of royal apologia ("Ammiṣaduqa's Edict," 101). This reading is fueled by the recognition that the contents of the prologue and epilogue of the collections are as significant to our understanding of these works as that of the laws themselves, if not more so (on this point, see Roth, "Mesopotamian Legal Traditions," 15–19). My focus here, however, is on the particular use of the cluster format as it appears in the Near Eastern law collections vis-à-vis Deuteronomy.

74. See Pakkala, "Influence of Treaties," 178–79. Pakkala suggests that the individuals who put the treaty language to new use were "professionals or scribal families" who were familiar with the treaties in their original language (Aramaic and/or Akkadian), as well as with legal traditions. Given the revolutionary use of treaty language for theological purposes, he situates this development in the post-monarchic period, when institutions had collapsed (180–81).

3

Echoes of Contracts in the Hebrew Legal Fictions

He who possesses many things is constantly on guard.

—Sumerian Proverb

IN CHAPTER 2, I PROPOSED that a handful of units in Exodus and Deuteronomy once functioned as a set of "Hebrew Legal Fictions" (HLFs), or fictional cases that played a role in scribal education in ancient Israel/Judah.[1] Like the Sumerian fictional cases, several of the HLFs (Exod 21:7–11, Deut 21:15–17, and Deut 25:5–10) are marked by terminology and themes that appear in Near Eastern contracts: respectively, the sale of daughters by fathers in debt, the bequeathal of inheritance shares to multiple sons, and the obligation to care for widowed women. Deuteronomy 25:5–10 makes for a paradigmatic case, in that it exhibits a striking set of parallels to wills from the ancient city of Emar (modern-day Tell Meskene, Syria, on the Euphrates River). Not only do the Emarite wills shed fresh light on the origins and interpretation of Deut 25:5–10, but they also reveal what is to be gained when we examine other biblical "laws" in the context of Near Eastern contracts.

1. The proverb in the epigraph is from Collection 1, Segment A (https://etcsl.orinst.ox.ac.uk/cgi-bin/etcsl.cgi?text=t.6.1.01#).

Making a Case. Sara J. Milstein, Oxford University Press. © Oxford University Press 2021.
DOI: 10.1093/oso/9780190911805.003.0004

THE STABILITY OF CONTRACT FORMULAS IN THE ANCIENT NEAR EAST

Because Israelite/Judahite scribes utilized the media of parchment and papyrus in a harsh climate, any written contracts that they produced are unlikely to surface.[2] Certain references in the Bible, however, do suggest that such documents were in circulation. Jeremiah 32:6–15, for instance, refers to Jeremiah "writing and sealing a contract" (וָאֶכְתֹּב בַּסֵּפֶר וָאֶחְתֹּם) for the purchase of his cousin's land, and Deut 24:1–4 features a husband writing "a divorce contract" (וְכָתַב לָהּ סֵפֶר כְּרִיתֻת) for his wife. Abraham's purchase of a burial plot in Genesis 23 shares striking parallels with the terminology that appears in Neo-Babylonian land sale documents.[3] Nonetheless, actual documents from Israel/Judah reflecting such agreements are unavailable. In contrast, due to the preference of cuneiform scribes for the more durable medium of clay, thousands of contracts of all types have been discovered: marriage and divorce contracts, adoptions, wills, property sales, loans, rental agreements, manumissions, and so on. These diverse contracts date from the third through the first millennium BCE and derive from a variety of locations throughout Syria and Mesopotamia, including Babylonia, Assyria, Emar, Nuzi, Alalakh, and Ugarit.[4] To this list can be added Aramaic contracts, whether written on

2. One exception is an ostracon from Yavneh Yam that preserves a legal plea written by an unnamed individual to a commander. The speaker states that after he had finished reaping, his master, Hosha'yahu, son of Shobay, took his garment and did not return it. The speaker asks for the official's intervention. The text has attracted much interest, in part because of its resonances with biblical texts that problematize the confiscation of an individual's garments for ethical reasons, such as Exod 22:26-27 and Amos 2:8. While most take the ostracon to reflect an authentic legal plea, Annelies Kuyt and Jeremias W. Wesselius suggest that it could represent a scribal exercise ("The Yavne-Yam Ostracon: An Exercise in Classical Hebrew Prose?" *BiOr* 48 [1991]: 726–35). They base this on the combination of the text's precise literary structure and the absence of relevant details of the case. Their intriguing suggestion dovetails with my proposals in this chapter.

3. See Herbert Petschow, "Die neubabylonische Zwiegesprächsurkunde und Genesis 23," *JCS* 19.4 (1965): 103–20.

4. Emarite and Hittite scribes used both clay and (waxed) wood; the latter appears to have been the medium for private contracts in Anatolia, given that none of them has survived (Haase, "Hittite Kingdom," 641).

clay or (more commonly) on papyri in drier climates, including the fifth-century BCE archives that were discovered on the island of Elephantine in Egypt and the fourth-century BCE Wadi ed-Daliyeh (Samaria) papyri.[5]

The contracts produced by these ancient Near Eastern societies both diverge from and overlap with the form and function of modern contracts. Near Eastern contracts differ most notably from modern contracts in that they describe oral transactions or agreements that have already transpired before witnesses. By extension, scholars surmise that in the case of a dispute, these documents tended to carry less weight than the testimony of the witnesses who were present at the transaction.[6] At the same time, Near Eastern contractual documents do have a fair amount in common with their modern counterparts. In modern legal systems, the "law of contract" is about undertakings or promises between contracting parties. It determines which promises are binding in law and stipulates remedies for a party who should claim that a promise has been broken.[7] Similarly, Near Eastern contracts outline the terms of the agreement and frequently include contingency clauses and/or penalty clauses for the party who breaks the agreement. Unlike the past-oriented clauses of the agreement, these subsequent clauses are future-oriented and presented in casuistic format,

5. See Andrew Gross's helpful overview of the available Aramaic legal documentation (*Continuity and Innovation in the Aramaic Legal Tradition*, Supplements to the Journal for the Study of Judaism 128 [Leiden: Brill, 2008], 8–20).

6. Gross, *Continuity and Innovation*, 3; Raymond Westbrook, "Anatolia and the Levant: Emar and Vicinity" (henceforth, "Emar and Vicinity"), in *HANEL* 1:662; Ignacio M. Rowe, "Anatolia and the Levant: Ugarit" (henceforth, "Ugarit"), in *HANEL* 1:723. An interesting OB trial record attests to the importance of both types of evidence in a dispute (Charpin, "Lettres et procès paléo-babyloniens," 93–95). A certain Geme-Asalluḫi is sent to prison because of her father's debt. After a *mīšarum* edict releasing her from prison, she returns home to find her husband remarried. She demands the contents of her dowry, which apparently included slaves and some movable property, but the slaves are dead and her husband claims that he sold the goods to release her from prison. The judge orders her to bring both the witnesses to the dowry and the tablet of the dowry itself. Unfortunately for Geme-Asalluḫi, the witnesses no longer remember the contents of the dowry and the dowry appears to be missing. After her husband refuses to take an oath, however, Geme-Asalluḫi is awarded a modified settlement.

7. J. C. Smith, *The Law of Contract*, Fundamental Principles of Law (London: Sweet & Maxwell, 1989), 3.

much like the provisions in the law collections.[8] It is worth adding that the majority of agreements would not have required documentation, as is likewise the case today. In fact, the very existence of certain types of ancient contracts may itself be an indicator of unusual circumstances, as scholars suggest.[9]

Like modern contracts, ancient Near Eastern contracts also feature recurring formulas, or in some cases, follow templates. Thus, for example, many OB marriage contracts open with some version of the statement that "PN_1, son of PN_2, has taken PN_3, daughter of PN_4, from PN_4 for marriage."[10] A number of these contracts include penalties for one or both parties for dissolving the marriage; one standard formulation is "If PN_1 says to her husband, 'You are not my husband,' they will bind her and

8. Bezalel Porten examines a set of Elephantine deeds of conveyance and observes that they can be understood in terms of "a brief tale" that operates chronologically: the contracts state the past transaction, confirm the person's present right to the property, and guarantee the person's rights in the future in the form of penalty clauses. In his estimation, the scribes who composed them were thus "steeped in a legal-literary tradition" ("Structure and Chiasmus in Aramaic Contracts and Letters," in *Chiasmus in Antiquity: Structures, Analyses, Exegesis*, ed. John W. Welch [Hildesheim: Gerstenberg Verlag, 1981], 169–70, 177).

9. In an oft-cited article on the subject, Samuel Greengus claims that written OB marriage contracts were tied to special circumstances of adopted, manumitted, or other legally vulnerable people ("The Old Babylonian Marriage Contract," *JAOS* 89.3 [1969]: 512). This claim belongs to a broader argument that the term *riksātum* need not indicate a written contract and can simply indicate an agreement in the abstract sense (510 and *passim*). Both Westbrook ("Emar and Vicinity," 677) and Sophie Démare-Lafont ("Éléments pour une diplomatique juridique des textes d'Émar," in *Trois millénaires de formulaires juridiques*, ed. Sophie Démare-Lafont and André Lemaire, Hautes Études Orientales - Moyen et Proche-Orient 48 [Geneva: Librairie Droz, 2010], 153), similarly characterize the Emarite wills as reflecting unusual circumstances. In a similar vein, Josué Justel notes that the recording of legal cases in the ancient Near East usually reflects atypical situations ("Women and Family in the Legal Documentation of Emar [with Additional Data from Other Late Bronze Age Syrian Archives]," *KASKAL* 11 [2014]: 75).

10. See, e.g., CT 48 56, in Westbrook, *OBML*, 124. (N.B.: all of the references in notes 10–12 derive from *OBML*; the first number indicates the reference listing in *OBML* and the latter indicates the page number[s].) There is, of course, some variation in the formula: some name both the father and mother (e.g., CT 8 7b and 22b [119], CT 47 40 [121], CT 48 48 [121–22], TCL 1 61 [130], TIM 4 47 [131], TIM 4 49 [32], TLB 1 229 [132], UET 5 87 [133], VAS 8 4–5 [134], and VAS 8 92 [134]); some do not name the parents (e.g., BE 6/2 48 [115], PBS 8/2 155 [128–29], and TCL 1 90 [131]); some involve the man taking two wives at once (e.g., TIM 4 46 and 47 [131], TIM 4 49 [132], and UET 5 274 [133]) and in at least one instance, the *woman* is said to take the man for marriage (e.g., BE 6/2 40 [114]).

cast her into the water'; if PN_2 says to his wife, 'You are not my wife,' he shall give X shekels of silver as divorce money."[11] Another subset of OB marriage contracts state that PN_1 is "a slave to PN_2 (the first wife); a wife to PN_3 (the husband)," and include the proverbial-like clause, "Whenever [the first wife] is angry, [the slave] will be angry; whenever [the first wife] is friendly, [the slave] will be friendly."[12] As J. Mervin Breneman has shown, various types of Nuzi marriage contracts also follow templates.[13] The same applies to what are known as "Syrian-style" wills, land sales, and loans from Emar.[14] OB manumission documents from Nippur feature the same set of eight elements, beginning with a clause that establishes the individual's freedom and concluding with an oath, witnesses, and date.[15] Likewise, OB loan documents include up to twelve common components, beginning with the object of the loan and similarly closing with an oath, witnesses, and the date.[16]

11. On death by drowning, see, e.g., CT 8 7b (119), CT 48 50 and 51 (122–23), CT 48 55 (123), Meissner BAP 89 and 90 (127), PBS 8/2 252 (129), PRAK 1 B 17 (129–30), TIM 4 49 (132), TLB 1 229 (132), and YOS 12 371 (137). Other contracts threaten to throw the woman from a tower (e.g., CT 2 44 [116–17], CT 6 26a [117], CT 48 52 [123], CT 48 56 [124], and VAS 8 4–5 [134]); a softer penalty clause states that one or both parties "shall forfeit house, field, and orchard/property" (e.g., ARN 37 [112], BIN 7 173 [116], PBS 8/2 155 [128–29], and YOS 15 73 [138]). A set of ten Babylonian marriage contracts from Sippar, Opis, Dilbat, and Larsa dating to the late seventh to late sixth century BCE include the same uniquely worded penalty clause for a woman who commits adultery ("She will die by the iron dagger"). Curiously, as Martha T. Roth notes, this clause does not appear in the extant contemporaneous marriage agreements from Borsippa or Babylon ("'She Will Die by the Iron Dagger': Adultery and Neo-Babylonian Marriage," *JESHO* 31.2 [1988]: 198).

12. Several follow this maxim up with the statement that the slave (or subordinate) shall carry the first wife's chair to the temple, wash her mistress's feet, and/or that any children that she bears will belong to the first wife (see, e.g., CT 2 44 [116–17], CT 4 39a [117], CT 48 57 [124], CT 48 67 [125], Meissner BAP 89 [127], and TIM 4 47 [131]).

13. J. Mervin Breneman, "Nuzi Marriage Tablets" (PhD diss., Brandeis University, 1971), 18–26 and 81–84.

14. On the land sales and loans, see Westbrook, "Emar and Vicinity," 682 and 684; the wills (and the designation "Syrian") are discussed at length below.

15. Spada, *Sumerian Model Contracts*, 19. The same pattern occurs in the model contracts, save for the omission of witnesses and the date (n. 26).

16. Skaist, *Old Babylonian Loan Contract*, 26.

Notwithstanding regional variations, ancient Near Eastern contractual clauses exhibit an enormous amount of stability across space and time. This continuity is especially striking with respect to the cuneiform, Aramaic, and Demotic contracts, as illustrated in Yochanan Muffs's foundational study of the Aramaic legal documentation from Elephantine.[17] According to Muffs, every Aramaic legal term and clause is "like a palimpsest," in that it preserves layers of cuneiform legal history.[18] Subsequent scholars of continuity across Near Eastern contracts include Douglas M. Gropp, who details the parallels between the Wadi ed-Daliyeh papyri and Neo-Babylonian and Late Babylonian cuneiform deeds; and Eleonora Cussini, who examines the Aramaic sale formulary in the light of first millennium BCE cuneiform traditions.[19] Taking an "Egyptological perspective," Alejandro Botta probes the relationship between legal formulas in Aramaic and Demotic deeds.[20] In *Continuity and Innovation in the Aramaic Legal Tradition*, Andrew Gross highlights a set of core clauses in Aramaic deeds of conveyance. As Gross shows here and elsewhere, not only do the Aramaic contracts exhibit internal continuity over time across locations, but they also show continuity with cuneiform contracts,

17. Yochanan Muffs, *Studies in the Aramaic Legal Papyri from Elephantine*, Studia et Documenta ad Iura Orientis Antiqui Pertinentia 8 (Leiden: Brill, 1969), reprint with Prolegomenon by Baruch Levine, HdO, Section 1 The Near and Middle East 66 (Leiden: Brill, 2003).

18. Ibid., 33–34. In particular, Muffs highlights the recurrence of the "satisfaction clause" ("his heart is satisfied") in the cuneiform corpus, the Elephantine documents, and the Egyptian Demotic deeds. In the cuneiform corpus, this clause is to be found in what Muffs called "provincial" and what is now sometimes referred to as the "upstream" tradition, i.e., Sippar and points further north, including Alalakh (Old Babylonian) and Kanesh (Old Assyrian). (It is worth adding, however, that the phrase is already attested several times in Sumerian, including once in the aforementioned inheritance model case published by Hallo; see Levine's Prolegomenon to *Aramaic Legal Papyri*, xxviii.) Muffs published his study before the Emar materials became available, and the presence of the clause there adds further support to his theory of a continuous tradition from the upstream tradition to the Aramaic one.

19. Douglas M. Gropp, *Wadi Daliyeh II: The Samaria Papyri from Wadi Daliyeh*, DJD 28 (Oxford: Clarendon Press, 2001); Eleonora Cussini, "The Aramaic Law of Sale and the Cuneiform Legal Tradition" (PhD diss., The Johns Hopkins University, 1992).

20. Alejandro F. Botta, *Aramaic and Egyptian Legal Traditions at Elephantine: An Egyptological Approach*, LSTS 64 (London: T&T Clark, 2009).

especially those from sites outside of southern Mesopotamia, including Nuzi, Emar, and Alalakh.[21] Other contract corpora preserve further evidence of continuity. The phenomenon of a testator conferring "male" status on either his wife or daughter, for example, appears in Old Assyrian, Emarite, and Nuzi wills.[22] Middle Assyrian and Emarite wills both include a clause restricting a widowed woman from giving her possessions to "an outsider."[23] Similarly worded divorce clauses are attested in OB and Elephantine marriage contracts, corpora separated by over a millennium.[24] Cuneiform contracts from Ugarit, Alalakh, Emar, and Ekalte open with the standard phrase *ištu ūmi annîm* ("On this day . . .").[25] Given the widespread durability of contractual clauses in the ancient Near East over space, time, and language, it is plausible that Israelite/Judahite contracts would have borne resemblances to those produced by their Near Eastern neighbors, especially to those outside of southern Mesopotamia.

21. Gross focuses on three clauses that are represented in all of the Aramaic deeds: the acknowledgment of receipt, the investiture clause, and the warranty clause (*Continuity and Innovation*, 3; see also Andrew Gross, "Emar and the Elephantine Papyri," in *In the Shadow of Bezalel: Aramaic, Biblical, and Ancient Near Eastern Studies in Honor of Bezalel Porten*, ed. Alejandro F. Botta, CHANE 60 [Leiden: Brill, 2013], 333–49). Sophie Démare-Lafont likewise differentiates between two juridical systems in the "north" (northern Mesopotamia, Syria, Assyria) and the "south" (Babylonia). As an illustration of these distinct systems, she points out that no wills to date have been found in Babylonia ("Inheritance Law of and through Women in the Middle Assyrian Period," in *Women and Property in Ancient Near Eastern and Mediterranean Societies*, Proceedings of the Center for Hellenic Studies colloquium, Washington, D.C., ed. Deborah Lyons and Raymond Westbrook [Cambridge, MA: Center for Hellenic Studies, Harvard University, 2003]).

22. Sophie Démare-Lafont, "The King and the Diviner at Emar," in *The City of Emar among the Late Bronze Age Empires: History, Landscape, and Society. Proceedings of the Konstanz Emar Conference, 25.–26.04.2006*, ed. Lorenzo d'Alfonso, Yoram Cohen, and Dietrich Sürenhagen, AOAT 349 (Münster: Ugarit Verlag, 2008), 207 n. 3. A woman at Nuzi could be appointed *abbūtu* over her sons, a term that indicates that she held the legal status and power of a father (Carlos Zaccagnini, "Mesopotamia: Nuzi," [henceforth, "Nuzi"] in *HANEL* 1:601).

23. For the former, see *KAJ* 9 and TR 2037 in Démare-Lafont, "Inheritance Law"; see below for discussion of the Emarite wills.

24. Markham J. Geller, "The Elephantine Papyri and Hosea 2,3: Evidence for the Form of the Early Jewish Divorce Writ," *JSJ* 8.2 (1977): 140–41. Geller points also to the recurrence of the clause in Hosea 2–3.

25. Gross, *Continuity and Innovation*, 21 n. 76.

"DECIDING THE FATE OF THE HOUSE": MAKING WILLS AT EMAR

With respect to legal documentation, the fourteenth- to twelfth-century BCE Hittite vassal city of Emar is particularly rich, with two-thirds of its 700+ published cuneiform tablets pertaining to legal matters.[26] The nearby town of Ekalte (Tell Munbaqa) yielded an additional sixty-seven tablets with legal interests.[27] The legal documents from Emar (and Ekalte, to a lesser degree) include a range of land sales, adoptions, divisions of property, labor contracts, manumission contracts, records of debts, marriage contracts, and wills. Although the material from Emar is more removed in time from Israel/Judah than the first-millennium BCE documentation from Babylonia and Assyria, it arguably belongs to a cultural matrix that is closer to the world of ancient Israel and Judah. The social and political setting of Emar was diverse and relatively decentralized, and thus presents a view of law as practiced on a small scale, often without recourse to the authority of kings and their representatives.

Legal documents at Emar exhibit two distinct formats, what Daniel Arnaud first dubbed "Syrian" and "Syro-Hittite," or what Sophie Démare-Lafont and Daniel Fleming more recently distinguish as "Conventional Format" (CF) and "Free Format" (FF).[28] CF (Syrian) tablets, as the name implies, are more conservative in formulation and display links to earlier

26. To be precise, Emar only becomes a Hittite vassal at the end of the fourteenth century, with the first sign of real Hittite activity in the archives closer to the 1260s. The archives thus straddle the time before the arrival of the Hittites, throughout Hittite activity, and likely after a partial withdrawal of Hittite presence at the very end.

27. On the Ekalte tablets, see Walter Mayer, *Ausgrabungen in Tall Munbāqa-Ekalte*, vol. 2, *Die Texte*, ed. Dittmar Machule, WVDOG 102 (Saarbrücken: Saarbrücker Druckerei und Verlag, 2001). Westbrook notes that the law as represented in the Ekalte tablets is virtually indistinguishable from that at Emar ("Emar and Vicinity," 659).

28. Daniel Arnaud, "Catalogue des textes cunéiformes trouvés au cours des trois premières campagnes à Meskéné-Qadimé Ouest," *AAAS* 25 (1975): 87–93; Sophie Démare-Lafont and Daniel Fleming, "Ad Hoc Administration and Archiving at Emar: Free Format and Free Composition in the Diviner's Text Collection," *AuOr* 36.1 (2018): 29–63 and "Emar Chronology and Scribal Streams: Cosmopolitanism and Legal Diversity," *RA* 109 (2015): 45–77. Ekalte legal tablets are not attested in the Syro-Hittite type (Westbrook, "Emar and Vicinity," 659).

Babylonian practice, while FF (Syro-Hittite) tablets are marked by innovations in script, shape, and layout.[29] CF tablets are inscribed across the horizontal dimension, while FF tablets are inscribed on the vertical dimension. The two groups also display differences with respect to their content and the parties involved. All transactions involving the Emarite king use CF; all sales of land in the name of the god ᵈNIN.URTA and the town elders are CF; and only CF texts feature a group of individuals known as "the brothers" who witness certain legal transactions.[30] By contrast, the scribes who drew up FF tablets functioned completely outside of the local king's social orbit.[31] All texts that feature a foreign Regional Overseer, Royal Kinsman or involve the Karkemiš royal court are FF.[32] Given the lack of overlap in onomastics across CF and FF tablets, Yoram Cohen and Lorenzo d'Alfonso conclude that the two reflected chronologically distinct sets of texts. Démare-Lafont and Fleming instead suggest that the two sets of documents represent coexisting legal alternatives that were produced for distinct populations.[33]

The nearly fifty available Emarite wills are split evenly across the two groups.[34] Most wills have male testators, though several are attributed to women.[35] The wills are intrinsically oral, with the document presented as a transcription of the direct speech of the testator before witnesses. Given

29. Daniel Fleming, "Reading Emar's Scribal Traditions against the Chronology of Late Bronze History," in d'Alfonso, Cohen, and Sürenhagen, *City of Emar*, 28.

30. On the brothers, see esp. Claus Wilcke, "AḪ, die 'Brüder' von Emar: Untersuchungen zur Schreibtradition am Euphratknie," *AuOr* 10 (1992): 115–50; and Nicoletta Bellotto, "I LÚ.MEŠ. *aḫ-ḫi-a* a Emar," *AoF* 22.2 (1995): 210–28.

31. Fleming, "Reading Emar's Scribal Traditions," 42–43.

32. Ibid., 28.

33. Yoram Cohen and Lorenzo d'Alfonso, "The Duration of the Emar Archives and the Relative and Absolute Chronology of the City," in d'Alfonso, Cohen, and Sürenhagen, *City of Emar*, 3–25; Démare-Lafont and Fleming, "Emar Chronology and Scribal Streams," 49.

34. Démare-Lafont, "Éléments," 52; for the references, see Justel, "Women and Family," 64 n. 51.

35. Démare-Lafont, "Éléments," 53. Though it is not a will per se, Justel cites in full a text in which a woman takes a man as her husband, establishes him as her son's father, provides property to her uncles, ensures money for her daughters' dowries, and prevents future claims against the stipulations ("Women and Family," 60–61). This document is a good example of

that a number of them ensure special legal rights for women, it is possible, as Démare-Lafont considers, that their existence in writing reflects deviation from common law.[36] CF wills open with the formulaic statement (with some variation) that "on this day" (*ištu ūmi annîm*), PN_1, son of PN_2, "in his lifetime" (*ina balṭūtīšu/bulṭūtīšu*), "seated his 'brothers' (*aḫḫīšu ušēšibma*). He decided the fate of the house (and) of his sons (*šīmti bītīšu mārīšu išīm*). Thus he said as follows . . ." (*kīam iqbi*).[37] As Démare-Lafont notes, the designation of "brothers" (lú-meš*aḫ*hi.a) refers not to the testator's own brothers but rather to a collective entity, as indicated by the plural determinative that precedes it.[38] In over twenty cases, the man protects his wife and daughters by pronouncing them "father and mother," "male and female," or in one case, "the male son," legal fictions that granted them full capacity to manage the inheritance and the family cult.[39] The testator then specifies what he bequeaths to his wife and children, with larger portions typically allotted to the firstborn male. Démare-Lafont observes that while CF (Syrian) wills are primarily interested in the distribution of property, FF (Syro-Hittite) wills are more concerned with issues involving people.[40] The children are often instructed to support—or serve—their

how practical legal documents do not fit neatly into our delineated categories of "marriage contract," "adoption," "will," etc., in that they commonly include features that pertain to a range of legal matters.

36. Démare-Lafont, "Éléments," 53.

37. See, e.g., Daniel Arnaud, *Recherches au pays d'Aštata, Emar VI/3: Textes sumériens et accadiens*, OBO 20 (Paris: Éditions Recherche sur les Civilisations, 1986) (henceforth Emar), 176, 180, 183, 188, and 189. The ubiquitous reference to "brothers sitting" is also featured in one Emar marriage contract and a division of property document (RE 61 and RE 94 in Gary Beckman, *Texts from the Vicinity of Emar in the Collection of Jonathan Rosen*, HANE/M II [Padova: Sargon srl, 1996]). Henceforth, all texts from this volume will be cited as RE. My translations of texts within these volumes are based on Arnaud and Beckman's transliterations.

38. Démare-Lafont, "Éléments," 54. Westbrook notes that at Ekalte each party apparently had its own "brothers" ("Emar and Vicinity," 676). Beckman, citing communication with John Huehnergard, labels the writing "pseudologographic" (*Texts from the Vicinity of Emar*, 15).

39. For examples, see RE 15, RE 46, RE 85, and Emar 185. For discussion, see Raymond Westbrook, "Social Justice and Creative Jurisprudence in Late Bronze Age Syria," *LTT* 2:123–24.

40. Démare-Lafont, "Éléments," 53. As Justel notes, the items specified for wives (e.g., animals, domestic items, movables) likely correspond to the contents of their dowries ("Women and Family," 64).

widowed mother until her death.[41] The document RE 15 neatly illustrates the standard opening section for CF wills. In this case, the testator has only daughters and no sons, and so alternatively, he "decides the fate" of his wife and assigns the property to her:

> Irib-Ba'alu, son of Amur-ša, in his lifetime, seated his "brothers" and decided the fate of Dagan-ni, his wife. He said the following: "Dagan-ni, my wife, is father and mother of my house. I give my house, my fields, and all of my possessions to Dagan-ni, my wife. Now I have granted Abinami and Išarte, my two daughters, male and female status. All of the days that Dagan-ni my wife lives, my two daughters shall support her."

After outlining the basic arrangement, both CF and FF wills then feature a range of contingencies and penalty clauses. Although the wills offer protection and even enhanced legal status to widowed women, they also impose restrictions on their legal rights. In RE 8, for example, Abī-li'mu, son of Baya, states, "If my wife Abnu goes after a strange man, she shall place her garment on the stool and go where she pleases."[42] Similar concerns regarding a widow giving her possessions to "an outsider" (*nakru*) or to a daughter marrying outside the family are attested elsewhere.[43] In RE 23, a man makes alternative arrangements for inheritance, should his son(s)

41. Justel, "Women and Family," 65. As Justel observes, the two groups of contracts employ different terms for the care of the widow: CF contracts feature *wabālu* ("to support"), while FF contracts feature *palāhu* ("to serve/honor," with connotations of fear and reverence). The same pattern is demonstrated across CF and FF adoption contracts (see, e.g., RE 13 and RE 25). With respect to the adoption tablets, Nicoletta Bellotto notes that *wabālu* stresses the material aspect of the adoptee's duties, while *palāhu* emphasizes the moral aspect ("Adoptions at Emar: An Outline," in d'Alfonso, Cohen, and Sürenhagen, *City of Emar*, 182–83). A parallel clause (using *palāhu* and/or *šemû*, "to listen to / obey") is attested in Nuzi wills (Zaccagnini, "Nuzi," 602).

42. This "garment clause," symbolizing the loss of rights to the property, is widely attested not only in the wills but also in other legal documents at Emar, Ugarit, Hana, and Nuzi; see Meir Malul, *Studies in Mesopotamian Legal Symbolism*, AOAT 221 (Kevelaer: Butzon & Bercker, 1988), 93–96.

43. For the former, see RE 15; for the latter, see Emar 176. In addition to *nakru*, the West Semitic term *ṣarrāru* occurs in nine documents at Emar and two at Ekalte. The Northwest Semitic term *sarru* is also attested (Justel, "Women and Family," 66). The term *za-ra-ri* (as in RE 8) or *sa-ar-ra*

and/or wife die without producing sons. In Emar 185, the testator stipulates that if his son becomes a widower, he must remarry and cannot leave the house. Some wills include adoptions, with clauses ensuring that the adoptee support his parents, lest he risk forfeiting his inheritance. In language typical of adoption contracts, RE 28 considers the consequences for a son who rejects his parents or for parents who reject their son, both of which are delivered as oral formulas (e.g., "You are not my father [and mother]," "You are not my son"). Once again, RE 15 serves as a useful example for the inclusion of these types of additional stipulations:

> "If my two daughters die and they have left behind no offspring, Dagan-ni, my wife, shall give [the inheritance] to whoever supports her among the offspring of my father. . . . If Abinami and Išarte, my two daughters, do not support Dagan-ni, their mother Dagan-ni shall strike their cheek and she shall give [the inheritance] to whoever supports her among the offspring of my father. She shall not give to a stranger."

In a form similar to other types of Emarite legal documents, the wills conclude with a list of male witnesses, the name of the scribe, and in some cases, seal impressions.[44] CF wills often feature the local king as the first witness. This detail is true for RE 15, which lists the first witness as Elli, the fifth king of what is known as the "Second Dynasty" (approx. 1250 BCE). First, however, the testator invokes a particularly unusual and harsh curse against anyone who challenges the terms of the will:

(as in Emar 176) is typically translated as "strange" or "stranger," though some translate "criminal," reading *sarrāru* as opposed to *zâru* (Marten Stol, *Women in the Ancient Near East*, trans. Helen and Mervyn Richardson [Boston/Berlin: De Gruyter, 2016], 289).

44. The son and grandson of Li'mi-šarra, a member of the "First Dynasty" and the highest representative of Emar in an international affair involving the King of the Land of Hurri, are listed as principal witnesses in several documents (Cohen and d'Alfonso, "Duration of the Emar Archives," 5; see also discussion in Fleming, "Reading Emar's Scribal Traditions," 33–35, 42). FF wills not only include seals but also name the individuals whose seals are affixed, using the word "seal."

> "Whoever rejects these words, may Dagan and [d]NIN.URTA destroy his offspring and his name and erect a stele in front of his house."[45]
>
> Witnesses: Elli, son of Pilsu-Dagan; Itūr-Dagan, son of Aḫī-malik; Baba, son of Rašap-ilī; Ba'al-ka, son of Aḫī-malik; Ba'al-bēlu, son of Mukna; Abī-Dagan, son of Zū-Asti (cylinder seal); Ea-damiq, scribe (cylinder seal).

Deuteronomy 25:5–10 displays a number of parallels to the Emarite testaments. Although these parallels are not limited to the Emarite wills and the biblical unit, the Emarite corpus allows for a targeted comparison between wills belonging to the "upstream tradition" and a biblical text that is likewise preoccupied with the fate of a deceased man's family and property.

WILL AND (OLD) TESTAMENT: THE ROOTS OF DEUTERONOMY 25:5–10

Deuteronomy 25:5–10 stipulates that if a man dies without a son, his brother-in-law should take the widowed woman as wife, resulting in the fact that the firstborn (or "seed," as in the LXX) whom she bears will carry on the name of the deceased. The bulk of the law outlines the legal protocol for a woman whose brother-in-law refuses to fulfill this obligation. First, the rejected woman is to approach the elders and make an official statement. The elders are then obliged to summon the negligent man, and if he confirms his refusal, he is to undergo a humiliating punishment. Within the context of the HLFs, the text is rather detailed, with multiple

45. Dagan is the chief god of Emar and [d]NIN.URTA is the god in whose name land is held at Emar. The deity indicated by the Sumerogram is uncertain but most likely not Ninurta. Two possibilities have been suggested by Daniel Arnaud and Daniel Fleming respectively: Aštar or Bēl māti ("Lord of the Land," as an epithet) (Gary Beckman, "Emar and Its Archives," in *Emar: The History, Religion, and Culture of a Syrian Town in the Late Bronze Age*, ed. Mark W. Chavalas [Bethesda, MD: CDL Press, 1996], 9 n. 44).

parties and direct speech, comparable to the case of the slandered bride in Deut 22:13–19.

The initial clause in v. 5, כִּֽי־יֵשְׁב֨וּ אַחִ֜ים יַחְדָּ֗ו ("If brothers sit/dwell together and one of them dies . . ."), is generally taken to represent a particular situation whereby actual brothers lost their father, inherited his property, and chose to live together on undivided land.[46] It may also be significant, however, that the CF wills at Emar universally open with reference to the testator causing "his 'brothers' to sit."[47] Likewise, in Ruth 4, the narrator states that Boaz "took ten men from among the elders of the city and said, '*Sit* here' and *they sat*" (וַיִּקַּ֞ח עֲשָׂרָ֧ה אֲנָשִׁ֛ים מִזִּקְנֵ֥י הָעִ֖יר וַיֹּ֣אמֶר שְׁבוּ־פֹ֑ה וַיֵּשֵֽׁבוּ). Of course, the "brothers" at Emar (and Ekalte) occupy a particular legal function, while the phrase כִּֽי־יֵשְׁב֨וּ אַחִ֜ים יַחְדָּ֗ו in Deut 25:5 may simply imply joint ownership among actual brothers. Nonetheless, as both the Emarite wills and Ruth 4 suggest, the combination of "brothers/men" and "sitting" has associations with small-scale legal gatherings witnessing the transfer of persons and property. Accordingly, its use in Deut 25:5 may reflect a relic of standard legal language.

As Deut 25:5 continues, it specifies that the dead man "has no son" (וּבֵ֣ן אֵֽין־ל֔וֹ). Within the Hebrew Bible, the phrase וּבֵ֣ן אֵֽין־ל֔וֹ occurs elsewhere in Num 27:4 and 8, Judg 11:34, Eccl 4:8, and 2 Sam 18:18.[48] The reference to a sonless man in all of these contexts signals an obstacle to the smooth and more standard transference of land from father to son. Several Emarite wills (e.g., RE 15, RE 23, and Emar 185) also include references

46. On this phenomenon, see David Daube, who likens the biblical situation to the Roman legal practice of *ercto non cito*, or undivided ownership ("*Consortium* in Roman and Hebrew Law," *Juridical Review* 62 [1950]: 71–91). The division of land after the father's death—evidently the standard practice—is referenced in LH §165 ("after the father goes to his fate . . . the brothers shall equally divide . . ."), LE §16 ("the son of a man who has not yet received his inheritance share [*la zīzu*, lit., "who is not divided]"), and MAL A §25 ("her husband's brothers have not yet divided"). MAL A §25 is particularly intriguing in the light of Deut 25:5–10, in that it also refers to a legal situation involving a childless widow and her husband's brothers. In that case, however, the woman lives not on their property but rather in her father's house.

47. See, e.g., RE 8, RE 15, RE 23, RE 28, RE 61, Emar 94, 176, 180, 181, 183, 188, and 189.

48. Benjamin Kilhör notes that only Num 27:8 preserves exactly the same wording ("Levirate Marriage in Deuteronomy 25:5–10 and Its Precursors in Leviticus and Numbers: A Test Case

to childlessness, whether of the testator's wife or of the testator's children. References to childlessness likewise are attested in Elephantine marriage contracts.[49]

Verse 5 further stipulates לֹא־תִהְיֶה אֵשֶׁת־הַמֵּת הַחוּצָה לְאִישׁ זָר ("the wife of the dead man shall not [marry] a strange man outside [the family]").[50] This restriction is almost identical to that which is specified in certain Emar wills (e.g., RE 8 and Emar 176), where repercussions are pledged for the wife who marries "a strange man." It is clear that both Deut 25:5 and the wills reflect the same interest, namely, to keep the property in the family. It is further significant that Deut 25:5 refers to the woman as אֵשֶׁת־הַמֵּת (lit., "the wife of the dead man") as opposed to the more widely attested term "widow" (אַלְמָנָה). In "Widows' Rights in Ur III Sumer," David Owen attributes significance to a similar formulation in an Ur III text, which makes reference to "the wife of (the deceased) PN" as opposed to NU.MU.SU/ *almattu* ("widow"). He concludes that *almattu* denotes a woman without

for the Relationship between P/H and D," *CBQ* 77.3 [2015]: 432). As noted in Chapter 2, the LXX instead features the gender-neutral term σπέρμα ("seed"). Interestingly, this term is also used in RE 15. A similar phrase appears in an unprovenanced Hebrew ostracon that features a letter from a widow to an official (see Pierre Bordreuil, Felice Israel, and Dennis Pardee, "Deux ostraca paléo-hébreux de la Collection Sh. Moussaïeff," *Semitica* 46 [1996]: 49–76, Pls. 7–8). In the letter, the widow states that her husband died childless (אישי לא בנם), and his brother was assigned a wheat field that was promised to her husband. She makes a case that she should be granted the field. Eberhard Bons suggests that the widow's plea is for possession of the property, not merely the usufruct, a proposal that he suggests is not contradicted by the documentation from Elephantine (Nahal Hever and Wadi Murabbaʿat, "Konnte eine Witwe die *naḥalāh* ihres verstorbenen Mannes erben?: Überlegungen zum Ostrakon 2 aus der Sammlung Moussaïeff," in *ZAR* 4 [1998]: 203–8). The authenticity of this document has been called into question, however. See discussion in Angelika Berlejung and Andreas Schüle, "Erwägungen zu den neuen Ostraka aus der Sammlung Moussaïeff," *ZAH* 11 (1998): 68–73; and Israel Eph'al and Joseph Naveh, "Remarks on the Recently Published Moussaïeff Ostraca," *IEJ* 48.3–4 (1998): 269–73. Eph'al and Naveh point especially to the substantial quantity of parallels between phrases in the letter and phrases from biblical verses (271).

49. See *TAD* B2.6 and B3.8 in Bezalel Porten, ed., *The Elephantine Papyri in English: Three Millennia of Cross-Cultural Continuity and Change*, 2nd ed., DMOA, Studies in Near Eastern Archaeology and Civilisation 22 (Atlanta: SBL Press, 2011), 178–84 and 227–32.

50. Cf. LXX, which prohibits the woman from marrying "a man who is not close" (ἀνδρὶ μὴ ἐγγίζοντι).

support, while the epithet "wife of PN" indicates a woman with financial security.[51] The two Hebrew phrases may reflect a similar distinction. In addition to Deut 25:5, Ruth and Abigail are not called "widows" but rather "wife of PN / the dead man," epithets that suit their long-term security in the hands of Boaz and David. In the context of Deut 25:5–10, the choice of the term "the wife of the dead man" (as opposed to "widow") thus appears to be deliberate, one designed to signal the woman's right to remain on the property after her husband's death.

The final section of v. 5 then states the terms of the agreement: יְבָמָהּ יָבֹא עָלֶיהָ וּלְקָחָהּ לוֹ לְאִשָּׁה וְיִבְּמָהּ ("Her husband's designate shall come to her and take her for himself as wife and support her").[52] The noun יבם, here translated "husband's designate," is a hapax legomenon in the Hebrew Bible, suggesting that it represents a special legal designation as opposed to the more generic "brother-in-law" or "husband's brother," as it is typically rendered.[53] The feminine form of the word is attested only in Deut 25:7 and 9 and Ruth 1:15, and the related verb occurs only here and in Gen 38:8.[54] The term is clearly tied to the role of the designated man; hence the *BDB* definition, "to do the duty of a brother-in-law." It is often assumed

51. David I. Owen, "Widows' Rights in Ur III Sumer," *ZA* 70.2 (1980): 174 n. 18. Owen surmises that widowed women in Ur III may have had primary right of inheritance unless their husbands had stipulated otherwise in their wills (175). Godfrey R. Driver and John C. Miles likewise distinguish the *almattu*, who has neither grown sons nor a father-in-law, from two other classes of widows in the Assyrian laws: women with sons and inchoately married brides (*The Assyrian Laws: Edited with Translation and Commentary*, Reprint of the Oxford 1935 Edition with Supplementary Additions and Corrections by Driver [Oxford: Clarendon Press, 1975], 246–47).

52. The verb יָבַם is rendered in the LXX as συνοικέω ("live with"). At the end of Deut 25:7, the same Hebrew verb is used, but the LXX notably leaves it untranslated: οὐκ ἠθέλησεν ὁ ἀδελφὸς τοῦ ἀνδρός μου ("my husband's brother does not want to"). In this case, it appears that the translator did not understand the import of the rare Hebrew verb.

53. See, e.g., the JPS translation and NRSV; see also Ludwig Koehler and Walter Baumgartner, "יבם" in *The Hebrew and Aramaic Lexicon of the Old Testament*, trans. M. E. J. Richardson, rev. Walter Baumgartner and Johann Jakob Stamm (Leiden: Brill, 2001), vol. 1, 383.

54. The term appears to have a parallel in Ugaritic, especially in its female form (*ybmt*), but as Aicha Rahmouni points out, there is no consensus with regard to its translation (*Divine Epithets in the Ugaritic Alphabetic Texts*, trans. J. N. Ford [Leiden: Brill, 2008], 185–92).

that the "duty" involves impregnation, with debate about the status of the relationship.[55]

It is possible, however, that the term יבם simply signifies obligatory protection. In Nuzi and Emarite wills, whenever wives are the object of a verb, the verb is linked to support or servitude. The equally rare Akkadian term (and West Semitic loanword) *yaba/āmum* is attested only in a single context, but its use suggests a male's legal obligation to care for a woman related to him by marriage, not to impregnate her. In a letter from Mari, the speaker refers to a woman who no longer wants to live with her husband and instead opts to go with her children to the house of her *yaba/āmum*.[56] The term in this letter is typically translated as either "brother-in-law" or "father-in-law," though it is possible that it refers more generically to a designated male relative who provides security for his in-law in the case of a dissolved marriage.[57] The letter represents an interesting case, in that the *yaba/āmum* is obligated to support his brother's wife in the case of divorce, not (only?) premature death. The fact that the letter uses the term *yaba/āmum*, as opposed to a proper name, seems to imply that the term also represents a designated legal role, though its paucity in documentation suggests a restricted set of circumstances.

Although the Emarite wills do not stipulate that the testator's brother marry his widow, it is notable that in more than one instance, the woman

55. This assumption is partly due to the use of the root בוא in v. 5 ("to come," with possible sexual connotations) and partly to the reference to offspring in the following verse. Ephraim Neufeld translates the verb as "impregnate" (*Ancient Hebrew Marriage Laws: With Special References to General Semitic Laws and Customs* [London: Longmans, Green, and Co., 1944], 23 n. 1). George W. Coats argues that marriage was not necessarily required; rather, the widow only had the right to expect conception of a child ("Widow's Rights: A Crux in the Structure of Genesis 38," *CBQ* 34.4 [1972]: 461–66). While it is evident that the term is tied to impregnation in Genesis 38, it remains a question as to whether or not the term originally had these associations in Deut 25:5.

56. An excerpt of the letter (OBTR 143) appears in Stol, *Women in the Ancient Near East*, 224.

57. The *AHw* translates "Schwager" (III, *jabāmum*, 1565a) and the *CDA* translates "father-in-law" (*yabamum*, 440a). The *CAD* does not list it, for the volume I/J was published before publication of the letter. See also Stol's translation (ibid.) and Jack Sasson, who translates "father-in-law" (*From the Mari Archives: An Anthology of Old Babylonian Letters* [Winona Lake, IN: Eisenbrauns, 2015], 328).

is obligated to give her possessions to "whoever supports her among her deceased husband's brothers" (see, e.g., RE 15, previously quoted). As scholars have noted, the notion of a widowed woman's in-laws taking her into their household is attested elsewhere in the ancient Near East. Both Middle Assyrian Laws (MAL) A §30 and §43 and Hittite Laws (HL) §193 refer to the transference of a widow into the care of her husband's agnates. In MAL A §30, this protection is designated by the legal term *ahūzatu*, defined in the *CAD* as "a marriage-like relationship of dependency and protection between an unprotected female and the head of a household."[58] If we interpret the final section of Deut 25:5 as the inverse of the preceding phrase, it appears that the woman is expected to marry not an *outsider* but rather her husband's *designate*, with all of the security that such a marriage entails. While this arrangement may result in a child, it is not necessary to assume that the act originally implied by the verb "יבם" was synonymous with intercourse or impregnation. More likely, comparable to the situations outlined in the Emarite wills, MAL, and HL, the verb and related nouns initially pertained to support or protection. The illogical sequence of the verse, which stipulates that the man "come to her" (יְבָ֣א עָלֶ֔יהָ) and then "take her as his wife" (cf. the reverse in Deut 22:13) may suggest that יְבָ֣א עָלֶ֔יהָ is a secondary insertion, one that either reads or reinterprets the role of the יבם in terms of impregnation.

While v. 5 centers on the designate's responsibilities to the woman, v. 6 is concerned with the potential offspring of the union and the child's ability to prevent his father's "name" from being wiped out from Israel. The verse states: וְהָיָ֗ה הַבְּכוֹר֙ אֲשֶׁ֣ר תֵּלֵ֔ד יָק֕וּם עַל־שֵׁ֥ם אָחִ֖יו הַמֵּ֑ת וְלֹֽא־יִמָּחֶ֥ה שְׁמ֖וֹ מִיִּשְׂרָאֵֽל ("The firstborn that she bears shall rise upon the name of his dead brother so that his name shall not be wiped out from Israel"). The concern with

58. *CAD* A/1 s.v. *ahūzatu*, 217. The term in MAL is not restricted to obligations through marriage, however. In A §32, a father whose daughter is raped is to give her into the household of the (married) man who raped her (a similarly disturbing scenario is represented in MT Exod 22:15–16 / LXX 22:16–17 and Deut 22:28–29). The reasoning, however, is the same: as noted in the *CAD* entry, "A woman who has lost her protector by death or her value through rape is handed over to the head of a household who, as relative or culprit, must assume responsibility for her."

a lost "name" also surfaces in Num 27:1–11, where Zelophehad's daughters make a plea to Moses that they should inherit their deceased father's holding. The women's concern, however, is set within the narrower context of the clan, not all Israel: לָ֣מָּה יִגָּרַ֤ע שֵׁם־אָבִ֙ינוּ֙ מִתּ֣וֹךְ מִשְׁפַּחְתּ֔וֹ כִּ֛י אֵ֥ין ל֖וֹ בֵּ֑ן ("Why should the 'name' of our father be taken away from his clan, [just] because he has no son?"). I concur here with Raymond Westbrook, who proposes that the "name" in Deut 25:6 is tied to the right to inherit property and is best translated as something akin to "title," a term that likewise carries dual connotations of a name and the right to property.[59]

The rest of the unit (vv. 7–10) outlines the protocol in the event that a man refuses to fulfill his obligation: "But if the man does not want to marry his sister-in-law, his sister-in-law shall go up to the gate, to the elders, and state, 'My husband's designate refuses to establish a name in Israel for his brother; he is not willing to support me.' And the elders of his city shall summon him and they shall speak to him; and if he takes a stand and states, 'I do not want to marry her,' his sister-in-law shall approach him before the elders, remove his sandal from his foot, spit in his face, testify, and say, 'Thus shall be done to the man who does not build up his brother's house.'[60] And his name in Israel shall [henceforth] be called 'The house of the one whose sandal was removed.'" As Meir Malul has shown, Near Eastern contracts concerning the severance of family ties and/or the loss of rights to the family's property likewise frequently include symbolic acts (e.g., "breaking a clod," "leaving the garment on the stool," "washing the hands and departing," "cutting the hem").[61] Furthermore, just as the man in Deut 25:5–10 must publicly declare his refusal, the refusal of certain

59. Raymond Westbrook, *Property and the Family in Biblical Law*, JSOTSup 113 (Sheffield: Sheffield Academic Press, 1991), 75. see also Eryl W. Davies, "Inheritance Rights and the Hebrew Levirate Marriage, Part 1," *VT* 31.2 (1981): 142.

60. It is possible that the phrase refers not to the man's duty to help produce an heir for his brother, but instead to his responsibility to his late brother's wife. Notably, the Laws of Hammurabi (LH) employs a similar phrase (*bīta*[*m*] *epēšu*, lit., "to build a/the house") in the context of laws that ensure continued rights to vulnerable individuals in the household (*CAD* s.v. *epēšu* 2c *bītu*). See LH §148 (with reference to a man's responsibility to his ill wife) and LH §191 (with respect to a father's responsibility to his adopted child after the birth of biological children).

61. Malul, *Studies in Mesopotamian Legal Symbolism*, 77–159.

parties to perform their duties in Emarite contracts is also represented by oral formulas: "You are not my father/mother/son" (e.g., RE 25, RE 28); "You are not my brothers" (e.g., Emar 181); "I will not honor you" (e.g., RE 13).[62] In addition, just as the man's refusal to support his sister-in-law is followed by a punishment, the anticipated negligence in the contracts is followed by penalties: most commonly, the loss of rights to the inheritance. It is notable that the "curse" and closing declaration in Deut 25:9–10 are similar to the divine curse in RE 15. In each case, a lack of compliance results in the permanent smearing of the "name" and "house" of the offender: the very assets that the wills and law are designed to protect.

In sum, Deut 25:5–10 is concerned with the fate of a man's wife after his death, the limits on her marital capacities, the man's (potential) progeny, and the destiny of the man's property after his death: precisely the concerns of Emarite (and other Near Eastern) wills. To some extent, the biblical unit echoes the format of contracts, in that a basic agreement is followed by a scenario in which the agreement is unfulfilled. This is not to say, however, that Deut 25:5–10 simply reflects a generalized form of an Israelite/Judahite will. The phrase "a name in Israel" would likely have had no place in a private legal document; thus, parts of vv. 6–7 may reflect the adaptation of older terminology and/or legal protocol from a broader perspective. Moreover, while the wills stipulate consequences for individuals who refuse to comply with their terms, the biblical unit reconstructs in detail the legal proceedings that such a refusal would entail. In this sense, it is closer in form to a (fictional) case, albeit one presented in general terms. Nonetheless, the parallels in terminology, interests, and structure between Deut 25:5–10 and the Emarite wills suggest that the scribe responsible for this HLF drew upon his knowledge of a comparable body of Israelite/Judahite wills; or alternatively, of a list of standard contractual clauses.

62. Such formulations are attested throughout the cuneiform and Aramaic corpora; Elephantine marriage contracts, e.g., likewise anticipate the potential dissolution of the marriage through *verba solemnia*: "If PN_1 says, 'I hated my wife PN_2 . . . or if PN_2 says, 'I hated my husband PN_1 . . . .'"

CONTRACT TERMINOLOGY IN DEUTERONOMY 21:15–17 AND EXODUS 21:7–11

Deuteronomy 21:15–17 and Exod 21:7–11 also demonstrate considerable overlap with practical legal documents. The first considers the unusual situation of a man who has two wives, one loved and the other hated.[63] Both of the wives have sons, and the firstborn belongs to the hated wife. The unit stipulates that the man "is not allowed to make the son of the loved one 'firstborn' over the son of the hated one, the (actual) firstborn" (v. 16). It is well known that the practice of assigning an extra share or double portion to the eldest son is attested throughout the ancient Near East. Wills from Emar and Ekalte indeed commonly reflect this practice.[64] Moreover, just as Deut 21:15–17 considers a situation in which a father might opt to render his younger son the firstborn, there is evidence in Nuzi and Emar wills that fathers could deviate from the custom of favoring the eldest.[65] This action was achieved by naming the younger sibling the "firstborn" or "primary heir," a legal fiction comparable to the "masculinization" of female heirs at Emar and Nuzi.[66] At the same time, like Deut 21:15–17, other contracts put limits on the patriarch's agency. As Bruce Wells notes, certain OB adoption contracts stipulate that if the adoptive father has additional sons, his adoptee must retain the status of his firstborn son (*aplum*).[67] Several Near Eastern contracts similarly prohibit a man from demoting his wife from first rank to second rank.[68] Again, given the close parallels in content,

63. As noted in Chapter 2, "loved" and "hated" are legal terms that reflect the status of each woman, not the husband's emotions toward each of his wives.

64. See RE 94, Ekalte 74, Emar 176, Emar 201, RE 28, and *TBR* 42.

65. On this phenomenon at Nuzi, see Zaccagnini, "Nuzi," 600–1; for the same at Ugarit, see Rowe, "Ugarit," 729–30. Raymond Westbrook identifies this choice as one of five powers that Near Eastern fathers could exercise as testators ("The Character of Ancient Near Eastern Law," in *HANEL* 1:59–60).

66. Wells, "Hated Wife," 133. Wells also cites a Ugaritic will (RS 94.2168) that enables a patriarch to grant more of his property to "the one among his sons whom [he] loves" (133).

67. Ibid.

68. These include contracts from Nuzi as well as a single attestation from Alalakh and a single Neo-Babylonian contract (ibid., 138).

terminology, and concerns across Deut 21:15–17 and the Near Eastern contracts, it appears that this HLF is also rooted in analogous documents of practice or lists of contractual clauses that pertain to inheritance.

Exodus 21:7–11 then considers a father's sale of his daughter as a slave-woman into another household, a position that is characterized as permanent but dependent on certain conditions.[69] The arrangement appears to allow for two potential target husbands for the young woman: the patriarch or his son.[70] The text is largely composed of a set of sub-clauses that outlines the conditions of the agreement. If the buyer designates the girl for himself but no longer wants her, he is not permitted to sell her.[71] If he designates her for his son, he must treat her כְּמִשְׁפַּ֥ט הַבָּנ֖וֹת ("according to the entitlement of daughters").[72] Finally, if "he" (presumably the buyer)

69. Verse 7 refers back to Exod 21:1–6 by stating that the girl is not to leave like the male slaves." Jackson notes the unusual nature of this "cross reference" within *Mishpatim*, along with the unusually elaborate nature of both the male and female slave laws (*Wisdom Laws*, 108).

70. See Pamela Barmash, who characterizes the relationship to the master as "vertical," in that the daughter is merely used for sexual relations and/or procreation, while the potential relationship to the son is "horizontal," in that the daughter would shift from slave status to that of wife/daughter-in-law ("The Daughter Sold into Slavery and Marriage," in *Sexuality and Law in the Torah*, ed. Hilary Lipka and Bruce Wells, Library of Hebrew Bible / OTS 675 [London: T&T Clark, 2020], 59 and 73).

71. This reading follows the MT *qere'*, the LXX, the Vulgate, and the Targum, all of which state that the master took the girl *for himself* (אֲשֶׁר־ל֥וֹ יְעָדָ֑הּ) as a slave-wife and then sought to expel her. The MT *ketiv*, however, indicates that the man neglected to arrange for the woman's marriage (אֲשֶׁר־לֹא יְעָדָ֑הּ). Most scholars prefer the *qere'* to the *ketiv*, given that it provides a closer structural counterpart to the designation of the woman for the son in the following verse. The confusion appears to stem from the unusual syntax of the verse: rather than state first that the master took the woman for himself, but then she became "bad," it begins with the man's dissatisfaction and only then refers to his relationship to the woman in a relative clause.

72. The phrase is elusive and attested only here. Near Eastern contracts feature similar terminology that may be useful in determining its meaning. Emarite contracts (e.g., RE 61), for example, refer to a husband divorcing his wife "like a daughter of Emar," a clause that Westbrook takes to refer to a divorce payment ("Emar and Vicinity," 670). In this light, it appears that the phrase indicates a payment of some sort. Two possibilities present themselves. The first is a dowry. This option would account for the fact that the phrase is only used with respect to the son. Alternatively, the phrase may allude to a bride-price. Here the Nuzi evidence may be useful. In certain cases, Nuzi patriarchs who sold their daughters received a partial payment at the time of sale (when the girl was young) and then the rest when the marriage was consummated. It is possible that the Exodus unit envisions a similar situation. See also the discussion in Gregory Chirichigno, *Debt-Slavery in Israel and the Ancient Near East*, JSOTSup 141 (Sheffield:

takes “another,” he is still obligated to provide for the first woman’s basic needs: food, clothing, and (possibly) oil.[73] If he does not do these things, he must allow the woman to go free. The situation outlined in this unit resonates to a certain extent with a subset of Nuzi contracts known as “marriage adoptions.”[74] These contracts involve a young girl being adopted into “daughterhood” (*ana mārtūti*), “daughter-in-law-hood” (*ana kallatūti*), and “daughterhood and daughter-in-law-hood” (*ana mārtūti u kallatūti*).[75] The three types differ somewhat, but all concern young women who are

JSOT Press, 1993), 250; and Shalom M. Paul, *Studies in the Book of the Covenant in the Light of Cuneiform and Biblical Law*, VTSupp 18 (Leiden: Brill, 1970), 55.

73. The text literally specifies that he must not withhold from the woman her “flesh, her clothing, or her *ʿonah*.” The final object is a hapax legomenon and has been assigned such varied definitions as “marital rights,” “oil/ointments,” and “shelter.” See discussion in William H. C. Propp, *Exodus 19–40: A New Translation with Introduction and Commentary,* Anchor Bible (New York: Doubleday, 2006), *Exodus*, 202–3.

74. The term was coined by Paulo Koschaker; see discussion in Guillaume Cardascia, “L’adoption matrimoniale à Babylone et à Nuzi,” *Revue historique de droit français et étranger* 36.4 (1959): 2 and Katarzyna Grosz, “On Some Aspects of the Adoption of Women at Nuzi,” in *General Studies and Excavations at Nuzi 9/1*, ed. David I. Owen and Martha A. Morrison, SCCNH 2 (Winona Lake, IN: Eisenbrauns, 1987), 131 n. 1. Although this phenomenon is best attested at Nuzi, it is also attested at Sippar (during the OB period) and Ugarit.

75. The first is known from thirty-five attestations; the second from seven; and the third from eighteen. The numbers are based on Jeanette Fincke, “Adoption of Women at Nuzi,” in *The Nuzi Workshop at the 55th Rencontre Assyriologique Internationale (July 2009 Paris)*, ed. Phillippe Abrahami and Brigitte Lion, SCCNH 19 (Bethesda, MD: CDL Press, 2012), 120–21. Given that separate tablets of “daughterhood” and “daughter-in-law-hood” exist, the question remains as to why a third type combines the two. At first, scholars assumed that the phrase referred to the two stages of the girl’s status: since she was adopted at a young age, she was first in the role of a daughter; then subsequently, she became a daughter-in-law. Cardascia, however, challenged the idea, claiming that the combination was instead used to provide the adoptive father with more flexibility. In other words, he could give her to someone in his house (and thus she would be a daughter-in-law), or he could marry her off to an outsider (and thus she would be a daughter) (“L’adoption matrimoniale,” 5). More recently, however, Lindsay Fraughton argues persuasively that there is no demonstrable significance to the tablet labels (“A New Approach to Ancient Archives: A Reevaluation of ‘Daughtership’ Adoption at Nuzi” [MA thesis, The University of British Columbia, 2021]). Fraughton observes that 40% of the known “combination” tablets derive from only two households: Teḫip-tilla, an evident real estate mogul; and Tulpun-naya, a wealthy businesswoman. Teḫip-tilla most often used the “combination” tablet, yet always assigned the “adoptee” to one of his slaves. As such, the notion that adopters used the “daughterhood and daughter-in-law-hood” type in order to have more flexibility does not appear to bear out.

adopted into another family, most likely due to debt, with the expectation that they will be married off in the future by the adoptive parent.

As scholars note, the third type, *ana mārtūti u kallatūti*, exhibits some overlap with the Exodus law (see appendix for a sample contract).[76] As with the Exodus unit, the target husband in these Nuzi arrangements can vary: as Katarzyna Grosz has shown, the girl can be married to a free citizen, someone outside the house, the head of the household, a son, a particular slave, any slave, or simply "according to [the master's] wish."[77] According to Guillaume Cardascia, an essential characteristic of these documents is the indetermination of the husband. Even if a specific man is named as the spouse, the contracts often stipulate that the woman could be given to someone else.[78] Marriage to a slave always included what Grosz calls a "consecutive marriage clause": if the husband died, she would be married to another man.[79] One contract states that the woman could be married as many as eleven times (!) if her first ten husbands die.[80] It seems that as long as the woman was fertile, she would be given to another partner.

76. The first to make this suggestion was Isaac Mendelsohn, "The Conditional Sale into Slavery of Free-Born Daughters in Nuzi and the Law of Ex. 21:7–11," *JAOS* 55.2 (1935): 190–95; see also Paul, *Studies in the Book of the Covenant*, 52–53; and Chirichigno, *Debt-Slavery in Israel*, 246–47. Barry Eichler points to both the parallels and divergences between the Nuzi practice and the biblical unit ("Nuzi and the Bible: A Retrospective," in *DUMU-E$_2$-DUB-BA-A: Studies in Honor of Åke Sjöberg*, ed. Hermann Behrens, Darlene Loding, and Martha T. Roth, Occasional Publications of the Samuel Noah Kramer Fund 11 [Philadelphia: University Museum, 1989], 116–17). This view is not without dissent, however; see, e.g., Raymond Westbrook, who rejects the link because slave terminology is not used in the Nuzi texts ("The Female Slave," in *LTT* 2:154). As I see it, however, the two phenomena need not be identical or related to be parallel.

77. Grosz, "On Some Aspects of the Adoption."

78. Cardascia, "L'adoption matrimoniale," 11. See, e.g., Breneman, "Nuzi Marriage Tablets," H IX 145 (pp. 114–16), JEN 50, JEN 26, JEN 437 (pp. 130–34); JEN 596, JEN 620 (pp. 136–37); AASOR XVI 30, AASOR XVI 23 (pp. 139–41); JEN 431 (p. 143); and AASOR XVI 42, JEN 433 (pp. 145–49).

79. Grosz, "On Some Aspects of the Adoption," 144–45.

80. Robert H. Pfeiffer and E. A. Speiser, *One Hundred New Selected Nuzi Texts*, The Annual of the American Schools of Oriental Research, vol. 16 for 1935–36 (New Haven, CT: American Schools of Oriental Research, 1936), 84; see also Breneman, "Nuzi Marriage Tablets," AASOR XVI 23 (pp. 140–41).

Although the terms of the Nuzi contracts differ from those in Exod 21:7–11, they illuminate the degree to which the latter mirrors the format of contracts. As outlined earlier, Near Eastern contracts typically include an agreement that is followed by a series of scenarios that consider potential invalidations of that agreement. The Nuzi contracts typically present an agreement between contracting parties, followed by one or more "consecutive marriage clauses." Likewise, in Exod 21:7–11, a basic agreement (v. 7) is followed by a series of casuistic clauses regarding the woman's spouse and the man's continued obligation to care for her if he takes another woman. Like the Nuzi contracts, the biblical unit allows for more than one target husband and casts the sale as permanent. It is further notable that the biblical law is preoccupied with money and restrictions on sale, that is, the "stuff" of contracts. It begins with a father selling his daughter into a slave-marriage arrangement, a situation that likely would have been due to debt. If the buyer who acquires the young woman no longer wants to retain her, she can only be redeemed by her family.[81] The final clause in v. 8 (בְּבִגְדוֹ־בָֽהּ, lit. "if he acts deceitfully") appears to refer directly to a breached contract.[82]

The reference in the biblical unit to the buyer's obligations in the case of a second "acquisition" also resonates with clauses that appear in regular Nuzi marriage contracts. At Nuzi, marriage contracts initiated by the bride's family include a clause stating that if the woman gives birth, the groom may not take another wife. Several other texts include a clause stating the opposite: that is, the groom may take another wife if the woman is barren. In addition, at least five documents include a penalty clause if the groom does take another wife.[83] Although Exod 21:10 does not refer explicitly to the young woman's infertility, that may be the implied subtext

81. It is worth noting that Nuzi contracts similarly state that a woman cannot be given to "the exterior" (*ana bābi*) (Elena Cassin, "Être femme à Nuzi: Remarques sur l'adoption matrimoniale," in *Épouser au plus proche: Inceste, prohibitions et stratégies matrimoniales autour de la Méditerranée*, ed. Pierre Bonte [Paris: Éditions de l'École des hautes études en sciences sociales, 1994], 131).

82. For this reading, see also Propp, *Exodus*, 199.

83. Jonathan Paradise, "Marriage Contracts of Free Persons at Nuzi," *JCS* 39.1 (1987): 7–11.

for acquiring "another." Once again, it appears that Exod 21:7–11 is also rooted in knowledge of a comparable body of Israelite/Judahite contracts and/or lists of standard contractual clauses.

CONCLUSION

Of the three HLFs, Exod 21:7–11 most closely echoes the format of a contract, in that a basic agreement is followed by a set of contingency and penalty clauses that echo those found in attested contracts. In form, it is thus closer to something like the first fictional case on the unicum edited by Klein and Sharlach and discussed in Chapter 1, a text that launches with a set of adoption contractual clauses. Though less elaborate, Deut 21:15–17 also mirrors a contract, in that the unit restricts a man from promoting his second-born son to firstborn status. The unusual nature of the situation (a man with *two* wives and *two* sons) suits the oft-observed pattern of abnormal circumstances in Near Eastern contracts. Deuteronomy 25:5–10 then exhibits a different tack. While it launches with a basic agreement that parallels the terms of attested contracts, the bulk of the unit details the protocol for dealing with a party who fails to fulfill that agreement. As such, it creatively brings to life the very concerns that contracting parties aimed to anticipate and assuage. To some degree, then, this unit more closely parallels something like Greengus's fictional case, which launched with a formula akin to those in marriage contracts and then spun out the circumstances and consequences of a breached agreement; or Hallo's fictional case, which likewise embedded a standard contractual clause (e.g., "His heart was satisfied at that time with that money") in the midst of a trial regarding a breach of contract.

Notwithstanding these stylistic differences, it is possible to conclude that the scribes who composed these HLFs drew on their knowledge of contracts and/or standard contractual clauses. As we saw with the Sumerian fictional cases, the pairing of contract terminology with a "court" setting makes sense: contracts anticipate and aim to assuage violations of the agreement, while trials—at least in some cases—reflect the real-life outcome of such breaches. The two styles, of course, varied: the Mesopotamians opted to use real names, casting their scenarios as actual cases; while the HLFs appear in generalized form. Nonetheless, the fictional cases and HLFs appear to reflect at least one common aim, namely, to teach (or practice) the format and/or terminology of contracts. Moreover, like the fictional cases, the situation of contractual clauses in the context of colorful "worst-case" scenarios would have been an effective strategy for teaching scribes the tricks (or terms) of the trade. In this light, although we lack access to comparable caches of contracts from ancient Israel and Judah, traces of these texts may well be at our fingertips, embedded in what we call biblical law.

4

Exodus 21–22

Old Law Collection or Scribal Exercise?

> Why this opposition to "Babel and Bible" when logic itself compels this sequence of the words?
>
> —Friedrich Delitzsch, "Babel und Bibel," Second Lecture, 1903

OF ALL OF the legal material in the Bible, Exod 21:18–22:16 stands out as the closest in content and form to the Near Eastern genre of the law collection. Unlike the "civil and criminal" casuistic units in Deuteronomy 19–25, which are interspersed with ethical precepts and cultic regulations, Exod 21:18–22:16 is an uninterrupted block of casuistic provisions. It features some of the same topics that are covered in the Near Eastern collections, including injury to a pregnant woman and the "goring" ox.[1] Moreover, unlike the "illusory" clusters of law in Deuteronomy 19–25 that were discussed in Chapter 2, the clusters in Exod 21:18–22:16 appear to belong to the same initial phase of composition. It is thus not surprising that Exod 21:18–22:16 (or, more broadly, the entirety of Exod 20:23–23:19, or what is called the Covenant Code [CC]) has been treated as a law collection, one

1. See, however, Martha T. Roth's article "Errant Oxen Or: The Goring Ox Redux," in *Literature as Politics, Politics as Literature: Essays on the Ancient Near East in Honor of Peter Machinist*, ed. David S. Vanderhooft and Abraham Winitzer (Winona Lake, IN: Eisenbrauns, 2013), in which she argues that the Mesopotamian laws and exercises feature not "goring oxen" but rather "errant" ones who go astray, something that she deems would have been a common sight in a premodern society (400).

Making a Case. Sara J. Milstein, Oxford University Press. © Oxford University Press 2021.
DOI: 10.1093/oso/9780190911805.003.0005

akin to—if not based on—the Laws of Hammurabi (LH). Compared to LH and other expressions of the genre, however, this so-called collection is much more narrowly focused, with laws that pertain only to physical and property damages. It is also far more disjointed and incomplete than its cuneiform counterparts, with a number of ambiguities and errors. Given these factors, I propose that there is a closer analogue to Exod 21:18–22:16 than the law collections. As outlined in Chapter 1, Mesopotamian scribes occasionally copied a limited series of laws in the context of their education, such as the Laws about Rented Oxen or the Sumerian Laws Exercise Tablet. These provisions were related to laws in the collections but not direct replicas of them. In the Laws about Rented Oxen, all of the provisions pertain to the theme of ox mishaps. The Sumerian Laws Exercise Tablet is marked by a number of ambiguities and errors. Given the limited focus of Exod 21:18–22:16, in addition to its disjointedness and ambiguities, I propose that this unit is rooted in a similar type of legal-pedagogical exercise.

"BABEL UND BIBEL," HAMMURABI AND MOSES

It is tough to overestimate the impact of Father Vincent Scheil's publication of what he dubbed the "Code of the Laws of Hammurabi" in 1902.[2] Almost immediately, translations appeared in German, English, and Italian; and the American weekly *The Independent* ran a complete translation of the "civil code of Hammurabi" over the course of three issues in 1903.[3] Recognition of the many parallels between LH and biblical law fueled a flurry of books, scholarly articles, and popular pieces on the

2. Scheil, *Textes élamites-sémitiques*, 11–162. It is clear that with this term, the Frenchman Scheil intended to identify Hammurabi's work as the long-lost ancestor to the Napoleonic Code.

3. The first German translations were Hugo Winckler, *Die Gesetze Hammurabis, Königs von Babylon um 2250 v. Chr. Das älteste Gesetzbuch der Welt* (Leipzig: J. C. Hinrichs, 1902) and Samuel Oettli, *Das Gesetz Hammurabis und die Thora Israels: Eine religions- und rechtsgeschichtliche Parallele* (Leipzig: A. Diechert, 1903); the first English translations were Claude Hermann Walter Johns, *The Oldest Code of Laws in the World: The Code of Laws Promulgated by Hammurabi, King of Babylon, B.C. 2285–2242* (Edinburgh: T&T Clark, 1903) and Robert F. Harper, *The Code of Hammurabi, King of Babylon, about 2250 B.C.* (Chicago: University

topic of "Hammurabi and Moses," with a number of charts presenting the "laws of Moses" alongside their Hammurabian analogues.[4] This is not to say that all contended that biblical law was dependent on Mesopotamian antecedents, however. While some deemed the parallels "overwhelming," others highlighted the numerous contrasts between the two, with special emphasis on the absence of certain areas of Hammurabian law within the biblical collections.[5] Much of this analysis was delivered in polemical terms, with an obvious interest in demonstrating the moral superiority of the Israelites over the Babylonians. Thus, for example, some used the comparison to claim that the Babylonians placed a lower estimate on life, or that in contrast to the Babylonians, the Israelites viewed slaves as humans, not merely chattel.[6]

It is important to put these arguments in context. At precisely the same time that LH was becoming available to the public, the high-profile Assyriologist Friedrich Delitzsch (Fig. 4.1) was in the midst of delivering a controversial series of lectures on the theme of "Babel und Bibel." The first two lectures were delivered at the prestigious Singakademie in Berlin before the Deutsche-Orient Gesellschaft, with none other than Kaiser

of Chicago Press, 1904); and the first Italian translation was Francesco Mari, *Il Codice di Hammurabi e la Bibbia* (Rome: Desclee, Lefebvre & C. Editori Pontifici, 1903). The publication of LH in *The Independent . . . Devoted to the Consideration of Politics, Social and Economic Tendencies, History, Literature, and the Arts* ran on January 8, 15, and 22, 1903.

4. See, e.g., George Ensor, *Moses and Hammurabi* (London: Religious Tract Society, 1903); George S. Duncan, "The Code of Moses and the Code of Hammurabi," *Biblical World* 23.3 (1904): 188–93; Stanley A. Cook, *The Laws of Moses and the Code of Hammurabi* (London: Adam & Charles Black, 1903); William Walter Davies, *The Codes of Hammurabi and Moses* (Cincinnati: Jennings and Graham, 1905); Johannes Jeremias, *Moses und Hammurabi* (Leipzig: J.C. Hinrichs, 1903); Chilperic Edwards, *The Oldest Laws in the World: Being an Account of the Hammurabi Code and the Sinaitic Legislation, With a Complete Translation of the Great Babylonian Inscription Discovered at Susa* (London: Watts & Co., 1906); and Hubert Grimme, *Das Gesetz Chammurabis und Moses: Eine Skizze* (Cologne: J.P. Bachem, 1903).

5. For the former stance, see Edwards, who concludes that biblical law derived from the Babylonian Code (*Oldest Laws in the World*, 52). In contrast, A. H. Sayce holds that despite the similarities between biblical law and LH, the two stand in strong contrast to one another ("The Legal Code of Babylonia," *American Journal of Theology* 8.2 [1904]: 256–66).

6. See Sara A. Emerson, "Hammurabi and Moses," *Zion's Herald* 81.15 (1903): 458.

Figure 4.1 Friedrich Delitzsch (1850-1922), Professor of Assyriology at the Friedrich-Wilhelms-Universität in Berlin and Director of the Royal Museum's Ancient Near East Department, whose lectures on "Babel und Bibel" provoked international controversy. Courtesy of Wikimedia Commons.

Wilhelm II in the audience.[7] In Delitzsch's first talk, he drew on data from recent excavations to demonstrate that the Israelites had borrowed myths, religious concepts, and laws from the Babylonians. Although the tone was celebratory, with Delitzsch delighting in the many insights that were to be gained by the illuminating light of Babylon, the public response was critical. The reaction prompted Delitzsch to take a more forceful stance in the second lecture.[8] In this second installment, he argued that

7. Bill T. Arnold and David B. Weisberg, "A Centennial Review of Friedrich Delitzsch's 'Babel und Bibel' Lectures," *JBL* 121.3 (2002): 441. As Arnold and Weisberg note, the Deutsche-Orient Gesellschaft was in the midst of launching major archaeological excavations at Assur, Babylon, and Hattusha (modern-day Boghazköy, Turkey) that would put Germany on equal footing with the British and French (444).

8. Friedrich Delitzsch, *Babel and Bible: Two Lectures Delivered before the Members of the Deutsche Orient-Gesellschaft in the Presence of the German Emperor*, trans. and ed. Claude

in certain arenas, the *Babylonians*, not the Israelites, occupied the moral high ground; and moreover, that the Babylonian finds showed that the "Hebrew Scriptures" did not constitute revelation.[9] These lectures were quickly made available outside of Germany: an English translation of the first two appeared already in 1903, and by 1906, a complete edition of the three lectures was published together with critiques.[10] It is apparent that people's conclusions about LH and the Bible were inextricable from their response to Delitzsch's remarks. Consider, for example, this caveat by the editors of *The Independent* in their article "Hammurabi and Moses": "In placing the name of Hammurabi before that of Moses we trust that we shall not seem guilty of that disrespect for holy things which was charged to Professor Delitzsch for putting '*Babel*' before '*Bibel*' in the title of his famous lecture."[11] Others, such as William Walter Davies, took a more veiled route: "These similarities (between Hammurabian and biblical law) prove to *the more liberal critics* that the Hebrews borrowed their religious ideas and laws wholesale from the Babylonians. This they maintain in spite of the

Hermann Walter Johns (New York: G.P. Putnam's Sons, 1903), 70. Delitzsch proceeds to lament the fact that people were rejecting the data in favor of "a narrow regard for dogmatic questions" (70). On the shift in tone from the first to second lecture, see also Arnold and Weisberg, "Centennial Review," 445.

9. As an example of the Babylonians' superiority, Delitzsch points to the privileges that women had in legal and ritual contexts in Babylonia. It is here that a whiff of anti-Semitism can also be detected, for he suggests that with this more egalitarian stance, the Babylonians were influenced by "the *non-Semitic* civilisation of the Sumerians" (*Babel and Bible: Two Lectures*, 108–9). He saves the matter of revelation for the end, where again, his remarks take on an anti-Semitic tone, as he positions Christianity as an evolutionary advancement over Judaism (*Babel and Bible: Two Lectures*, 112). Arnold and Weisberg highlight Delitzsch's anti-Semitic stance, particularly in the third lecture and in his final two-volume publication, *Die Grosse Täuschung* (1920–21) ("Centennial Review," 448–51). As Arnold and Weisberg point out, in vol. 1 of *Die Grosse Täuschung* ("The Great Deception," i.e., the Hebrew Bible), Delitzsch expresses concern about the "great, frightening danger" that the Jews pose for "all other peoples on earth" ("Centennial Review," 448–49).

10. Delitzsch, *Babel and Bible: Two Lectures*; Delitzsch, *Babel and Bible: Three Lectures on the Significance of Assyriological Research for Religion, Embodying the Most Important Criticisms and the Author's Replies*, trans. Thomas J. McCormack et al. (Chicago: Open Court Publishing, 1906). My references to Delitzsch's talks derive from Johns's translation.

11. "Hammurabi and Moses," *The Independent*, January 22, 1903. This essay appeared in the same issue that published the last section of LH.

great superiority of Hebrew institutions over those of the Babylonians."[12] Whatever the take, it is clear that the debate about the relationship between "Hammurabi and Moses" was regarded as having a direct bearing on beliefs about God and the divine origins of Scripture.

Although the interest in proving Israel's moral superiority over Babylonia has lost steam, the debate regarding the relationship between LH and biblical law (especially CC) continues. Positions range from those who champion the independent development of CC and LH to those who advocate for a direct relationship between the two.[13] Intermediate positions include the postulation of a shared common source or of Canaanite intermediaries.[14] Such disparate positions are not surprising, given the mixed nature of the evidence. While there are twenty-five to thirty laws that parallel provisions in LH, there are likewise entire areas of law in LH that are "missing" from CC, as scholars have observed. Moreover, the quality of the parallels is uneven, as I indicate in the appendix.[15] The most

12. Davies, *Codes of Hammurabi and Moses*, 9; emphasis mine.

13. The position that CC depends directly on LH is advanced most strongly by Wright, *Inventing God's Law*, who situates this influence in the Neo-Assyrian period; see also Van Seters, *Law Book for the Diaspora*; and for critique of Van Seters, see Bernard M. Levinson, "Is the Covenant Code an Exilic Composition? A Response to John Van Seters," in *"The Right Chorale": Studies in Biblical Law and Interpretation* (Winona Lake, IN: Eisenbrauns, 2011), 300–6. While Wright allows for the additional reliance of CC on other cuneiform sources, he focuses mainly on the reuse of LH by the authors of CC. In his reconstruction, the many differences between CC and LH most commonly reflect the CC authors' efforts to revise their source. When CC displays "inconsistencies" that some identify as secondary additions, Wright explains them in terms of the authors' use of multiple precepts in LH (see, e.g., *Inventing God's Law*, 207–9). On the other end is Otto, who contends that the laws in *Mishpatim* have "indigenous" origins in Israelite legal practice, though he proposes that the laws were later influenced by the cuneiform collections at the redactional level ("Town and Rural Countryside," 17–21).

14. For an outline of the different positions, see William Morrow, "Legal Interactions: The *Mišpāṭîm* and the Laws of Hammurabi," *BiOr* 70.3–4 (2013): 310–12; and Wright, *Inventing God's Law*, 16–24 and 92–96. The postulation of Canaanite intermediaries long preceded the publication of Hazor 18 in 2012. Already in 1934, Albrecht Alt claimed that the casuistic content in CC derived from Canaanite codes, while the apodictic material constituted indigenous law ("The Origins of Israelite Law," in *Essays on Old Testament History and Religion*, trans. R. A. Wilson [Garden City, NY: Doubleday, 1967], 101–71).

15. Bruce Wells likewise states that "the degree of closeness can vary widely" and advocates for more precision in categorizing parallels. He proposes the following terms for assessing the

striking similarities are between laws in Exod 21:18–36 and LH, though even here, differences abound in order and content, especially with respect to the penalties.[16] The laws in Exod 21:37–22:16 display some parallels with provisions in LH, but these parallels are looser with respect to content and order.[17] The units in Exod 21:2–17 are even more dissimilar from LH. The male and female slave laws in Exod 21:2–11 share more in common with Late Bronze Age slave contracts than with precepts in LH.[18]

relationship between CC and other legal traditions (in increasing order of closeness): "resemblance," "similarity," "correspondence," and "point of identicalness" ("The Covenant Code and Near Eastern Legal Traditions: A Response to David P. Wright," *Maarav* 13.1 [2006]: 87–89). In a related vein, Morrow presents a helpful set of criteria for determining allusions: translation or close paraphrase; textual organization (i.e., content that appears in the same order); density of criteria (i.e., multiple points of contact); and uniqueness, as opposed to coincidence ("Legal Interactions," 312–13).

16. For different reasons (i.e., apart from the question of parallels to LH), Otto proposes that CC is rooted in a number of once-independent shorter collections, including Exod 21:12–17, 21:18–32, 21:33–22:14, and 23:1–8; for discussion, see "Aspects of Legal Reforms," 182–86; see further, Otto, "The History of the Legal-Religious Hermeneutics of the Book of Deuteronomy from the Assyrian to the Hellenistic Period," in Hagedorn and Kratz, *Law and Religion*, 212.

17. On the limitations of correspondences between some of these laws and LH, see Wells, "Covenant Code," 93–99 and 106–11. For Ralf Rothenbusch, the different relationships to Mesopotamian law in Exod 21:18–32 and Exod 21:33–22:16 apply both to "der Einzelsätze" (the individual sentences) and to "die redactional Zusammenordnung verschiedener Rechtsgegenstände" (the redactional organization of the different legal articles) (*Die kasuistische Rechtssammlung im "Bundesbuch" [Ex 21,2–11.18–22,16] und ihr literarischer Kontext im Licht altorientalischer Parallelen*, AOAT 259 [Münster: Ugarit Verlag, 2000], 394).

18. Cf. Wright, who contends that the individuals responsible for CC created Exod 21:2 and 7 on the basis of LH §117 and then drew upon the contents of LH §§119, 148–49, 154–56, 175, 178, and 282 to formulate Exod 21:3–6 and 8–11 (*Inventing God's Law*, 133–48). Yet the question remains as to whether any similarity between a *portion* of a law and a *portion* of another law is better explained by borrowing (or what Wright calls "cross-referencing") than by coincidence/convergent evolution. Thus, for example, as Wright points out, both Exod 21:8–11 and LH §149 require a man to support his first wife if he marries another. Yet the situation in LH §149 is in the context of a man's obligation to his ill wife (as Wright acknowledges) for the duration of her life, while the biblical unit pertains to an entirely different situation, a young woman sold as a slave-wife, with no explanation as to why her husband would take "another." Moreover, the threefold obligation of providing flesh, covering, and oil(?) in Exod 21:10–11 indeed surfaces with some variation in LH §178, as Wright notes, but this obligation refers to brothers' obligation to their priestess sister after their father's death, and these basic allowances correspond specifically to her inheritance share. LH §178 is far more detailed, moreover, and is primarily concerned with the problem of a woman's father failing to indicate in writing that she has the authority to give her estate to the person of her choosing. This trifold obligation, moreover, is

The apodictic laws in vv. 12–17 are too general to correlate directly with precepts in LH.[19] It is further notable that not all of the parallels within the biblical block correspond most closely to LH. Thus, for example, the unit with the closest parallel to Near Eastern law—the ox that gores another ox in Exod 21:35—corresponds most closely to a precept in the Laws of Eshnunna (LE).[20] The data thus suggest that we should account for the similarities between Mesopotamian law and CC in a different way.

also a common phrase in contracts, as discussed in Chapter 3, and as such, it is not necessary to assume that it derives from LH §178.

19. See, e.g., Wright's discussion of the "child rebellion" laws in Exod 21:15 and 17 and LH §§192–93 and 195 (*Inventing God's Law*, 35–36). Both Exod 21:15 and LH §195 indeed deal with striking a parent, yet the biblical unit deals with both parents and prescribes the death penalty, while the provision in LH pertains only to the father, prescribes cutting off the child's hand, and precedes the long series of injury laws in §§196–214. The case for borrowing and adaptation with respect to Exod 21:17 and LH §§192–93 is then less persuasive. The biblical law refers to cursing one's father or mother, an act that merits the death penalty; while LH §192 concerns a child who tells his non-biological parent (a "courtier or *sekretu*") that he or she "is not my father/mother," an act that is punished with cutting out the tongue. (The next law in LH then concerns a child who leaves his guardian's house for his biological father's house.) The verbal formula "You are not my father/mother" is not unique to LH but instead is a standard feature of Babylonian adoption contracts. While Wright acknowledges some of the specifics of the LH precept, he places more emphasis on what he deems to be parallel. Wright further argues that the apodictic regulations concerning cult, ethics, and justice in the outer frame (Exod 20:23–26 and 22:20–23:19) exhibit a host of correlations to the prologue and epilogue of LH. For a general critique of this argument, see Morrow, "Legal Interactions," 314–16, 319, and 323. Morrow focuses in particular on the use of the second-person singular in the apodictic laws, an unusual choice if the writer intended to imitate the epilogue of LH. For Morrow, these have a better parallel in treaty rhetoric (314–15). Alt was the first to draw a strong distinction between the casuistic format of laws (as known from the Near Eastern collections) and "apodeictic" laws, which he viewed as native to Israel ("Origins of Israelite Laws," 109–10). It is important to note that Alt distinguished the two types not only in terms of their grammatical constructions, but also with respect to their content: he observed, e.g., that "apodeictic law" covered serious crimes, while the casuistic laws dealt with practical realities (124–25).

20. The parallels between the goring ox sequence and its Mesopotamian counterparts (not only LE §§53–55 but also LH §§250–52) are often touted as the parallel par excellence (Morrow, "Legal Interactions," 320; Meir Malul, *The Comparative Method in Ancient Near Eastern and Biblical Legal Studies*, AOAT 227 [Kevelaer: Butzon und Bercker, 1990], 113–52, esp. 141–42). Malul concludes that the biblical author "knew first-hand the Mesopotamian work" (152). Jackson observes that the biblical unit is nearly a translation of its predecessor (*Wisdom Laws*, 280); and for Raymond Westbrook, the parallel is "virtually identical" (*Studies in Biblical and Cuneiform Law*, Cahiers de la Revue Biblique 26 [Paris: J. Gabalda et Cie, 1988], 40 n. 4). Roth, however, expresses hesitation about dependence across LH, LE, and Exodus 21, given the commonplace nature of oxen in society ("Errant Oxen," 403–4).

BACK TO (LAW) SCHOOL: INSIGHTS FROM MESOPOTAMIAN SCRIBAL EDUCATION

As discussed in Chapter 1, Mesopotamian scribes copied short sets of laws in the context of their training. On certain occasions, this practice involved copying an extract from a "canonical" law collection: most commonly, from LH. On other occasions, however, certain scribes copied a short series of laws that paralleled laws in the collections but did not replicate them precisely. The Laws about Rented Oxen (LOx) and the Sumerian Laws Exercise Tablet (SLEx) belong to this second category: while they exhibit parallels to the law collections, neither one constitutes an extract per se. Scribes also copied some precepts in the context of longer pedagogical works. Thus, for example, the Sumerian Laws Handbook of Forms (SLHF) includes about a dozen laws on boat mishaps and rented oxen, and *ana ittišu* (Ai) likewise preserves a handful of laws alongside verbal paradigms and contractual clauses. In a similar fashion to LOx and SLEx, the provisions preserved in SLHF and Ai do not precisely reproduce "canonical" law, but they do parallel this content. It is worth taking a closer look at this phenomenon, as it has the potential to facilitate a reassessment of Exod 21:18–22:16.[21]

The Sumerian exercise LOx (Fig. 4.2) is known from six copies and preserves about nine laws in total. All of the laws concern mishaps that could befall a rented ox. The first five provisions consider injuries to specific body parts of an ox, while the remaining ones concern the death of an ox by natural causes. The provisions overlap most closely with a set of provisions in the Laws of Lipit-Ishtar (LL) and to a lesser degree with precepts in LH. At the same time, LOx is not an exact replica of content from either collection. As is evident in Table 4.1, LOx §§1–5 and LL §§34–37 exhibit the closest parallels, though the two still differ in certain ways.[22]

21. As per the discussion in the prior section, I focus in this chapter specifically on Exod 21:18–22:16.

22. See also the chart exhibiting the differences among LOx, LL, and LH in Spada, "New Fragment," 13. The citations in this section primarily rely on Roth (*Law Collections from Mesopotamia*, 33, 40–41) but also incorporate the new readings in Spada ("New Fragment").

Figure 4.2 Two copies of the OB scribal exercise known as the Laws about Rented Oxen. Courtesy of the Penn Museum, objects N 4938 (https://cdli.ucla.edu/P228949) and N 5119 (https://cdli.ucla.edu/P231270).

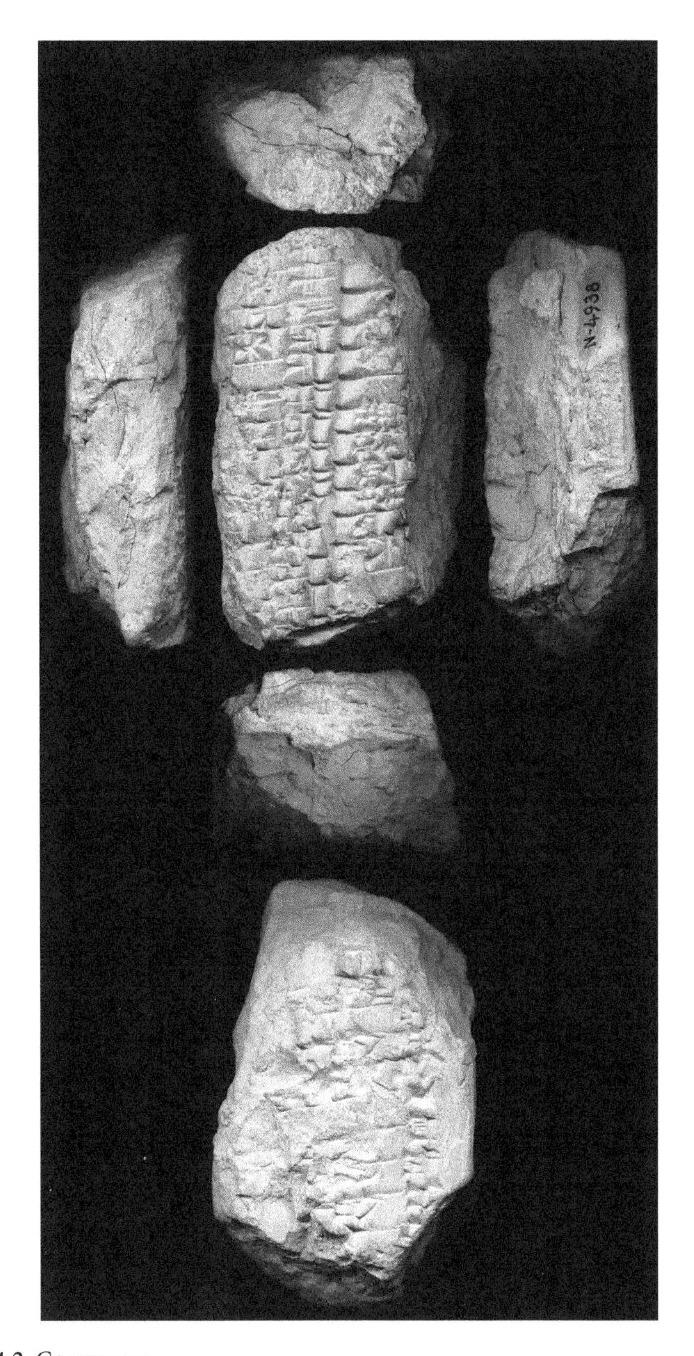

Figure 4.2 Continued

Table 4.1 Comparison of the Laws about Rented Oxen, the Laws of Lipit-Ishtar, and the Laws of Hammurabi

LOx	LL	LH
§1 If he destroys the eye of the ox, he shall weigh and deliver *one-half* of its value (in silver).	§34 If a man rents an ox and cuts the hoof tendon, he shall weigh and deliver *one-third* of its value (in silver).	§244 If a man rents an ox or a donkey and a lion kills it in the open country, it is the owner's loss.
§2 If he cuts off the horn of the ox, he shall weigh and deliver *one-third* of its value (in silver).	§35 If a man rents an ox and destroys its eye, he shall weigh and deliver *one-half* of its value (in silver).	§245 If a man rents an ox and causes its death either by negligence or by physical abuse, he shall replace the ox with an ox of comparable value for the owner of the ox.
§3 If he severs(?) the hoof tendon of the ox, he shall weigh and deliver *one-quarter* of its value (in silver).	§36 If a man rents an ox and breaks its horn, he shall weigh and deliver *one-quarter* of its value (in silver).	§246 If a man rents an ox and breaks its leg or cuts its neck tendon, he shall replace the ox with *an ox of comparable value* for the owner of the ox.
§4 If he cuts off the tail of the ox, [he shall weigh and deliver *one-*. . . of its value (in silver)].	§37 If a man rents an ox and breaks its tail, he shall weigh and deliver *one-quarter* of its value (in silver).	§247 If a man rents an ox and blinds its eye, he shall give silver equal to *one-half* of its value to the owner of the ox.

Table 4.1 CONTINUED

LOx	LL	LH
§5 If he [. . .]-s the . . . of the ox, he shall weigh and deliver *one-quarter* of its value (in silver).	—	§248 If a man rents an ox and breaks its horn, cuts off its tail, or injures its hoof tendon, he shall give silver equal to *one-quarter* of its value.
—	—	§249 If a man rents an ox, and a god strikes it down dead, the man who rented the ox shall swear an oath by the god and he shall be released.

It is first of all clear that the order is different: while LOx outlines injuries to an ox's eye, horn, hoof tendon, tail, and tendon, the sequence in LL is hoof tendon, eye, horn, and tail. Second, the penalties differ: whereas in LOx, the renter must pay one-third of the ox's value for a broken horn, the penalty is only one-quarter of its value in LL. The opposite then applies in the case of a cut tendon: in LOx, the fine is one-quarter of the ox's value and one-third of its value in LL.[23] Third, the wording varies: LL specifies "If a man has rented an ox" (tukum-bi lu$_2$-u$_3$ gud in-ḫun) while LOx omits the agent (e.g., tukum-bi gud X) and launches immediately with the injurious act. LOx and LL also display some variations in spelling.[24] It is also notable that the sequence in LOx differs from LL in that it includes an additional set of mishaps: the death of an ox while crossing a river (§6), a

23. See Spada, "New Fragment," for a new proposal regarding the verb used in the provision regarding the damaged tendon. The new fragment of LOx features a different verb for this particular provision, which Spada reads as ab-bu-us$_2$ ("tears out").

24. E.g., sa-sal-bi, "tendon" (LOx §3) vs. sa-sal (LL §34); šam$_2$-ba-ka, "its value" (LOx §§2, 3, 5) vs. šam$_2$-ma-kam (LL §§34, 35, 36, 37); and šu-ri, "one-half" (LOx §1) vs. šu-ri-a (LL §35).

lion that kills a yoked ox (§7), possibly a lion that kills an ox (§8), and another fragmentary situation (§9).[25]

The provisions in LOx also overlap to a lesser degree with LH §§244–49. Like LOx (but unlike LL), LH includes both ox fatalities and injuries to specific body parts. In contrast, however, it appears that LH includes additional injuries; and on two occasions, it also combines multiple body parts in a single precept.[26] We see a similar preference for combining injuries with identical penalties in LH §§198–99 (e.g., "If he blinds the eye of a commoner or breaks the bone of a commoner . . ."). The order in LH also diverges from that of LOx (and LL, for that matter). Finally, LH includes two additional situations that are not apparently represented in LOx or LL. One of these makes reference to an oath that the renter must swear, a theme that comes up elsewhere in LH. Given that (a) LL is the oldest attestation, (b) the provisions in LOx are closest to those in LL, and (c) both LL and LOx are in Sumerian while LH is in Akkadian, I suggest that the sequence in LL served as a source for LOx. It then appears that the scribes responsible for LH adapted the provisions in LOx (or another exercise like it) for inclusion in LH.[27] This adaptation also would have involved newly rendering the provisions in Akkadian. If this posited reconstruction is correct, the relationship between pedagogical exercises and the law collections went in both directions: that is, a law collection could spawn an exercise, but an exercise could potentially provide fodder for a law collection.

The provisions in SLEx are then less similar to provisions in the collections. SLEx is attested in only one copy (Fig. 4.3), and in this case, we even know the name of the scribe who drafted it: Bēlšunu.

25. Roth expresses uncertainty that §§8–9 belong to the composition (*Law Collections from Mesopotamia*, 40). While absent from LL, the contents of LOx §§6–7 do appear in two other legal-pedagogical texts: SLEx and SLHF.

26. It remains possible, however, that one of the fragmentary laws from LOx or LL included one or more of these additional injuries.

27. It is possible that the scribes responsible for LH also drew on something like SLHF as a source. Like LH §§236–49, SLHF follows boat mishaps with mishaps concerning rented oxen. Unlike LOx and LH, however, SLHF does not include injuries to specific body parts of the ox.

Figure 4.3 The Sumerian Laws Exercise Tablet (YOS I 28/YBC 2177), copied by the scribe Bēlšunu, dates to approximately 1800 BCE. Courtesy of the Yale Babylonian Collection; photograph by Klaus Wagensonner.

The ten laws and contractual clauses on the reverse of SLEx cover a variety of topics: damage to a fetus, boat mishaps, clauses related to adoptions, assault, and liabilities concerning rented oxen. These contents do not line up precisely with any one sequence in the collections. As such, SLEx is not an extract but instead more like a miscellany of "classic" laws. The provisions do exhibit some parallels to provisions known from the collections (and in one case, to a provision in LOx), however, as can be seen in Table 4.2.

Thus, the laws on striking a pregnant woman and another concerning a boat loss (SLEx §§2–3) correspond to precepts in LL (§§d and 5); and SLEx §9, a law regarding a lion that devours an ox, overlaps with LH §244 and LOx §8. Other laws, however, such as the assault laws in SLEx §§7–8, exhibit only loose parallels to precepts in other collections (Laws of Ur-Namma [LU] §6 / LH §130); and SLEx §§1 and 10 are not represented in other extant sources. Beyond the parallels, it is also notable that the

Table 4.2 Comparison of Provisions in the Sumerian Laws Exercise Tablet (SLEx) with Mesopotamian Laws

SLEx	Parallel provisions
§1 If he jostles the daughter of a man and causes her to miscarry her fetus, he shall weigh and deliver 10 shekels of silver.	—
§2 If he strikes the daughter of a man and causes her to miscarry her fetus, he shall weigh and deliver 20 shekels of silver.	LL §d If [a . . .] strikes the daughter of a man and causes her to lose her fetus, he shall weigh and deliver 30 shekels of silver (see also LH §209).
§3 If he alters his agreed route and thus causes the loss of the boat, until he restores the boat he shall measure and deliver one-half of its hire in grain to its owner.	LL §5 If a man rents a boat and an agreed route is established for him, but he violates its route and the boat . . . in that place—he has acted lawlessly; the man who rented the boat shall replace the boat and [he shall measure and deliver in grain its hire].
§§7–8 If he deflowers in the street the daughter of a man, her father and her mother do not identify(?) him, (but) he declares, "I will marry you"—her father and her mother shall give her to him in marriage. If he deflowers in the street the daughter of a man, her father and her mother identify(?) him, (but) the deflowerer disputes the identification(?)—he shall swear an oath . . . at the temple gate.	LU §6 If a man violates the rights of another and deflowers the virgin wife of a young man, they shall kill that male. LH §130 If a man pins down another man's virgin wife who is still residing in her father's house, and they seize him lying with her, that man shall be killed; that woman shall be released.
§9 If a lion devours a wandering ox, the misfortune falls to its owner.	LH §244 If a man rents an ox or a donkey and a lion kills it in the open country, it is the owner's loss. LOx §8 If a lion kills an ox or an ass(?) [. . .] in that place, he (the renter) will not replace (the ox).
§10 If a wandering ox is lost, he shall replace ox for ox.	—

tablet is "replete with ambiguities and mistakes," in Roth's estimation. For example, Bēlšunu tried to write tukum-bi ("If"), a compound logogram composed of five signs (ŠU.GAR.TUR.LÁ.BI), but he wrote the word incorrectly three times (ŠU.GAR.LÁ.BI).[28] He then copied the logogram correctly three times—possibly at the teacher's behest—as a way of reinforcing his knowledge. It is worth adding that the same pattern of omission that marks LOx is evident in SLEx, with the lack of reference to a specific agent (i.e., "If *he* jostles the daughter of a man . . ." versus "If a man jostles . . .").

The data thus point to an OB scribal practice of copying a limited set of laws, either on one theme (as in LOx) or a range of topics (as in SLEx); and either as an independent sequence (LOx, SLEx) or embedded in a larger work (SLHF, Ai). Although the provisions in these texts are related to the law collections to varying degrees, they do not constitute extracts, and it is also not apparent that copying these laws constituted a first step toward producing a collection. To some degree, this phenomenon reflects the general OB practice of scribes mastering Sumerian. Yet at least in the case of LOx, there also appears to have been a practical legal interest at work, in that some of the provisions overlap with clauses in actual animal rental contracts.[29] In a similar vein, the combination of laws and contractual clauses in both SLHF and Ai suggest that these two text-types were perceived as belonging together and as enhancing similar skill sets. As such, copying a limited series of casuistic laws appears to have been one more aspect of law-oriented training in Mesopotamia, at least for some scribes. At the same time, given the overlap of provisions from LOx (and SLEx, to a lesser degree) with provisions in LH, it is conceivable that Hammurabi's scribes drew upon some of this content in their composition of certain units in LH.

28. These translations rely on Roth, *Law Collections from Mesopotamia*, 42.

29. Spada, "New Fragment," 11.

PEDAGOGICAL INDICATORS IN EXODUS 21:18–22:16

It is now worth examining Exod 21:18–22:16 in the context of this Mesopotamian legal-pedagogical phenomenon. The unit covers damages of various types: a brawl between men that leads to a non-fatal injury, fatal and non-fatal injuries that a man inflicts upon his slave, a brawl that results in injury to a pregnant woman and/or her fetus, a man who damages his slave's eye or tooth, a variety of fatal accidents involving animals and people, animal theft and bloodguilt regarding a murdered thief, agricultural damage, the loss of goods during safekeeping, damage to borrowed animals, and a case of assault. The provisions are mostly presented in clusters, with the modification of certain factors, such as the severity of the injury or the status of the victim, used to generate different outcomes. Three features point to the origins of the unit in a legal-pedagogical exercise, comparable to LOx and SLEx: its limited focus on physical and property damages, its incomplete and disjointed nature, and its inclusion of ambiguities and errors. This latter feature is most apparent in the MT and appears to have prompted a number of modifications in the LXX and Samaritan Pentateuch (SP).

The Limited Nature of the Unit

One of the decisive arguments against the categorization of LH as a "code" was its lack of comprehensiveness. Bottéro referred to "disturbing lacunae in legislative matters," noting that there were numerous problems that remained unaddressed in the so-called Code.[30] Rather than cover general situations, LH tends to feature highly specific scenarios. This particularizing tendency is exemplified by the first provision: "If a man brings an accusation of murder against another man with no proof, the accuser shall be killed." While the "Code" addresses this specific situation, it features no law regarding the actual act of murder itself. But that is not the only

30. Bottéro, "'Code' of Ḫammurabi," 161.

omission. As Bottéro points out, nowhere does LH deal with criminality, the social hierarchy, political obligations, administration, or fiscal policy. To his mind, these omissions called into question the normativity of the so-called Code.[31]

Although the composers of LH did not cover every aspect of society, however, their efforts were nonetheless substantial. The work features nearly three hundred precepts on a wide range of topics, including the rental and cultivation of land, debts and interest-bearing loans, property safekeeping, marriage and divorce, inheritance, torts, ox rentals, hiring fees, slavery, and so on. Even the shorter collections, such as LL or LE, cover a comparable range of legal topics. In this company, the length and the limited focus of Exod 21:18–22:16 stand out. Exodus 21:18–21:36 deals exclusively with fatal and non-fatal injuries to free persons, slaves, and animals. Exodus 21:37–22:16 is almost entirely concerned with property damage.[32] In comparison with LH and the other collections, then, the biblical unit is both substantially shorter (fewer than thirty casuistic laws) and far more limited in coverage. It is further notable that the contents of Exod 21:18–22:16 parallel provisions known from the collections (mostly LH, but not entirely), but also diverge from their counterparts in the collections with respect to the order of the laws, the number of scenarios covered, and the contents of the laws themselves.[33] While these characteristics speak against the identification of Exod 21:18–22:16 as a law collection akin to those from Mesopotamia, they do resonate with the legal-pedagogical exercises in a number of ways. LOx was limited to the theme of damages to rented oxen and of limited length. SLEx likely included a limited set of

31. Questions about the aptness of the term "code" are not confined to the Mesopotamian collections; see, e.g., Karl-Joachim Hölkeskamp, "What's in a Code? Solon's Laws between Complexity, Compilation and Contingency," *Hermes* 133 (2005): 280–93, esp. 282–88.

32. The exception to the rule is the case of the assaulted virgin in Exod 22:15–16 (LXX 22:16–17). Its lack of connection to the units that precede and follow it suggest that it has independent origins, as discussed in Chapter 2.

33. A number of these parallels are addressed in the next two sections. See also the appendix for reference to the Mesopotamian parallels.

provisions and contractual clauses.[34] SLHF featured about a dozen laws. As discussed previously, LOx and SLEx overlap with but do not precisely replicate the order and contents of provisions from the collections. The notion that Exod 21:18–22:16 is rooted in some sort of analogous exercise would account for both the nature of its parallels to Mesopotamian law and its limited focus on the theme of damages.

Although the evidence is fragmentary, it appears that Hazor 18 may reflect a similar phenomenon from the same region. The two cuneiform fragments that make up Hazor 18 preserve about seven injury laws that overlap with but do not precisely replicate LH §§196–205. As noted in Chapter 1, its editors suggest that the fragments belonged to a larger tablet that may have contained as many as twenty or thirty additional laws, but also contend that the number was "most likely fewer."[35] Although the possibility remains that the tablet belonged to a series, it also may well have constituted the extent of the work. Hazor 18 is one of more than ninety objects inscribed with cuneiform that have been discovered in twenty-eight sites in Canaan, a phenomenon that is mirrored outside of Mesopotamia in the mid- to late second millennium BCE, when scribes in the region had to learn Akkadian for the purposes of international communication. As noted in Chapter 1, several of the attestations of cuneiform tablets in Canaan are Babylonian school-texts, including fragments of lexical lists at Aphek, Ashkelon, and Hazor; a mathematical prism from Hazor; and a fragment from Megiddo with content from the Gilgamesh Epic.[36] These data match the evidence at Ugarit, Emar, and Tell el-Amarna, Egypt, all of which have likewise yielded Babylonian school-texts. In general, it does not appear that these non-Babylonian scribes had access to these works

34. Based on Roth's discussion of the line subtotals for each column, the total appears to be in the vicinity of thirty provisions and contractual clauses (*Law Collections from Mesopotamia*, 45 n. 5).

35. Horowitz, Oshima, and Vukosavović, "Hazor 18," 159.

36. The Megiddo fragment corresponds to Tablet VII of the Standard Babylonian Version of the Gilgamesh Epic yet also differs from it (for discussion, see Karel van der Toorn, "Cuneiform in Syria-Palestine: Texts, Scribes, and Schools," in *God in Context: Selected Essays on Society and Religion in the Early Middle East*, FAT 123 [Tübingen: Mohr Siebeck, 2018], 140–41 n. 14).

in their entirety. Rather, the evidence suggests that they copied excerpts or simplified and/or truncated versions of "classic" texts.[37] In this context, it seems plausible that Hazor 18 reflects the copying of a limited set of Babylonian laws in Canaan in the context of scribal education. Although Hazor 18 and Exod 21:18–22:16 are not related directly, it is striking that the two are the only known attestations of Babylonian law in the "west" and that moreover, both feature talionic injury laws.

The Incomplete and Disjointed Nature of the Unit

The incomplete and disjointed nature of Exod 21:18–22:16 is apparent at various points, especially in comparison with the corresponding laws in the collections. Let us begin with the sequence of provisions on fatal and non-fatal injuries in Exod 21:18–27. This sequence corresponds most closely to LH §§199–201, 206, and 209–10, a set of laws that belong to an extended block of injury laws in LH §§196–214. Although the series in LH §§196–214 is not comprehensive, it does cover an impressive number of scenarios in a systematic fashion:

§196: *awīlum* blinds eye of *awīlum*
§197: *awīlum* breaks bone of *awīlum*
§198: *awīlum* blinds eye or breaks bone of a commoner
§199: *awīlum* blinds eye or breaks bone of *awīlum*'s slave

37. Compare, for example, the version of Adapa that was discovered at Tell el-Amarna, Egypt (for an excellent edition, see Shlomo Izre'el, *Adapa and the South Wind: Language Has the Power of Life and Death,* MC 10 [Winona Lake, IN: Eisenbrauns, 2001]). The Amarna version is considerably shorter than both its preceding Sumerian version and (apparently) from the Neo-Assyrian "version" known from fragments found at Assurbanipal's libraries, both of which feature a lengthy introduction and an epilogue that is not in the Amarna version (see Sara Milstein, *Tracking the Master Scribe: Revision through Introduction in Biblical and Mesopotamian Literature* [New York: Oxford University Press, 2016], 90–108). As such, it may reflect a truncated version of the myth, developed for pedagogical purposes. In a similar vein, the last line of the Amarna version of Nergal and Ereshkigal ends abruptly with the phrase *adu kīnanna* ("Until here"). In another publication, Izre'el surmises that the phrase reflects the teacher's oral instruction to his student (*Amarna Scholarly Tablets*, 60–61).

§200: *awīlum* knocks out tooth of *awīlum*
§201: *awīlum* knocks out tooth of commoner
§202: *awīlum* strikes cheek of *awīlum* of higher status
§203: *awīlum* strikes cheek of *awīlum* of equal status
§204: commoner strikes cheek of commoner
§205: *awīlum*'s slave strikes *awīlum*
§206: *awīlum* strikes *awīlum* during a fight and inflicts wound
§207: *awīlum* strikes *awīlum* and he dies
§208: *awīlum* strikes commoner and he dies
§209: *awīlum* strikes pregnant daughter of *awīlum* and she miscarries
§210: *awīlum* strikes pregnant daughter of *awīlum* and she dies
§211: *awīlum* strikes pregnant daughter of commoner and she miscarries
§212: *awīlum* strikes pregnant daughter of commoner and she dies
§213: *awīlum* strikes pregnant slave and she miscarries
§214: *awīlum* strikes pregnant slave and she dies

Certain scenarios are indeed missing from the LH sequence. There are no provisions, for example, regarding an *awīlum* knocking out a slave's tooth, striking the cheek of a commoner, or striking and killing the slave of another *awīlum*. Nonetheless, the relative coverage of the LH sequence is apparent in comparison with the biblical sequence. In contrast to the nineteen laws in LH, the sequence in Exod 21:18–27 covers only seven scenarios: a man strikes and injures his fellow man but he does not die (// §206); a man strikes his own slave/slave-woman and he/she dies either on the spot or shortly thereafter (~//§208); brawling men knock into a pregnant woman, causing two alternative outcomes (//§§209–10); a man strikes his own slave's eye (//§199); and a man knocks out his own slave's tooth.

The numerous differences from LH are not just a reflection of the fact that ancient Israel and Judah were less stratified. A number of expected counter-cases are missing from Exod 21:18–27. Thus, for example, Exod 21:18–19 refers to a case in which a man strikes his fellow in the context of a fight but "he does *not* die." Unlike the corresponding pair of laws in LH

§§206–7, however, there is no counter-case in which the victim *does* die.[38] Similarly, while LH §§196–99 prescribes penalties for an *awīlum* who damages the eye/bone of an *awīlum*, commoner, and slave, Exod 21:26–27 only considers a man who damages his own slave's eye or tooth, with no reference to a man who damages another man's (or slave's) eye or tooth. These gaps are all in addition to the lack of reference to other injuries or to pregnant victims of lesser status, as we see in LH. The biblical sequence is also more disjointed than its Babylonian comparand. LH begins with injuries to free men, commoners, and slaves and then logically moves to the unique circumstances of injury to a pregnant woman. The biblical unit, however, begins with a man who strikes his slave/slave-woman (Exod 21:20–21), then moves to the laws concerning an injured pregnant woman (21:22–25), and then *returns* to the matter of a man who strikes his slave/slave-woman (26–27). A similar pattern of disjointedness is attested in Exod 21:28–36. Exodus 21:28–32 and 35–36 address the matter of a goring ox, with both units assigning a harsher penalty if the owner knew of his ox's aggressive tendencies. While Exod 21:28–32 concerns human victims, vv. 35–36 feature a decimated ox. Unlike its closest cuneiform parallel in LE, the biblical unit interrupts this sequence with a law regarding a man who opens up a pit and inadvertently causes the death of an animal.[39] This has prompted some to regard either the intervening verses or the final unit as a secondary addition.[40]

38. According to Propp, "What the law implies but does not state is that, should the victim fall to bed and then die without having left his house, then the attacker is not 'cleared'" (*Exodus*, 216). Some (e.g., Jackson, *Wisdom Laws*, 172) instead propose that the case of a fatal blow is already "covered" in Exod 21:12–14. One would have to explain, however, why Exod 21:12–14 is separated from vv. 18–19 and why Exod 21:12 is delivered in a completely different style. It is also notable that Exod 21:12–14 is not set within the context of a brawl.

39. In LE §§53–55, a law concerning an ox that gores another ox appears back-to-back with that concerning an ox that gores a man and slave.

40. Rothenbusch treats vv. 33–34 as an insertion within vv. 28–37 that introduces a new emphasis on the *perpetrators* as opposed to the victims; he also notes its lack of a cuneiform parallel vis-à-vis the surrounding units (*Die kasuistische Rechtssammlung*, 326–36). David Daube likewise regards vv. 35–36 as a later addition ("Direct and Indirect Causation in Biblical Law," *VT* 11.3 [1961]: 261).

The theft unit in Exod 21:37–22:3 is also highly disjointed. In Exod 21:37, a man who steals an ox or sheep and slaughters or sells it must pay fivefold for the oxen and fourfold for the sheep. As indicated below in roman font, the situation covered in this law then appears to continue in Exod 22:2b–3:

> If a man steals an ox or sheep and slaughters it or sells it, he must pay five cattle for the ox and four sheep for the sheep. [*If the thief is caught in the midst of the break-in and he is struck*[41] *and dies, there is no bloodguilt for him. But if it is daylight (lit., the sun has risen on him), there is bloodguilt.*] He must pay, and if he has nothing, he shall be sold for his stolen object. If the stolen object is actually found in his hand—whether ox, donkey, or sheep, he shall pay with two live animals.

The continuation of the law states that if the thief cannot pay for the loss, he will be sold into slavery. If the animal is still alive and in the thief's possession, however, he only pays twofold (22:3).[42] Exodus 22:1–2a then interrupts this sequence with a different set of legal concerns. In Exod 22:1, the thief is said to be caught in the midst of the break-in; he is then struck and dies. This situation does not induce bloodguilt. In Exod 22:2a, however, the scribe clarifies that if "the sun has risen on him" (i.e., the manslaughter transpired in broad daylight), there *is* bloodguilt. Thus, while the external laws are concerned with the pecuniary penalties for a thief, the internal laws are concerned with the innocence/guilt of the owner. Not only does this interlude disrupt the logic of Exod 21:37 + 22:2b–3, but it also results in a nonlinear sequence, with unclear referents for the pronouns. After prescribing a penalty for a thief who disposes of his stolen animal (Exod 21:37), Exod 22:1 returns to the scene of the crime,

41. Cf. the SP, which states, "and he strikes him."

42. Penalties in multiples for animal theft indeed come up elsewhere in the Near Eastern collections; see, e.g., LH §8, which likewise deals with the problem of an insolvent thief.

stating that there is bloodguilt "for him" (presumably the owner of the house, though he is not mentioned). Then, after prescribing a penalty for killing the thief in daylight (22:2a), the culprit is again alive and well in Exod 22:2b–3.[43] This lack of logic has prompted many to regard vv. 1–2a as a secondary insertion.[44] Others suggest that the disjointedness is the result of scribal error.[45] As Bernard Levinson observes, the NEB goes so far as to "impose a text-critical solution," rearranging the sequence so that Exod 22:1–2a follows 22:3.[46] Whatever the case, the final form of the unit is disjointed to the point of incoherence.[47]

The Ghost of Bēlšunu: Ambiguities and Errors in Exodus 21:18–22:16

Exodus 21:18–22:16 is plagued by a number of other ambiguities and/or scribal errors. The focus of this section is the sequence of injury laws in

43. The phrase שַׁלֵּם יְשַׁלֵּם ("he shall surely pay"), which also occurs in 21:36 and 22:13, serves as a convenient connector between v. 2a and vv. 2b–3. Bernard M. Levinson viewed the phrase as "the elegant signature of [the scribe's] handiwork" ("The Case for Revision and Interpolation within the Biblical Legal Corpora," in Levinson, *Theory and Method*, 52).

44. See Levinson, "Case for Revision," 51 n. 40; and Cornelis Houtman, *Exodus*, vol. 3: *Chapters 20–40*, HCOT (Leuven: Peeters, 2000), 186. Paul takes vv. 1–2a to be a footnote, on analogy to Talmudic constructions (*Studies in the Book of the Covenant*, 110 n. 1); similarly, J. J. Finkelstein reads vv. 1–2a as an intentional, parenthetical thought (*The Ox That Gored*, TAPS 71.2 [Philadelphia: The American Philosophical Society, 1981]: 39). Cf. David Daube, who instead contends that v. 3 is a secondary addition (*Studies in Biblical Law* [Cambridge: Cambridge University Press, 1947], 74–101).

45. Schwienhorst-Schönberger, *Das Bundesbuch*, 162f; Joe M. Sprinkle, *'The Book of the Covenant': A Literary Approach*, JSOTSup 174 (Sheffield: Sheffield Academic Press, 1994), 130.

46. Levinson, "Case for Revision," 49.

47. In classic form, Westbrook attempts to save the coherence of the unit by means of a creative solution. To his mind, the unit has a threefold focus, which logically suits the nature of theft in the cuneiform collections (*Studies in Biblical and Cuneiform Law*, 115–19). According to this reasoning, Exod 21:37 pertains to the thief; 22:1–2a to the owner, and 22:3 to the buyer. The solution is creative in both senses of the word, in that it cleverly solves the problem and also invents a third party. For critique, see Levinson, "Case for Revision," 48–51.

Exod 21:18–25.[48] Not only is this unit rife with ambiguities and errors in the MT, but these issues also appear to have generated a set of corrections in the LXX and SP. The substantial number of variants in the text-critical evidence suggests that these details were already viewed as problematic or ambiguous by the ancients.

I begin with the highly ambiguous unit on the pregnant woman in Exod 21:22–25.[49] It is well known that this issue was a "popular" topic in the Near Eastern law collections: the quandary appears in various expressions in LH §§209–14, LL §§d–f, MAL A §§50–52, HL §§17–18, and the student exercise SLEx §§1–2. The matter is covered most systematically in LH. In a cluster of six related laws, LH assigns different penalties for a man who strikes (a) the pregnant daughter of a free man and causes a miscarriage; (b) the pregnant daughter of a free man and causes her death; (c) the pregnant daughter of a commoner and causes a miscarriage; (d) the pregnant daughter of a commoner and causes her death; (e) a slave-woman and causes a miscarriage; and (f) a slave-woman and causes her death. The other versions are less elaborate but for the most part similarly straightforward.[50]

In this wider legal-literary tradition, the opacity of Exod 21:22–25 stands out. It is first important to note that the biblical unit is the only version that features *two* men fighting and knocking into a pregnant woman.[51]

48. Outside of this sequence, however, see also MT Exod 22:13–14: "And if a man asks his fellow man—and it is maimed or dies and its owner was not with it, he shall surely pay." As noted in the appendix, the law appears to be missing the clause "to borrow an animal."

49. Schwienhorst-Schönberger likewise stresses the ambiguous nature of the unit (*Das Bundesbuch*, 82–87).

50. LL §§d–e is similar in that it prescribes different penalties according to the severity of the injury (miscarriage/maternal death) and the status of the woman (free/slave). MAL A §§50–52 likewise distinguishes between miscarriage and maternal death, but also considers other scenarios: §50 prescribes different penalties based on the gender of the fetus; §51 appears to refer to an injured surrogate, and §52 involves a pregnant prostitute who suffers miscarriage. The other Mesopotamian laws are only concerned with miscarriage. SLEx §§1–2 is distinct in its focus on intentionality. In the first case, a man "jostles" a pregnant woman and induces miscarriage; in the second, he "strikes" a woman and causes the same result. In HL §§17–18, in addition to the matter of the woman's status (free/slave), the law takes into account the stage of the pregnancy (fifth month / tenth month).

51. This peculiarity led Samuel E. Loewenstamm to suggest that Exod 21:22–25 had undergone textual corruption, in that the law dealing with a blow to a pregnant woman had gotten "mixed

This detail results in some confusion, for both men push the woman (וְנָגְפוּ אִשָּׁה הָרָה) but only one of them pays (עָנוֹשׁ יֵעָנֵשׁ), with no introduction of a new subject and no indication of how the guilty party is determined.[52] The blow then results in an unexpected phrase in the MT: literally, "her *children* come out" (וְיָצְאוּ יְלָדֶיהָ). Although Hebrew nouns are occasionally rendered in the plural to denote abstraction, it is difficult to say why an abstract noun would be intended, and the phrase may be a scribal error.[53] It is thus not surprising that both the LXX and SP render the noun and verb in the singular. This apparent modification is admirably economical in the SP: the redactors simply shifted the final letter of the verb וְיָצְאוּ to the front of the next word to read ויצא ולדה ("and the child came out"), a change that only required the elimination of a single *yod*.

More ambiguity in the MT then results from the use of the rare term אסון. In the first case, the "children" come out but there is *no* אסון, and the fine is thus determined by the woman's husband.[54] In the countercase, however, there *is* אסון, and in such a situation, "you shall give life (in exchange) for life" (וְנָתַתָּה נֶפֶשׁ תַּחַת נָפֶשׁ).[55] Outside of this text, the

up" with that of another law concerning the consequences of injury in a brawl ("Exodus 21:22–25," *VT* 27 [1977]: 357). He does not, however, provide a specific rendering of the two proposed laws. In reconstructing Loewenstamm's argument, Jackson clarifies that this would have involved an accidental transposition: the opening of v. 22 would have originally concluded with vv. 24–25, while the remaining content would have originally pertained to one man's blow to a pregnant woman (*Wisdom Laws*, 211–13).

52. As Schwienhorst-Schönberger points out, one would expect either that both parties should pay or an explicit indication that the actual striker shall pay (*Das Bundesbuch*, 82).

53. Jackson notes scholars' various efforts to account for the plural: the "original" case on which the law was based involved multiples; the fetus was amorphous and thus rendered as a plurality; or the loss pertained not only to the child but also to the loss of fertility (*Wisdom Laws*, 215–16 n. 22).

54. The first case also includes another rare term: the guilty party is to pay בִּפְלִלִים, a hapax legomenon that has been variously interpreted (cf. the LXX, which reads "court settlement" [ἀξιώματος]). Rothenbusch ventures that the term denotes a "Schiedrechter" (arbitrator) (*Die kasuistische Rechtssammlung*, 277). Loewenstamm takes it as belonging to the same "dialect" as אסון and denoting "some procedure of objective assessment" ("Exodus XXI 22–25," 358). For discussion, see Jackson, *Wisdom Laws*, 223–27; and Wright, *Inventing God's Law*, 180.

55. It is first of all unclear as to why the 2MS voice is used in the apodosis. Alt proposed that the use of the second-person voice represented an insertion of an Israelite law into "the old casuistic

term אסון occurs only three times in the Bible, and always with respect to Jacob's fear that אסון will "happen" (קרא) to his son Benjamin if he sends him to Egypt.[56] The typical understanding is that אסון connotes serious harm, so that the two cases in Exod 21:22–25 treat miscarriage and maternal death, much like LH §§209–10.[57] If the woman's death is implied, however, it is strange that Exod 21:22–25 does not refer directly to it, as in LH §210.[58] Some have thus proposed alternative interpretations. For Bernard Jackson, the first case refers to *premature* birth (but a viable fetus), while the second refers to miscarriage. In this reading, אסון thus connotes serious damage to the fetus alone. The advantage of this proposal is that it explains the lack of reference to the woman in the countercase. The disadvantage, however, is that it would make Exod 21:22–25 the only case in which a fetus is ejected but survives the blow.[59] Raymond Westbrook instead proposes that אסון signals uncertainty regarding the *culprit's* identity. In the first scenario, the culprit is known (וְלֹא יִהְיֶה אָסוֹן) and must pay, while in the second, he is unknown (וְאִם־אָסוֹן יִהְיֶה) and the *community* (lit. "you") shall give "life for life" (וְנָתַתָּה נֶפֶשׁ תַּחַת נָפֶשׁ). The advantage of this proposal is that it accounts both for the abrupt shift to

code" ("Origins of Israelite Law," 105). Wright suggests that the reason for the second-person voice is to introduce "a general law of wider applicability than just miscarriage" (*Inventing God's Law*, 177). In the context of reading this unit as rooted in a pedagogical exercise, however, it is possible to consider that the shift simply reflects a mistake.

56. The term occurs in Gen 42:4, 42:38, and 44:29. LXX Gen 42:4 and 44:29 both read μαλακία ("sickness"), a well-attested word that most often corresponds to Hebrew nouns deriving from the root חלה ("to be sick").

57. See, e.g., Wright, *Inventing God's Law*, 178. Rothenbusch notes that there are two main readings of the term: either it indicates a fatal accident or a serious but nonfatal injury. To his mind, the first option works better with the ancient Near Eastern parallels, while the second suits the use of the talionic formula (*Die kasuistische Rechtssamlung*, 295).

58. For Sophie Démare-Lafont, "Incrimination for two different offenses by means of a single, rarely used word goes against the usual concern of the legislator for terminological precision" ("Ancient Near Eastern Laws: Continuity and Pluralism," in Levinson, *Theory and Method*, 113).

59. As Jackson points out, however, Exod 21:22–25 is also the only case that features a brawl and an unfixed financial penalty, so it is theoretically possible that it is also distinct in this way (*Wisdom Laws*, 218–20).

the 3MS in v. 22 (עָנ֣וֹשׁ יֵעָנֵ֗שׁ) and for the abrupt shift to the 2MS in v. 23. It is unclear, however, how this reading suits the use of אסון in Genesis.[60] Moreover, if "unknown culprit" were implied by the term אסון, one would expect it to appear in Deut 21:1–9, the case of perpetrator unknown par excellence. Instead, the text refers to a corpse that is found in an open field and states "it is not known who struck him" (לֹ֥א נוֹדַ֖ע מִ֥י הִכָּֽהוּ).

More recently, Nicole Tombazzi has argued persuasively that אסון is best understood in terms of an intentional attack, a reading that also suits its use in Genesis 42 and 44. As such, the first scenario, with its lesser penalty, would refer to an unintended shove while the second would indicate an intentional act of harm on the part of one of the men. Accordingly, the two cases would be comparable to other biblical and Near Eastern provisions that are concerned with the presence or absence of *mens rea* (e.g., Deut 19:4–13; LH §§206–8; HL §§1–4). Tombazzi's solution helps account for the unusual appearance of *two* men fighting in the biblical unit, in that such a scenario would be more likely to yield an accidental injury to a bystander.[61] A similar concern with intent is also apparent in SLEx §§1–2, moreover, in that the first case concerns someone "jostling" a pregnant woman while the second involves a man "striking" a pregnant woman.

However one translates it, it is clear that the opacity of אסון was also a problem for the ancients. The LXX sidesteps the term, presenting an entirely different set of circumstances. Here the distinguishing factor is not injury but rather the viability of the fetus. In the first, the fetus is "not fully formed" (μὴ ἐξεικονισμένον), while in the second, it is "fully formed" (ἐξεικονισμένον). It is possible that this reading was fueled by something more than confusion about the Hebrew term. As Sophie Démare-Lafont points out, there was an active discussion in Greek thought regarding the point at which an embryo could be viewed as imbued with life, and this,

60. Raymond Westbrook, "Lex Talionis and Exodus 21:22–25," in *LTT* 2:345–47.

61. Nicole Tombazzi, "'If There Was an Attack': A Reinterpretation of *ʾason* as Intentional Assault" (BA Honours Thesis, The University of British Columbia, 2021). My translation in the appendix adopts Tombazzi's reading.

too, may have influenced the Greek translation.[62] Intriguingly, a similar distinction appears in HL, which assigns different penalties depending on the stage of fetal development: ten shekels for a miscarriage if a free woman is injured in her tenth month and five shekels if the woman is injured in her fifth month (§§17–18).

The unit finally concludes with a refrain that does not suit the context: "Eye for eye, tooth for tooth, hand for hand, foot for foot, burn for burn, wound for wound, blow for blow." This "talionic refrain" resonates with the physical injury laws in LH §§196–205, but there are a number of differences. The LH precepts do not include "hand," "foot," "burn," or "wound"; they *do* include broken bones and cheek-slapping; and none of them features a talionic formula divorced from action. With respect to Exod 21:22–25, it is unclear how the formula follows from the preceding cases. If the injuries refer to the fetus alone, the loss of a tooth would be irrelevant. If the woman herself is the referent, however, it is unclear as to why her pregnant state would be relevant in the context of an injured eye or tooth. The inclusion of a burn is also out of place in the context of a street fight.[63] It seems instead that the refrain represents a playful pedagogical formula, tacked on due to free association with the original conclusion of the apodosis, "life for life."[64]

MT Exod 21:18–19 also features various ambiguities and potential errors, several of which again appear to have generated variants. As discussed earlier, Exod 21:18–19 mandates a penalty for one who strikes another during a brawl but the individual does not die. The unit stipulates that the striker shall pay only for שִׁבְתּוֹ ("his period of inactivity," or lit., "his sitting") and וְרַפֹּא יְרַפֵּא ("he shall fully heal"). Both stipulations are

62. Démare-Lafont, "Ancient Near Eastern Laws," 111–12. Démare-Lafont cleverly proposes that the LXX reading was fueled by the translators' assimilation of אסון (*'ason*) to the Greek *asoma* ("without any body"), a process that she identifies as "homophonic contagion." It is unclear, however, how she determines that this process has occurred, given the absence of the term *asoma* in LXX Exod 22:22–25.

63. Regarding the disconnect between the woman's pregnant state and the loss of an eye, see Loewenstamm, "Exodus XXI 22–25," 358.

64. See also Van Seters, *Law Book for the Diaspora*, 112–18.

ambiguous.[65] Although the rare noun שֶׁבֶת can be associated with two roots—שבת or ישב—the vocalization implies the latter, as William Propp points out.[66] Most often, however, ישב literally denotes sitting or dwelling, and the notion of "sitting" due to injury (as opposed to lying, or שכב) seems unlikely. As such, some derive the noun instead from שבת ("to rest/cease," so, he shall pay for "his cessation," presumably from work), but this implication is more elliptical than one would expect from a penalty.[67] The construction of the second phrase (וְרַפֹּא יְרַפֵּא, "he shall fully heal") is also grammatically awkward. In all other contexts, the *piel* of רפא has an active meaning; as such, the phrase implies that the striker himself is to heal the victim.[68] Aside from the peculiarity of this proposition, the absence of a pronominal suffix ("him") is conspicuous in this context. Some early Jewish traditions tried to modify the phrase by stating that the culprit had to pay the medical fees, a proposal that actually brings the law closer to the corresponding precept in LH.[69] Similarly, the LXX states that the culprit shall pay for the victim's "remedy" (ἰατρεῖα).

The next pair of laws also exhibits ambiguities. Exodus 21:20–21 stipulates that if a man strikes his male or female slave with a rod and he dies on the spot, he (or "it," as in "the crime") is either "to be avenged" or "to suffer vengeance."[70] If the slave survives a day or two, however, he/it is not to be

65. Citing HL §10 as a parallel, Jackson proposes that שִׁבְתּוֹ refers to the provision of a substitute worker who can do the labor while the victim recovers (*Wisdom Laws*, 181). On the parallel with HL §10, see also Wright, *Inventing God's Law*, 168 and Schwienhorst-Schönberger, *Das Bundesbuch*, 57–58.

66. Propp, *Exodus*, 216. For the derivation from שבת, Propp notes that we would expect the vocalization **šobtô*.

67. This appears to be how the LXX reads it, however: ἀργίας, "idleness/rest."

68. Propp, *Exodus*, 217. Chirichigno is one of the few to uphold this reading: "The assailant is required to take care of the injured person until he is completely healed" (*Debt-Slavery in Israel*, 173).

69. Propp, with reference to *Targums*, the Syriac Bible, and *b. Baba Qamma* 85a–b (*Exodus*, 217). In LH §206, the striking man is to "satisfy the physician" (Roth, *Law Collections from Mesopotamia*, 122).

70. For the reading "it (i.e., the thing/matter) must be avenged," see Schwiehnhorst-Schönberger, *Das Bundesbuch*, 72. Taking into account the SP variant מות יומת that takes the master as the

avenged/suffer vengeance because "he is his silver" (כַּסְפּוֹ הוּא). As indicated by my translation, the subject of the two avengement phrases is unclear. Typically, an apodosis pertains to the penalty for the *culprit*; as such, the notion that the victim is the subject would be atypical. In an apparent response to this ambiguity, the SP changes both references to לא יומת ("he shall [not] be killed"), in turn making the striker the obvious subject. The phrase כַּסְפּוֹ הוּא (lit., "he is his silver") is also unusual. Generally, scholars extend it to mean that the slave is the owner's *property*, and while such an implication would be logical, it does not suit the concrete meaning of the term כסף ("silver/money") in all other contexts.[71]

***

Exodus 21:18–22:16 (especially the MT) is thus marked by a limited scope, disjointedness and ambiguity, and possible scribal errors. In comparison with the closest sequences of provisions in the Mesopotamian collections, the biblical unit is noticeably incomplete and disjointed, at times to the point of unintelligibility. The text-critical variants suggest that these points of incoherence were already perceived in antiquity. Given this cluster of features, I suggest that the MT text is rooted in a school exercise. Although the unit demonstrates awareness of some Mesopotamian laws, its narrow scope suggests that the scribes did not have access to a collection per se but rather to a limited set of provisions on damages. As for when Israelite/Judahite scribes would have had access to this proposed exercise, and in which language the exercise would have been written, one can only speculate. Hazor 18 does indicate that Babylonian law—on the topic of physical

subject, Henri Cazelles instead proposes that the master is also the subject in this phrase ("he must undergo vengeance") (*Études sur le code d'Alliance* [Paris: Letouzey et Ané, 1946], 54). What precisely is implied by vengeance is unclear; while some assume that the person is to be put to death (e.g., Wright, *Inventing God's Law*, 174), other proposals have been ventured. For thorough discussion, see Chirichigno, who concludes that the expression was used to implore the judge to issue strict recompense, given the slave's lack of representation in the community (*Debt Slavery in Israel*, 149–69).

71. It is worth noting that the Nuzi daughtership contracts regularly include the term KU_3.BABBAR-*šu* or KU_3.BABBAR^{meš}-*šu* ("his silver") to signify the bride-price that the adoptive guardian is to receive. Yet even in these cases, where the term "silver" likewise appears with a pronominal suffix, the interpretation of *kaspum* ("silver") is literal.

damages no less—was copied within the region of Canaan in Akkadian in the Middle Bronze Age. How one connects the dots between Hazor 18 and the Hebrew text of Exod 21:18–22:16, however, remains an open question.[72]

CONCLUSION

Altogether, it appears that Exod 21:18–22:16 shares more in common with Mesopotamian legal-pedagogical exercises such as LOx or SLEx than with the law collections. The classification of a biblical text as a scribal exercise, however, requires some further elaboration. Scholars have been able to identify Mesopotamian texts as scribal exercises thanks to a range of external/physical indicators and internal features. These include the archaeological context of the find; the tablet type; the handwriting on the tablet; the presence of mistakes; the doxology to Nisaba, the goddess of the scribes; the multiple attestations of a given text; the combination of works on a single tablet; the limited extent of the composition, and so on. Obviously, there are no external/physical features that can confirm the pedagogical origins of a biblical text. Nonetheless, scholars have regularly relied on internal factors to claim that certain biblical texts originated in pedagogical contexts and/or served a pedagogical function. It is widely recognized, for instance, that acrostic texts, such as certain psalms, likely played a role in scribal education.[73] William Schniedewind has recently suggested that various lists of nouns that are now embedded in narrative

72. Though Rothenbusch writes prior to the publication of Hazor 18, he stresses the presence of Akkadian texts—including a legal contract—at Hazor, as well as at other Middle Bronze Age / Late Bronze Age sites in Palestine, and emphasizes the cultural continuity between Late Bronze Age Palestine and Israel (*Die kasuistische Rechtssamlung*, 481–509). He identifies the city of Tyre as a plausible place at which Canaanite legal traditions could have been preserved and transferred; unlike Ugarit and Emar, both of which were destroyed in the Late Bronze Age, Tyre survived and could have been a "Vermittler kanaanäischer Kulturkenntnisse" (a mediator of Canaanite cultural knowledge") (511–12).

73. The acrostic psalms are Pss 25, 34, 37, 111, 112, 119, and 145. Marc Brettler has suggested to me that Psalm 112 may in fact constitute a poorly crafted school exercise (personal communication). See discussion in Schniedewind, *Finger of the Scribe*, 60–69.

contexts likely have pedagogical roots.[74] The fact that Exod 21:18–22:16 displays incompleteness, disjointedness, ambiguities, and potential errors adduces internal support for its roots in a scribal exercise. In addition, the evident derivation of Exod 21:18–22:16 from a work with foreign origins—much like the copy of the Babylonian myth of Adapa discovered at Tell el-Amarna or the excerpts from the Babylonian Gilgamesh Epic found at Megiddo, Emar, and Ugarit—adduces further support for its pedagogical origins.

Finally, there may be some extra-biblical evidence that Israelite school-texts were similar to those that were copied by Mesopotamian scribes. Schniedewind also makes a compelling case that the famous inscriptions that were found on two large pithoi at Kuntillet ʿAjrud should be understood first and foremost as pedagogical exercises. These inscriptions include a proverbial saying, several "model" letters, fragments of lexical lists, numerical exercises, and short literary texts with religious themes: all text-types with cuneiform pedagogical parallels. For Schniedewind, the Kuntillet ʿAjrud evidence strongly indicates that the cuneiform school tradition had a direct influence on the development of the Israelite alphabetic curriculum.[75] He situates this influence at the end of the Late Bronze Age, given the obligation of Near Eastern scribes during this period to learn Akkadian. To his mind, the fact that Akkadian texts were found in Canaan further indicates that this was the period during which such knowledge was transferred. Since curricula are notoriously slow to change, elements of this curriculum would have been preserved and adapted over centuries, into the Iron Age.[76] According to this reconstruction, it is at least plausible that an old Babylonian legal exercise could have been transmitted to Canaanite scribes and subsequently adapted into Hebrew.

While the later repurposing of Exod 21:18–22:16 as "law" is akin to the proposed trajectory for the Hebrew Legal Fictions (HLFs), there are some

74. Ibid., 88–94.

75. Ibid., 11, 165–66.

76. Ibid., 10–22.

key differences. The scribes who recast the HLFs added more freely to them, with the production of counter-cases (e.g., Deut 22:20–21) and additional "laws" in the style of the HLFs (e.g., Deut 21:18–21). As such, they put the classic Near Eastern method of modifying factors in a law so as to generate additional precepts to radical new ends. In the case of Exod 21:18–22:16, however, it appears that the inherited exercise was more or less retained and reframed. In part, these different editorial processes reflect the nature of the sources themselves. As I argue in Chapter 2, the HLFs were originally standalone cases, and as such, they lent themselves more readily to supplementation. In contrast, if LOx and SLEx are any indication, the exercise on which Exod 21:18–22:16 is based was likely a block of provisions, already in cluster format. As such, the scribes who recast it logically confined their contributions to the front and back ends. Yet the nature of the sources is only part of the picture. The heavy-handed agenda of the scribes who repurposed the HLFs is not at all on display in Exod 21:18–22:16 or in CC for that matter. In this case, it simply appears that scribes supplemented an old legal-pedagogical exercise on damages with their own ethical stipulations, cultic regulations, and judicial protocol, mostly at the end (Exod 22:17–23:19). In conclusion, Exod 21:18–22:16 indeed points to evidence of "Babel" before "Bible," but only insofar as it is rooted in a (lost) scribal exercise, not a Babylonian law collection.

5

The Distinct Nature of "Biblical Law"

Let be be the finale of seem.

—WALLACE STEVENS, "THE EMPEROR OF ICE-CREAM"

IN 1872, GEORGE SMITH, a young British Assyriologist, chanced upon a Babylonian precursor to the biblical flood story in the basement of the British Museum.[1] As the story goes, Smith was reportedly so overcome with amazement that he began to disrobe.[2] His discovery—what would later be identified as Tablet XI of the Gilgamesh Epic—indeed sparked such a stir that even Prime Minister William Gladstone was in the audience when Smith read his translation to the Society of Biblical Archaeology

1. Decades ago, my father introduced me to this playful and enigmatic poem by Wallace Stevens. Even though much of the poem eludes straightforward meaning (Stevens himself said that the poem captured "something of the essential gaudiness of poetry"), this particular line seems to permit application (Austin Allen, "Wallace Stevens: The Emperor of Ice-Cream," accessed March 12, 2021 at https://www.poetryfoundation.org/articles/70138/wallace-stevens-the-emperor-of-ice-cream). I thank Bernard Levinson for rousing fond memories of my own initiation into Stevens' oeuvre ("*The Right Chorale*," 3).

2. According to Vybarr Cregan-Reid, however, this oft-cited anecdote is only stated in a single source ("The Tragic Tale of Gilgamesh and George Smith," available at http://www.telegraph.co.uk/history/10321147/The-tragic-tale-of-George-Smith-andGilgamesh.html); for further details, see Vybarr Cregan-Reid, *Discovering Gilgamesh: Geology, Narrative and the Historical Sublime in Victorian Culture* (Manchester: Telegraph, 2013).

Making a Case. Sara J. Milstein, Oxford University Press. © Oxford University Press 2021.
DOI: 10.1093/oso/9780190911805.003.0006

later that year. Not only did Smith's find mark the beginning of serious investigation into the non-Israelite origins of the Bible, but it also threw into question beliefs about the age of the earth that were rooted in biblical notions.[3] It is not difficult to see the similarities in the responses to the "Code" of Hammurabi just a few decades later. Once the "Code" was made public, comparisons between it and biblical law were unavoidable, even if the comparison led to fierce debate regarding how to evaluate the parallels. Just as the Babylonian flood story called into question the uniqueness of biblical lore, the discovery of the "Code" would forever complicate notions of the distinctiveness of biblical law.

These responses may require redress, however (no pun intended). Tablet XI indeed revealed that the biblical flood story did not emerge ex nihilo, but its existence does not entail that the Israelites had access to Tablet XI per se, let alone the Gilgamesh Epic in its entirety. And likewise, while the discovery of the Laws of Hammurabi (LH) revealed that the Israelites/Judahites did not create the provisions in Exod 21:18–22:16 from scratch, its existence does not entail that they had access to LH or even an extract from LH per se. We can see that the scribes of Israel/Judah *did* have access to a set of Babylonian precepts on damages that overlapped to a certain degree with some Hammurabian provisions, and as a second step, that they rendered them in Hebrew, apparently with some adjustment. Without Hazor 18, we would be hard-pressed to prove that Babylonian law—at least in some limited form—made its way to Canaan, but the two fragments of Hazor 18 demonstrate that this transfer indeed transpired, at least with respect to provisions concerning physical damages. As I argue in Chapter 1, though, rather than assume that Hazor 18 reflects remnants of a "Code of Hazor," akin to the Mesopotamian law collections, it is crucial to take stock of what we have: paltry fragments of a sequence of talionic laws that echo but do not replicate Hammurabian law. In general, cuneiform fragments of Babylonian literary texts outside of Babylonia in the mid-second millennium BCE reflect pedagogical usage, and although we do not have the source for Exod 21:18–22:16, it appears that something

3. Cregan-Reid, "Tragic Tale of Gilgamesh."

comparable to Hazor 18 lies behind it: a limited set of Babylonian laws on damages, originally copied for pedagogical purposes.

* * *

One of the overlooked advantages of Martha Roth's essential edition, *Law Collections from Mesopotamia and Asia Minor*, is that she included several pedagogical texts alongside the major Mesopotamian and Hittite law collections: the Sumerian Laws Handbook of Forms, the Laws about Rented Oxen, and the Sumerian Laws Exercise Tablet. This choice was surely fueled by her own interest in the legal-pedagogical content, as attested in her dissertation on the Sumerian Laws Handbook of Forms. Yet she also must have believed that there was something to be gained by viewing the law collections together with the legal-oriented content that played a role in scribal training. These exercises preserve casuistic laws, but they constitute neither extracts nor law collections in the Near Eastern sense of the genre. The distinction is important. Copying a short set of laws—whether independently or as part of a larger pedagogical exercise, alongside other text-types—played a role in early Babylonian education, at least to some degree. Whether these laws were copied because of their repetitive structure and content, making it easy to learn for budding scribes; or because "law" belonged to the "classics" of Sumerian literature, alongside myths, debates, and hymns; or because it would help them write actual legal documents in the future; or because it provided fodder for intellectual debates about legal quandaries, we will never know. What we can say is that copying limited sets of casuistic precepts belonged to the realm of scribal education, just as the copying of sample contracts, legal clauses, and fictional cases belonged to Old Babylonian scribal training. And while the copying of this content would have aided scribes in mastering Sumerian, the overlap between this material and law in the "real world" suggests that language acquisition was not the only intention.

What does this material have to do with what we call biblical law? Not only does the legal-pedagogical material give us a sense as to how law functioned in a Near Eastern educational context, but the text-types themselves illuminate aspects of "biblical law" that otherwise would not be visible. With respect to Exod 21:18–22:16, the limited scope of the unit, combined with its ambiguities and errors, suggest origins in a scribal exercise, not a law collection per se. As for the "Hebrew Legal Fictions" (HLFs), these texts reflect not derivation from Mesopotamian sources but rather native efforts by Israelite/Judahite scribes both to practice contractual clauses and contemplate legal dilemmas. Although they employed the basic casuistic format of Near Eastern law (unless this is a secondary adaptation), their textual products were distinct: they featured direct speech and various legal parties, in certain cases, re-enacting legal proceedings; and they did not include spin-off scenarios (or "clusters") at the first stage. As such, they appear to be closer in form and function to the Mesopotamian fictional cases than to the genre of Mesopotamian law. One can imagine a quasi-"law school" setting, where young scribes debated the merits of limiting a patriarch's inheritance rights or contemplated why a *levir* would fail to fulfill his obligation, discussions that might have prepared the boys for careers as judges or court scribes. Unfortunately, as attractive as this picture is, certainty regarding the practical application of these pursuits remains beyond our grasp.

The trajectories of Exod 21:18–22:16 and the HLFs were broadly parallel, in that they were each taken up and recast as divine law, but they were also distinct. The damages exercise (Exod 21:18–22:16) was simply incorporated into a larger narrative context, with additions at the front and back ends. To a certain degree, this trajectory is not surprising: if the scribes originally inherited and copied the exercise as a unit, it is logical that they would have preserved it intact, down to the ambiguities and errors (at least in the tradition behind the MT). As for the HLFs, however, these units were originally independent, even if they were copied and/or learned alongside one another. It is thus not surprising that they do not appear in sequence in Deuteronomy. What is curious, though, is that the incorporation of the HLFs into a work primarily concerned with cult centralization involved the production of additional "laws" of a fundamentally different nature, laws such as Deut 19:11–13, 22:20–21, and 22:23–27. This use of the cluster method—something they likely picked up from Exodus 21–22—made the HLFs resemble fragments of an old law collection, as scholars have long surmised. Yet appearances can be deceiving. Once the new units are separated from the HLFs, it becomes clear that they were not composed in the interest of law, but rather of a brand of exclusive and uncompromising monolatry—as indicated by their overt overlap with Deut 13:2–19 and 17:2–7. By prescribing the same punishment of collective stoning to death for adultery, the disrespect of parents, and the worship of other gods, these later scribes brought the worship of Yahweh into the legal sphere. The result was the innovative notion that people could be legally bound to venerate Yahweh alone. And by reiterating more than two dozen times in Deuteronomy 4–17 and 27–30 that "these are the statutes, laws/judgments, and/or commandments," the scribes responsible for the final form of Deuteronomy rebranded the HLFs as belonging to the same category as ethical regulations, cultic precepts, and the "crimes" of non-Yahwistic worship.

Yet repeating this claim ad nauseam does not magically make Deuteronomy or part of it a law collection, just as the header "These are the *mišpatîm*" does not render Exodus 21–22 one. The genre of the law collection originated in the Sumerian city of Ur and flourished in southern Mesopotamia, and its adaptation in the ancient Near East remained a Mesopotamian / Greater Mesopotamian phenomenon: one inscribed in cuneiform, on clay tablets, by major powers largely for political purposes. In contrast, the Israelites and Judahites started with pedagogical building blocks and ended up with two distinct final products: in the case of Exodus 20–23, an old legal exercise framed with ethical and cultic regulations and imbued with divine authority; and in the case of Deuteronomy, a pseudo-"law collection" that had as its primary interest not law but instead the mandate of exclusive monolatry. This model helps explain why the provisions in Exod 21:18–22:16 do not recur in revised form in Deuteronomy: put simply, the nighttime thief, the goring ox, and the injured pregnant woman were of no interest to any of the scribes who contributed to Deuteronomy, for none of them had intentions of producing a law collection qua law collection. Although the final contributors to Deuteronomy chose to preserve and even supplement the HLFs, this choice was due to the HLFs' potential to be marshalled as fodder for promoting loyalty to Yahweh.

* * *

Returning to the debate about the distinctiveness of biblical law, it is possible to say that what we call "biblical law" is indeed distinct—but not for the reasons that certain intellectuals of the early 1900s advanced. It is unique because it is neither rooted in old law collections nor composed with the aim of producing an Israelite/Judahite expression of the genre. It is unique because its building blocks are rooted in legal-pedagogical exercises that originated in the sphere of scribal education. And it is unique because even though its final contributors cast it as "law," these scribes were ultimately more interested in the *application* of law to the sphere of worship and ethics than in the intricacies of law itself.[4] Contrary to popular belief, then, it is not that the Israelites/Judahites merely attributed their laws to Yahweh while the Mesopotamians credited kings with the collections. Rather, the Israelites/Judahites never had law collections in the first place. With respect to Exodus 20–23, the scribes repurposed an old legal exercise on damages, framing it at the front and back ends with non-legal content. As for Deuteronomy, the scribes' contribution was even more pronounced, in that they produced new "laws" and legal clusters, leaving the impression that parts of Deuteronomy 19–25 were rooted in an old law collection. But here we must finally let "be" be the finale of seem. When we examine what we call "biblical law" in the context of Mesopotamian legal-pedagogical texts, it becomes clear that its longstanding placement among the Babylonian, Assyrian, and Hittite law collections is inapt. In recognizing the practical roots of "biblical law," we can begin to reconstruct both the impetus for its emergence and the uniqueness of its trajectory.

4. The development of the Hebrew term *dat*, adapted from the Persian term *data*, neatly exemplifies this shift. As Adele Berlin points out, the term is employed repeatedly throughout the Book of Esther, where it has the semantic range of "law," "practice," or "custom." In later Hebrew, then, the term evolves to mean "religion," a term that is not covered as a distinct linguistic concept in earlier phases of Hebrew ("Esther," in *The Jewish Study Bible*, ed. Adele Berlin and Marc Zvi Brettler [New York: Oxford University Press, 2004], 1627).

APPENDIX

CHAPTER 1

Nippur Homicide Trial

Translated by Martha T. Roth, "Gender and Law: A Case Study from Ancient Mesopotamia," in *Gender and Law in the Hebrew Bible and the Ancient Near East*, ed. Bernard M. Levinson, Tikva Frymer-Kensky, and Victor H. Matthews, JSOTSup 262 (Sheffield: Sheffield Academic Press, 1998), 176–77. Used by permission of Bloomsbury Publishing Plc.

(1–5) Nanna-sig, son of Lu-Suen; Ku-Enlilla, son of Ku-Nanna the barber; and Enlil-ennam, servant of Adda-kalla, the orchard man—killed Lu-Inanna, son of Lugal-uru-du, the *nešakku* (official of the Enlil cult in Nippur).

(6–12) When Lu-Inanna, son of Lugal-uru-du, the *nešakku*, had been killed, they told Nin-Dada, daughter of Lu-Ninurta, wife of Lu-Inanna, that her husband Lu-Inanna had been killed.

(13–14) Nin-Dada, daughter of Lu-Ninurta, did not open her mouth, she covered it with a cloth.

(15–19) Its case was taken to Isin (for a hearing) before the king. King Ur-Ninurta ordered its case accepted for trial in the Assembly of Nippur.

(20–29) Ur-gula, son of Lugal-ibila; Dudu, the bird-catcher; Ali-ellati, the *muškēnu*; Puzu, son of Lu-Suen; Eluti, son of Tizqar-Ea; Shesh-kalla, the potter; Lugal-kam, the orchard man; Lugal-azida, son of Suen-andul; and Shesh-kalla, son of Shara-har, addressed (the Assembly).

(30–34) They declared: "As men who have killed men, they should not be allowed to live. Those three males and that woman shall be killed before the chair of Lu-Inanna, son of Lugal-uru-du, the *nešakku*."

(35–37) Shuqallilum, the chief of the troops, the soldier from Ninurta; and Ubar-Suen, the orchard man, addressed (the Assembly).

(38–41) "Given even that Nin-Dada, daughter of Lu-Ninurta, might have killed her husband—but a woman, what can she do, to warrant that she be killed?"

(42–43) The Assembly of Nippur addressed them.

(44–48) They declared: "A woman who does not value her husband might surely know his enemy; he might kill her husband; he might then inform her that her husband has been killed.

(49) Why should he not make her keep her mouth shut about him?

(50–52) It is she who (as good as) killed her husband, her guilt exceeds even that of those who (actually) kill a man."

(53–59) The Assembly of Nippur resolved the matter: Nanna-sig, son of Lu-Suen; Ku-Enlilla, son of Ku-Nanna the barber; and Enlil-ennam, servant of Adda-kalla the orchard man; and also Nin-Dada, daughter of Lu-Ninurta, wife of Lu-Inanna—were delivered up to be killed.

(60) Case accepted for trial in the Assembly of Nippur.

CHAPTER 2

Hebrew Legal Fictions (HLFs)

Exodus 21:7–11[1]

If a man sells his daughter as a slave-woman, she may not leave like the male slaves. If [she] loses favor in the eyes of her lord (אִם־רָעָ֞ה בְּעֵינֵ֧י

1. All of the translations of the biblical texts in the appendix are my own, with recurring and/or significant phrases indicated in Hebrew. Some of the ambiguous terms and phrases in Exod

אֲדֹנֶ֫יהָ) who designated her for himself, he must let her be ransomed. He does not have the jurisdiction to sell her to an outsider (לְעַ֥ם נָכְרִ֛י), for he has breached [his contract with] her. If he designates her for his son, he must do for her according to the right of daughters (כְּמִשְׁפַּ֥ט הַבָּנ֖וֹת). If he takes another, he cannot withhold her flesh, her clothing, or her oil. And if he does not do these three (things) for her, she may leave freely, for no silver (אֵ֥ין כָּֽסֶף).

MT Exodus 22:15–16 / LXX 22:16–17

If a man lures an unengaged virgin (בְּתוּלָ֛ה אֲשֶׁ֥ר לֹא־אֹרָ֖שָׂה) and lies with her, he must surely acquire her by means of a bride-price (מָהֹ֛ר יִמְהָרֶ֥נָּה) [to make] her his wife (ל֖וֹ לְאִשָּֽׁה). If her father flat-out refuses (אִם־מָאֵ֥ן יְמָאֵ֛ן אָבִ֖יהָ) to give her to him, he must pay silver (כֶּ֣סֶף) according to the bride-price of virgins (כְּמֹ֥הַר הַבְּתוּלֹֽת).

Deuteronomy 19:4–6*

This is the case of the manslayer who strikes his fellow unintentionally, and was not an enemy of his (לֹא־שֹׂנֵ֥א ל֖וֹ) in the past: [if] he goes with his fellow to the thicket to chop wood and swings the axe to cut down the tree, and then the axe-head slips off from the wood (i.e., the handle) and strikes his fellow and he dies, there is no death penalty for him (וְלוֹ֙ אֵ֣ין מִשְׁפַּט־מָ֔וֶת), for he was not an enemy of his in the past.

Deuteronomy 21:15–17

If a man has two wives (כִּֽי־תִהְיֶ֨יןָ לְאִ֜ישׁ שְׁתֵּ֣י נָשִׁ֗ים), one loved and one hated (וְהָאַחַ֣ת שְׂנוּאָ֔ה)—and the loved one and the hated one (both) bear sons, and the firstborn son belongs to the hated—on the day that [the man] bequeaths his inheritance to his sons, he is not allowed (לֹ֣א יוּכַ֗ל) to make the son of the loved one "firstborn" over the son of the hated one, the (actual) firstborn. For he must acknowledge the son of the hated (wife) as the firstborn [and] give him a double portion of all that he possesses,

21:7–11 are discussed in Chapter 3; for further discussion, see Sara Milstein, "Insights from Tradition into the Biblical Law of the Slavewoman (Exodus 21,7–11)," *BN* 189 (2021): 29–44.

for he is the first of his vigor. To him belongs the right of the firstborn (לוֹ מִשְׁפַּט הַבְּכֹרָה).

Deuteronomy 22:13–19

If a man takes a wife (כִּי־יִקַּח אִישׁ אִשָּׁה), has intercourse with her, and hates her (וּשְׂנֵאָהּ); and he makes an incendiary claim[2] against her and gives her a bad name, stating: "I married this woman, [but when] I approached her, I did not find within her [proof of] virginity (בְּתוּלִים)," the father of the young woman and her mother shall take and bring out the [proof of] virginity of the young woman before the elders of the city at the gate (אֶל־זִקְנֵי הָעִיר הַשָּׁעְרָה). And the father of the young woman (אֲבִי הַנַּעֲרָ) shall say to the elders, "I gave my daughter to this man for a wife and he has hated her, and now he has made an incendiary claim against her, saying, 'I did not find [proof of] virginity in your daughter,' but this is the [proof of] my daughter's virginity," and they shall spread out the cloth before the elders of the city. And the elders of that city (זִקְנֵי הָעִיר־הַהִוא) shall take the man and discipline him:[3] they shall fine him one hundred shekels (מֵאָה כֶסֶף) and give it to the father of the young woman because he brought a bad name on a virgin of Israel; and she shall (remain) his wife. He is not allowed to divorce her (lit. "send her out") during his lifetime (וְלוֹ־תִהְיֶה לְאִשָּׁה לֹא־יוּכַל לְשַׁלְּחָהּ כָּל־יָמָיו).

Deuteronomy 22:28–29

If a man comes upon a young woman (נַעֲרָ)— an unengaged virgin (בְתוּלָה אֲשֶׁר לֹא־אֹרָשָׂה)—and seizes her and lies with her (וְשָׁכַב עִמָּהּ) and they are found, the man who lay with her shall give fifty shekels (חֲמִשִּׁים כָּסֶף) to the father of the young woman (לַאֲבִי הַנַּעֲרָ), and she shall be his wife (לוֹ־תִהְיֶה לְאִשָּׁה) on account of the fact that he raped her. He is not

2. Wells notes that this singular expression (עֲלִילֹת דְּבָרִים) has been interpreted as pertaining to a formal accusation ("Sex, Lies, and Virginal Rape," 58).

3. Cf. Wells, who interprets יסר instead as "flogging" and in turn understands the man to receive a threefold punishment: flogging, a fine, and the loss of divorce rights ("Sex, Lies, and Virginal Rape," 43).

allowed to divorce her (lit., "send her out") during his lifetime (לֹא־יוּכַל שַׁלְּחָהּ כָּל־יָמָיו).

Deuteronomy 24:1–4a

If a man takes a wife (כִּי־יִקַּח אִישׁ אִשָּׁה) and marries her (וּבְעָלָהּ), and if she (then) no longer finds favor in his eyes (אִם־לֹא תִמְצָא־חֵן בְּעֵינָיו), for he finds something repulsive[4] about her, and he writes her a divorce contract, puts it in her hand, and sends her out of his house (וְשִׁלְּחָהּ מִבֵּיתוֹ), and she leaves his house and goes and marries another man, and the subsequent man hates her (וּשְׂנֵאָהּ הָאִישׁ הָאַחֲרוֹן) and writes her a divorce contract, puts it in her hand, and sends her out of his house—or if the second man who took her for himself as a wife (לְקָחָהּ לוֹ לְאִשָּׁה) dies—the first husband who divorced her is not allowed (לֹא־יוּכַל) to take her as his wife again.[5]

Deuteronomy 25:5–10

If brothers dwell together and one of them dies and he has no son, the wife of the dead man shall not marry a strange man outside [the family]; [rather] her husband's designate shall come to her and take her for himself as a wife (וּלְקָחָהּ לוֹ לְאִשָּׁה) and support her. And it shall be that the first-born (הַבְּכוֹר) that she bears shall rise upon the name of his dead brother so that [the brother's] name shall not be wiped out from Israel. But if the man does not want to marry his sister-in-law, his sister-in-law shall go up to the gate, to the elders (הַשַּׁעְרָה אֶל־הַזְּקֵנִים), and state, "My husband's designate refuses to establish a name in Israel for his brother; he is not willing to support me." And the elders of his city (זִקְנֵי־עִירוֹ) shall summon him and they shall speak to him, and if he takes a stand and states, "I do not want to marry her," his sister-in-law shall approach him before the

4. The rare phrase עֶרְוַת דָּבָר (lit., "nakedness of a thing") occurs elsewhere only in Deuteronomy 23:15, with reference to excrement. The first term (עֶרְוָה) is most commonly translated "nakedness" and occurs more frequently in construct form, usually in the context of forbidden sexual unions (e.g., עֶרְוַת אָבִיךָ, "the nakedness of your father," as in Lev 18:7) or with a possessive suffix (e.g., עֶרְוָתְךָ, "your nakedness," as in Lev 18:10).

5. I take the rest of v. 4 to be secondary; see discussion in Chapter 2.

elders, remove his sandal from his foot, spit in his face, testify, and say, "Thus shall be done to the man who does not build up his brother's house." And his name in Israel shall [henceforth] be called "The house of the one whose sandal was removed."

Secondary Additions to the HLFs

Deuteronomy 17:2–7

If there is found in your midst (כִּֽי־יִמָּצֵ֤א בְקִרְבְּךָ֙)—in one of your gates that Yahweh your God is giving to you—a man or woman who does what is evil in the eyes of Yahweh your God, transgressing his covenant—and he goes and serves other gods and bows down to them—to the sun or to the moon or to any celestial body that I did not command—and it is reported to you, and you hear [it] and investigate well and if it is true, the claim is established, this abomination occurred in Israel, you shall take this man or this woman who did this evil thing to your gates and you shall pelt them to death with stones (וְהוֹצֵאתָ֣ אֶת־הָאִ֣ישׁ הַה֡וּא א֣וֹ אֶת־הָאִשָּׁ֨ה הַהִ֜וא אֲשֶׁר֩ עָשׂ֨וּ אֶת־הַדָּבָ֥ר הָרָ֛ע הַזֶּ֖ה אֶל־שְׁעָרֶ֑יךָ אֶת־הָאִ֕ישׁ א֖וֹ אֶת־הָאִשָּׁ֑ה וּסְקַלְתָּ֥ם בָּאֲבָנִ֖ים וָמֵֽתוּ). The man who is to die (lit. "the dead man") shall be put to death on the testimony of two or three witnesses; he shall not be put to death on the testimony of one witness. The hand of the witnesses shall be upon him first to kill him, and the hand of all the people [shall be] afterward; and you shall exterminate the evil from your midst (וּבִעַרְתָּ֥ הָרָ֖ע מִקִּרְבֶּֽךָ).

Deuteronomy 19:11–13

And if there is a man who *is* the enemy of his fellow man and lies in wait for him, rises up against him, and fatally strikes him, and he escapes to one of these cities, the elders of his city shall send for and take him from there and hand him over into the hand of the blood avenger to be put to death.[6] And you shall not look with compassion on him; you shall exterminate

6. Here I follow the SP (והומת) as opposed to the MT (ומת).

the innocent blood from Israel (וּבִעַרְתָּ דַם־הַנָּקִי מִיִּשְׂרָאֵל) and it shall go well for you.

Deuteronomy 21:18–21

If a man has a rebellious and disobedient son who does not listen to his father or his mother, and they discipline him (וְיִסְּרוּ אֹתוֹ) but he [still] does not listen to them, his father and mother shall seize him (וְתָפְשׂוּ בוֹ) and take him to the elders of his city (וְהוֹצִיאוּ אֹתוֹ אֶל־זִקְנֵי עִירוֹ), and to the gate of his place (וְאֶל־שַׁעַר מְקֹמוֹ). And they shall say to the elders[7] of his city, "This son of ours is rebellious and disobedient. He does not listen to us. He is a glutton and a drunkard." And all the men of his city shall stone him to death with stones (וּרְגָמֻהוּ כָּל־אַנְשֵׁי עִירוֹ בָאֲבָנִים וָמֵת), and you shall exterminate the evil from your midst (וּבִעַרְתָּ הָרָע מִקִּרְבֶּךָ), and all Israel shall hear and be afraid.

Deuteronomy 22:20–21

But if this claim was true, evidence of the young woman's virginity was not found, they shall take the young woman to the entrance of her father's house and the men of her city shall pelt her to death with stones (וְהוֹצִיאוּ אֶת־הַנַּעֲרָ אֶל־פֶּתַח בֵּית־אָבִיהָ וּסְקָלוּהָ אַנְשֵׁי עִירָהּ בָּאֲבָנִים וָמֵתָה), for she did a scandalous thing in Israel—having illicit sex [while in] her father's house—and you shall exterminate the evil from your midst (וּבִעַרְתָּ הָרָע מִקִּרְבֶּךָ).

Deuteronomy 22:22

If a man is caught (כִּי־יִמָּצֵא אִישׁ) lying with a woman who is married to a husband (עִם־אִשָּׁה בְעֻלַת־בַּעַל), both of them shall die (וּמֵתוּ גַּם־שְׁנֵיהֶם): the man who lay with the woman and the woman; and you shall exterminate the evil from your midst (וּבִעַרְתָּ הָרָע מִיִּשְׂרָאֵל).

7. The SP and LXX instead read "to the men [of his city]," apparently anticipating the people in v. 21.

Deuteronomy 22:23–27

If there is a young woman, a virgin engaged to a man, and a man comes upon her in the city and lies with her, you shall take the two of them to the gate of that city and pelt them to death with stones (וְהוֹצֵאתֶם אֶת־שְׁנֵיהֶם אֶל־שַׁעַר ׀ הָעִיר הַהִוא וּסְקַלְתֶּם אֹתָם בָּאֲבָנִים)—the young woman because she did not cry out in the city and the man because he debased the wife of his fellow man—and you shall exterminate the evil from your midst (וּבִעַרְתָּ הָרָע מִקִּרְבֶּךָ).

But if the man comes upon the engaged young woman in the field, and the man overpowers her and lies with her, only the man shall die. As for the young woman, you shall not do a thing. The young woman has not committed a sin deserving of death (אֵין לַנַּעֲרָ חֵטְא מָוֶת), for this is like a man who rises up against his fellow man and murders him: so is this case. For he came upon her in the field, the engaged girl cried out, and she had no savior.

CHAPTER 3

Sample Nuzi Contract of "Daughterhood and Daughter-in-Law-Hood"

Text II (N 26), from Nuzi

The tablet of daughterhood and daughter-in-law-hood[8]

of ^{m}Teḫip-tilla, son of ^{m}Puhi-šenni.[9]

^{m}Iuki, son of ^{m}Mazi-ili,

8. I base my translation on the Akkadian transliterations provided in Breneman, "Nuzi Marriage Tablets," 132–33.

9. The "buyer" in this text, Teḫip-tilla, was one of the richest men at Nuzi: over two hundred texts feature him acquiring land; and he adopts people into his household on at least seven occasions. Teḫip-tilla's house was excavated during one of the initial excavation seasons (Jeanette Fincke, "The Nuzi Collection of the Harvard Semitic Museum," in *Nuzi at Seventy-Five*, ed. David I. Owen and Gernot Wilhelm, SCCNH 10 [Bethesda, MD: CDL Press, 1999], 14). The superscript ^{m} corresponds to the male determinative, and the superscript ^{f} corresponds to the female determinative.

gave his daughter fŠiluya,

for daughterhood and for daughter-in-law-hood (*ana mārtūti u ana kallatūti*)

to mTeḫip-tilla.

And mTeḫip-tilla gave [her] into wifehood (*aššūtu*)

to mAkip-šarri, his slave.[10]

If mAkip-šarri dies,

then mTeḫip-tilla shall give fŠiluya

to another [of] his slaves.

And as long as fŠiluya lives,

she shall not go out from the house of mTeḫip-tilla.

And mTeḫip-tilla gave forty-five shekels of silver

to mIuki.

CHAPTER 4

Exodus 21:18–22:14

Exodus 21:18–19 // LH §206 // HL §10

And if men are fighting, and one man strikes his fellow man with a stone or fist and he does not die but takes to (his) bed, if he gets up and walks about outside on his staff, the striker is free from guilt; he shall pay only for his (period of) inactivity and he shall fully heal.[11]

10. Cf. Cyrus Gordon ("Fifteen Nuzi Tablets Relating to Women," *Le Muséon* 48 [1935]: 113–32), who instead transliterates *a-na* m*a-kip-šarri a-na amti-šu* (reading GEME$_2$-*šu*) and translates: "to Akipšarri, as his handmaid." The signs ÌR-*šu* (*wardīšu*, "his slave") are clear, however (Brigitte Lion, personal communication).

11. The reader is encouraged to consult Roth's volume, *Law Collections from Mesopotamia*, for the referenced Near Eastern parallels. "Loose" parallels are indicated by the sign ~ and closer parallels are preceded by //. As should be clear from Chapter 4, I do not suggest that the biblical unit reflects firsthand knowledge of these collections per se. It is important to note that the parallels are looser from Exod 21:37 on, and not all closest parallels derive from LH.

Exodus 21:20–21 ~ HL §2

If a man strikes his slave or his slave-woman with a club and he dies on the spot, he shall be avenged. But if he survives a day or two, he shall not be avenged because he is his silver.

Exodus 21:22–25 // LH §§209–10 // MAL A §50 // SLEx §§1–2 // HL §§17–18

And if men are wrestling with each other and they push a pregnant woman and her children come out but it is not an (intentional) attack, he shall be strictly fined, according to what the woman's husband determines, and he shall pay with judges. But if it is an attack, you shall give life for life.

Eye for eye, tooth for tooth, hand for hand, foot for foot, burn for burn, wound for wound, blow for blow.

Exodus 21:26–27 // LH §199 // HL §8

And if a man strikes the eye of his male slave or the eye of his slave-woman and ruins it, he shall set him free on account of his eye. And if (he knocks out) the tooth of his slave or the tooth of his slave-woman, he shall set him free on account of his tooth.

Exodus 21:28–32 // LH §§250–52 // LE §§54–55

If an ox gores a man or woman and he dies, the ox shall be stoned and its flesh should not be eaten, but the owner of the ox is innocent. But if the ox had gored previously, and its owner was admonished but did not guard it,[12] and a man or woman is killed, the ox shall be stoned and also its owner shall die. But if a ransom is set upon him, he shall give a ransom (for) his life, in accordance with all that is set upon him. If it gores a boy or girl, (the same) shall be done for him according to this law. If it gores a male slave or female slave, he shall give thirty shekels of silver to his owner and the ox shall be stoned.

12. Cf. the LXX, which reads ". . . did not destroy it."

Exodus 21:33–34 ~ LH §263

If a man opens a pit or if a man digs a pit and does not cover it up, and an ox or donkey falls into it, the owner of the pit must pay; he shall restore silver to his owner and the carcass shall belong to him.

Exodus 21:35–36 // LE §53

And if a man's ox strikes the ox of his fellow and it dies, they shall sell the living ox and divide the money, and they shall also divide the carcass. But if it was known that the ox had gored previously and its owner did not guard it, [the owner] shall surely pay, ox for ox; the carcass shall belong to him.

Exodus 21:37–22:3 ~ LH §8 ~ LE §13 ~ HL §§59ff + 70

If a man steals an ox or sheep and slaughters it or sells it, he must pay five cattle for the ox and four sheep for the sheep. If the thief is caught in the midst of the break-in and he is struck and dies, there is no bloodguilt for him. But if the sun has risen on him, there is bloodguilt. He must pay, and if he has nothing, he shall be sold for his stolen object. If the stolen object is actually found in his hand—whether ox, donkey, or sheep—he shall pay with two live animals.

Exodus 22:4 ~ HL §§104–6

If a man causes a field or vineyard to be consumed by letting forth his cattle, and it consumes another's field, he must pay from the choice[13] of his field or the choice of his vineyard.[14]

13. Following Rashi ("the best of his field he shall pay"); similarly, the Syriac reads ומטוב.

14. The ambiguity of this law is compounded by the closeness of the terms "cattle" and "burning." The primary definition of the root בער carries the double meaning of "burn" and "consume" (similar to the use of "consume" in English), and is also used in the recurring formula in Deuteronomy ("you shall exterminate the evil . . ."). *BDB* then lists a second denominative verb "to be brutish," with only this verse listed as a use of the proposed meaning of a *hiphil* form, "to be grazed over." The proposed verb derives from the somewhat rare noun "cattle" (בְּעִיר), a term that is close to the hapax legomenon "burning" (בְּעֵרָה) that appears in the following verse. The term "his cattle" is also a *ketiv/qere*': [בְּעִירֹו] אֶת־בעירה. With different pointing in the *ketiv*, it could be read as "burning." In fact, with different pointing of the verbs, the same verse could be read, "If a man burned his field or vineyard, and (when) he set the fire,

Exodus 22:5

If a fire spreads and comes upon thorns, and a stack or the standing grain or the field is consumed, the one who started the fire shall fully pay.[15]

Exodus 22:6–8 ~ LH §§125–26 ~ LE §§ 36–37

If a man gives silver or property to his fellow man to guard, and it is stolen from the man's house, if the thief is caught, he shall pay twofold. If the thief is not caught, the owner of the house must be brought before the god and must swear that he did not touch his fellow man's property. Regarding any case of transgression, whether ox or donkey or sheep or garment or any lost item, where one states, "He is the one" (or "This is it") before the god, the case of the two parties shall come (for judgment); and whoever the god deems guilty shall pay his fellow man twofold.

Exodus 22:9–12 ~ LH §§244 + 266 ~ HL §75

If a man gives a donkey or ox or sheep or any animal to his fellow man to guard and it dies or is maimed or is taken captive, and there is no one who sees (it), an oath of Yahweh must transpire between the two of them, (swearing) that he did not touch the property of his fellow, and its owner shall accept (the oath) and he (the guard) does not have to pay. If it was stolen from him, he shall pay its owner. But if it was torn (by wild beasts), he shall bring the torn flesh as evidence, and he does not have to pay.

Exodus 22:13–14 ~ LH §263

And if a man asks his fellow man—and it is maimed or dies and its owner was not with it, he shall surely pay.[16] But if its owner was with it, he does not have to compensate. If it was hired, it came with the hire.

it burned another person's field, he shall pay . . . ." This alternative would work better contextually with the following verse.

15. This law is unusual in that the fire is the agent in the protasis, as opposed to "a man" or animal. It is possible that the term fire (אֵשׁ) intentionally plays on the similar term "man" (אִשׁ/אִישׁ).

16. Note the missing clause in the verse ("to borrow an animal"). The clause may be an intentional omission, assuming reference to the preceding provision, but it would constitute the only ellipsis in this block of material. I suggest instead that the omission is a scribal error.

BIBLIOGRAPHY

Alt, Albrecht. "The Origins of Israelite Law." Pages 101–71 in *Essays on Old Testament History and Religion*. Translated by R. A. Wilson. Garden City, NY: Doubleday, 1967.

Arnaud, Daniel. "Catalogue des textes cunéiformes trouvés au cours des trois premières campagnes à Meskéné-Qadimé Ouest." *AAAS* 25 (1975): 87–93.

Arnaud, Daniel. *Corpus des texts de bibliothèque de Ras Shamra-Ougarit (1936–2000) en sumérien, babylonien et assyrien*. Aula Orientalis Supplementa 23. Sabadell: Editorial Ausa, 2007.

Arnaud, Daniel. *Recherches au pays d'Aštata, Emar VI/3: Textes sumériens et accadiens*. OBO 20. Paris: Éditions Recherche sur les Civilisations, 1986.

Arnold, Bill T., and David B. Weisberg. "A Centennial Review of Friedrich Delitzsch's 'Babel und Bibel' Lectures." *JBL* 121.3 (2002): 441–57.

Barmash, Pamela. "The Daughter Sold into Slavery and Marriage." Pages 48–76 in *Sexuality and Law in the Torah*. Edited by Hilary Lipka and Bruce Wells. Library of Hebrew Bible / OTS 675. London: T&T Clark, 2020.

Barmash, Pamela. *Homicide in the Biblical World*. Cambridge: Cambridge University Press, 2005.

Bartor, Assnat. *Reading Laws as Narrative: A Study in the Casuistic Laws of the Pentateuch*. AIL 5. Atlanta: SBL Press; Leiden: Brill, 2010.

Beckman, Gary. "Emar and Its Archives." Pages 1–12 in *Emar: The History, Religion, and Culture of a Syrian Town in the Late Bronze Age*. Edited by Mark W. Chavalas. Bethesda, MD: CDL Press, 1996.

Beckman, Gary. *Texts from the Vicinity of Emar in the Collection of Jonathan Rosen*. HANE/M II. Padova: Sargon srl, 1996.

Bellotto, Nicoletta. "Adoptions at Emar: An Outline." Pages 179–94 in *The City of Emar among the Late Bronze Age Empires: History, Landscape, and Society. Proceedings of the Konstanz Emar Conference, 25.–26.04.2006*. Edited by Lorenzo d'Alfonso, Yoram Cohen, and Dietrich Sürenhagen. AOAT 349. Münster: Ugarit Verlag, 2008.

Bellotto, Nicoletta. "I LÚ.MEŠ.*aḫ-ḫi-a* a Emar." *AoF* 22.2 (1995): 210–28.

Berlejung, Angelika, and Andreas Schüle. "Erwägungen zu den neuen Ostraka aus der Sammlung Moussaïeff." *ZAH* 11 (1998): 68–73.

Berlin, Adele. "Esther." Pages 1623–39 in *The Jewish Study Bible*. Edited by Adele Berlin and Marc Zvi Brettler. New York: Oxford University Press, 2004.

Bodine, Walter R. *How Mesopotamian Scribes Learned to Write Legal Documents: A Study of the Sumerian Model Contracts in the Babylonian Collection at Yale University*. Lewiston, NY: Edwin Mellen Press, 2014.

Boecker, Hans Jochen. *Law and the Administration of Justice in the Old Testament and Ancient East*. Translated by Jeremy Moiser. Minneapolis: Augsburg Publishing House, 1980.

Bons, Eberhard. "Konnte eine Witwe die *naḥalāh* ihres verstorbenen Mannes erben? Überlegungen zum Ostrakon 2 aus der Sammlung Moussaïeff." *ZAR* 4 (1998): 197–208.

Bordreuil, Pierre, Felice Israel, and Dennis Pardee. "Deux ostraca paléo-hébreux de la Collection Sh. Moussaïeff." *Semitica* 46 (1996): 49–76, Pls. 7–8.

Botta, Alejandro F. *Aramaic and Egyptian Legal Traditions at Elephantine: An Egyptological Approach*. LSTS 64. London: T&T Clark, 2009.

Bottéro, Jean. "The 'Code' of Ḫammurabi." Pages 156–84 in *Mesopotamia: Writing, Reasoning, and the Gods*. Translated by Zainab Bahrani and Marc Van De Mieroop. Chicago/London: University of Chicago Press, 1992.

Braulik, Georg. *Das Deuteronomium*. ÖBS 23. Bern: Peter Lang, 2003.

Breneman, J. Mervin. "Nuzi Marriage Tablets." PhD diss., Brandeis University, 1971.

Cardascia, Guillaume. "L'adoption matrimoniale à Babylone et à Nuzi." *Revue historique de droit français et étranger* 36.4 (1959): 1–16.

Carr, David M. *Writing on the Tablet of the Heart: Origins of Scripture and Literature*. New York: Oxford University Press, 2005.

Cassin, Elena. "Être femme à Nuzi: Remarques sur l'adoption matrimoniale." Pages 129–47 in *Épouser au plus proche: Inceste, prohibitions et stratégies matrimoniales autour de la Méditerranée*. Edited by Pierre Bonte. Paris: Éditions de l'École des hautes études en sciences sociales, 1994.

Cazelles, Henri. *Études sur le code d'Alliance*. Paris: Letouzey et Ané, 1946.

Charpin, Dominique. "Chroniques bibliographiques 20: Pour une diplomatique des documents paléo-babyloniens." *RA* 111 (2017): 155–78.

Charpin, Dominique. *Hammurabi of Babylon*. London: I.B. Tauris, 2012.

Charpin, Dominique. "Lettres et procès paléo-babyloniens." Pages 69–111 in *Rendre la justice en Mésopotamie: Archives judiciaires du Proche-Orient ancien (IIIe–Ier millénaires avant J.-C)*. Edited by Francis Joannès. Temps et espaces. Saint-Denis: Presses universitaires de Vincennes, 2000.

Charpin, Dominique. *Writing, Law, and Kingship in Old Babylonian Mesopotamia*. Translated by Jane Marie Todd. Chicago: University of Chicago Press, 2010.

Chirichigno, Gregory. *Debt-Slavery in Israel and the Ancient Near East*. JSOTSup 141. Sheffield: JSOT Press, 1993.

Civil, Miguel. "Ancient Mesopotamian Lexicography." Pages 2305–14 in *Civilizations of the Ancient Near East*. Edited by Jack Sasson. New York: Charles Scribner's Sons, 1995.

Civil, Miguel. *Ea A = nâqu, Aa A = nâqu, with Their Forerunners and Related Texts*. Edited by Miguel Civil, with the collaboration of Wilfred G. Lambert and Margaret W. Green. MSL 14. Rome: Pontificium Institutum Biblicum, 1979.

Civil, Miguel. "The Law Collection of Ur-Namma." Pages 221–86 in *Cuneiform Royal Inscriptions and Related Texts in the Schøyen Collection*. Edited by Andrew R. George. CUSAS 17. Bethesda, MD: CDL Press, 2011.

Civil, Miguel. "Old Babylonian Proto-Lu: Types of Sources." Pages 24–73 in *The Series lú = ša and Related Texts*. Edited by Miguel Civil and Erica Reiner. MSL 12. Rome: Pontificium Institutum Biblicum, 1969.

Coats, George W. "Widow's Rights: A Crux in the Structure of Genesis 38." *CBQ* 34.4 (1972): 461–66.

Cohen, Yoram, and Lorenzo d'Alfonso. "The Duration of the Emar Archives and the Relative and Absolute Chronology of the City." Pages 3–25 in *The City of Emar among the Late Bronze Age Empires: History, Landscape, and Society. Proceedings of the Konstanz Emar Conference, 25.–26.04.2006*. Edited by Lorenzo d'Alfonso, Yoram Cohen, and Dietrich Sürenhagen. AOAT 349. Münster: Ugarit Verlag, 2008.

Cole, Steven W. "Chronology Revisited." Pages 3–6 in *Mesopotamian Pottery: A Guide to the Babylonian Tradition in the Second Millennium B.C.* Edited by James A. Armstrong and Hermann Gasche. Mesopotamian History and Environment, Series II, Memoirs VI. Ghent: University of Ghent; and Chicago: Oriental Institute of the University of Chicago, 2014.

Cook, Stanley A. *The Laws of Moses and the Code of Hammurabi*. London: Adam & Charles Black, 1903.

Cregan-Reid, Vybarr. *Discovering Gilgamesh: Geology, Narrative and the Historical Sublime in Victorian Culture*. Manchester: Telegraph, 2013.

Crüsemann, Frank. *The Torah: Theology and Social History of Old Testament Law*. Translated by Allan W. Mahnke. Minneapolis: Fortress Press, 1996.

Cussini, Eleonora. "The Aramaic Law of Sale and the Cuneiform Legal Tradition." PhD diss., The Johns Hopkins University, 1992.

D'Agostino, Franco. "Some Considerations on Humour in Mesopotamia." *RSO* 72 (1988): 273–78.

Daube, David. "*Consortium* in Roman and Hebrew Law." *Juridical Review* 62 (1950): 71–91.

Daube, David. "Direct and Indirect Causation in Biblical Law." *VT* 11.3 (1961): 246–69.

Daube, David. *Studies in Biblical Law*. Cambridge: Cambridge University Press, 1947.

Davies, Eryl W. "Inheritance Rights and the Hebrew Levirate Marriage, Part 1." *VT* 31.2 (1981): 138–44.

Davies, William Walter. *The Codes of Hammurabi and Moses*. Cincinnati: Jennings and Graham, 1905.

Delitzsch, Friedrich. *Babel and Bible: Three Lectures on the Significance of Assyriological Research for Religion, Embodying the Most Important Criticisms and the Author's Replies*. Translated by Thomas J. McCormack, William Herbert Carruth, and Lydia Gillingham Robinson. Chicago: Open Court Publishing, 1906.

Delitzsch, Friedrich. *Babel and Bible: Two Lectures Delivered before the Members of the Deutsche Orient-Gesellschaft in the Presence of the German Emperor*. Translated and edited by Claude Hermann Walter Johns. New York: G.P. Putnam's Sons, 1903.

Delnero, Paul. "Sumerian Extract Tablets and Scribal Education." *JCS* 62 (2010): 53–69.

Delnero, Paul. *The Textual Criticism of Sumerian Literature*. JCSSS 3. Boston: American Schools of Oriental Research, 2012.

Démare-Lafont, Sophie. "Ancient Near Eastern Laws: Continuity and Pluralism." Pages 91–118 in *Theory and Method in Biblical and Cuneiform Law: Revision, Interpolation and Development*. Edited by Bernard M. Levinson. Reprint. Sheffield: Sheffield Phoenix Press, 2006.

Démare-Lafont, Sophie. "Éléments pour une diplomatique juridique des textes d'Émar." Pages 43–84 in *Trois millénaires de formulaires juridiques*. Edited by Sophie Démare-Lafont and André Lemaire. Hautes Etudes Orientales—Moyen et Proche-Orient 48. Geneva: Librairie Droz, 2010.

Démare-Lafont, Sophie. "Inheritance Law of and through Women in the Middle Assyrian Period." In *Women and Property in Ancient Near Eastern and Mediterranean Societies*. Proceedings of the Center for Hellenic Studies colloquium, Washington, D.C. Edited by Deborah Lyons and Raymond Westbrook. Cambridge, MA: Center for Hellenic Studies, Harvard University, 2003.

Démare-Lafont, Sophie. "The King and the Diviner at Emar." Pages 207–17 in *The City of Emar among the Late Bronze Age Empires: History, Landscape, and Society. Proceedings of the Konstanz Emar Conference, 25.–26.04.2006*. Edited by Lorenzo d'Alfonso, Yoram Cohen, and Dietrich Sürenhagen. AOAT 349. Münster: Ugarit Verlag, 2008.

Démare-Lafont, Sophie. "Law Collections and Legal Documents." In *Handbook of Ancient Mesopotamia*. Edited by Gonzalo Rubio. Berlin: De Gruyter, forthcoming.

Démare-Lafont, Sophie. "Mesopotamia: Middle Assyrian Period." Pages 521–63 in vol. 1, *A History of Ancient Near Eastern Law*. Edited by Raymond Westbrook. HdO. Section 1 The Near and Middle East 72. Leiden: Brill, 2003.

Démare-Lafont, Sophie, and Daniel Fleming. "Ad Hoc Administration and Archiving at Emar: Free Format and Free Composition in the Diviner's Text Collection." *AuOr* 36.1 (2018): 29–63.

Démare-Lafont, Sophie, and Daniel Fleming. "Emar Chronology and Scribal Streams: Cosmopolitanism and Legal Diversity." *RA* 109 (2015): 45–77.

Driver, Godfrey R., and John C. Miles. *The Assyrian Laws: Edited with Translation and Commentary*. Reprint of the Oxford 1935 Edition with Supplementary Additions and Corrections by Driver. Oxford: Clarendon Press, 1975.

Driver, Godfrey R., and John C. Miles. *The Babylonian Laws*. Vol. 1, *Legal Commentary*. Oxford: Clarendon Press, 1952.

Driver, Samuel Rolles. *A Critical and Exegetical Commentary on Deuteronomy*. International Critical Commentary on the Holy Scriptures of the Old and New Testaments 3. New York: Charles Scribner's Sons, 1895.

Duncan, George S. "The Code of Moses and the Code of Hammurabi." *Biblical World* 23.3 (1904): 188–93.

Edenburg, Cynthia. "Ideology and Social Context of the Deuteronomic Women's Sex Laws (Deut 22:13–29)." *JBL* 128.1 (2009): 43–60.

Edwards, Chilperic. *The Oldest Laws in the World: Being an Account of the Hammurabi Code and the Sinaitic Legislation, With a Complete Translation of the Great Babylonian Inscription Discovered at Susa*. London: Watts & Co., 1906.

Eichler, Barry. "Examples of Restatement in the Laws of Hammurabi." Pages 365–400 in *Mishneh Todah: Studies in Deuteronomy and Its Cultural Environment in Honor of Jeffrey H. Tigay*. Edited by Nili Sacher Fox, David A. Glatt-Gilad, and Michael J. Williams. Winona Lake, IN: Eisenbrauns, 2009.

Eichler, Barry. "Literary Structure in the Laws of Eshnunna." Pages 71–84 in *Language, Literature, and History: Philological and Historical Studies Presented to Erica Reiner*. Edited by Francesca Rochberg-Halton. AOS 67. New Haven, CT: American Oriental Society, 1987.

Eichler, Barry. "Nuzi and the Bible: A Retrospective." Pages 107–19 in *DUMU-E$_2$-DUB-BA-A: Studies in Honor of Åke Sjöberg*. Edited by Hermann Behrens, Darlene Loding, and Martha T. Roth. Occasional Publications of the Samuel Noah Kramer Fund 11. Philadelphia: University Museum, 1989.

Eissfeldt, Otto. *The Old Testament: An Introduction*. Translated by Peter Ackroyd. Oxford: Basil Blackwell, 1965.

Emerson, Sara A. "Hammurabi and Moses." *Zion's Herald* 81.15 (1903): 458.

Ensor, George. *Moses and Hammurabi*. London: Religious Tract Society, 1903.

Eph'al, Israel, and Joseph Naveh. "Remarks on the Recently Published Moussaïeff Ostraca." *IEJ* 48.3/4 (1998): 269–73.

Fincke, Jeanette. "Adoption of Women at Nuzi." Pages 119–40 in *The Nuzi Workshop at the 55th Rencontre Assyriologique Internationale (July 2009 Paris)*. Edited by Phillippe Abrahami and Brigitte Lion. SCCNH 19. Bethesda, MD: CDL Press, 2012.

Fincke, Jeanette. "The Nuzi Collection of the Harvard Semitic Museum." Pages 13–24 in *Nuzi at Seventy-Five*. Edited by David I. Owen and Gernot Wilhelm. SCCNH 10. Bethesda, MD: CDL Press, 1999.

Finkelstein, J. J. "Ammiṣaduqa's Edict and the Babylonian 'Law Codes.'" *JCS* 15.3 (1961): 91–104.

Finkelstein, J. J. *The Ox That Gored*. TAPS 71.2. Philadelphia: The American Philosophical Society, 1981.

Finkelstein, J. J. "Sex Offenses in Sumerian Laws." *JAOS* 86.4 (1966): 355–72.

Fleming, Daniel. "Reading Emar's Scribal Traditions against the Chronology of Late Bronze History." Pages 27–43 in *The City of Emar among the Late Bronze Age Empires: History, Landscape, and Society. Proceedings of the Konstanz Emar Conference, 25.–26.04.2006*. Edited by Lorenzo d'Alfonso, Yoram Cohen, and Dietrich Sürenhagen. AOAT 349. Münster: Ugarit-Verlag, 2008.

Fraughton, Lindsay. "A New Approach to Ancient Archives: A Reevaluation of 'Daughtership' Adoption at Nuzi." MA thesis, The University of British Columbia, 2021.

Geller, Markham J. "The Elephantine Papyri and Hosea 2,3: Evidence for the Form of the Early Jewish Divorce Writ." *JSJ* 8.2 (1977): 139–48.

George, Andrew R. "The Gilgameš Epic at Ugarit." *AuOr* 25.2 (2007): 237–54.

George, Andrew R. "Old Babylonian School Letters." Pages 9–72 in Andrew R. George and Gabriella Spada, *Old Babylonian Texts in the Schøyen Collection, Part Two: School Letters, Model Contracts, and Related Texts*. CUSAS 43. University Park, PA: Eisenbrauns, 2019.

George, Andrew R., and Gabriella Spada. *Old Babylonian Texts in the Schøyen Collection, Part Two: School Letters, Model Contracts, and Related Texts*. CUSAS 43. University Park, PA: Eisenbrauns, 2019.

Gertz, Jan Christian. *Die Gerichtsorganisation Israels im deuteronomischen Gesetz*. FRLANT 165. Göttingen: Vandenhoeck & Ruprecht, 1994.

Gordon, Cyrus. "Fifteen Nuzi Tablets Relating to Women." *Le Muséon* 48 (1935): 113–32.

Greenberg, Moshe. "Some Postulates of Biblical Criminal Law." Pages 283–300 in *A Song of Power and the Power of Song: Essays on the Book of Deuteronomy*. Edited by Duane L. Christensen. Sources for Biblical and Theological Study 3. Winona Lake, IN: Eisenbrauns, 1993.

Greengus, Samuel. "The Old Babylonian Marriage Contract." *JAOS* 89.3 (1969): 505–32.

Greengus, Samuel. "A Textbook Case of Adultery in Ancient Mesopotamia." *HUCA* 40–41 (1969–70): 33–44.

Grimme, Hubert. *Das Gesetz Chammurabis und Moses: Eine Skizze*. Cologne: J. P. Bachem, 1903.

Gropp, Douglas M. *Wadi Daliyeh II: The Samaria Papyri from Wadi Daliyeh*. DJD 28. Oxford: Clarendon Press, 2001.

Gross, Andrew. *Continuity and Innovation in the Aramaic Legal Tradition*. Supplements to the Journal for the Study of Judaism 128. Leiden: Brill, 2008.

Gross, Andrew. "Emar and the Elephantine Papyri." Pages 333–49 in *In the Shadow of Bezalel: Aramaic, Biblical, and Ancient Near Eastern Studies in Honor of Bezalel Porten*. Edited by Alejandro F. Botta. CHANE 60. Leiden: Brill, 2013.

Grosz, Katarzyna. "On Some Aspects of the Adoption of Women at Nuzi." Pages 131–52 in *General Studies and Excavations at Nuzi 9/1*. Edited by Martha A. Morrison and David I. Owen. SCCNH 2. Winona Lake, IN: Eisenbrauns, 1987.

Haase, Richard. "Anatolia and the Levant: The Hittite Kingdom." Pages 619–56 in vol. 1, *A History of Ancient Near Eastern Law*. Edited by Raymond Westbrook. HdO. Section 1 The Near and Middle East 72. Leiden: Brill, 2003.

Hagedorn, Anselm C. "Gortyn—Utilising an Archaic Greek Law Code for Biblical Research." *ZAR* 7 (2001): 217–42.

Hallo, William W. Foreword. Pages i–ii in *How Mesopotamian Scribes Learned to Write Legal Documents: A Study of the Sumerian Model Contracts in the Babylonian Collection at Yale University*, by Walter R. Bodine. Lewiston, NY: Edwin Mellen Press, 2014.

Hallo, William W. "A Model Court Case Concerning Inheritance." Pages 141–54 in *Riches Hidden in Secret Places: Ancient Near Eastern Studies in Memory of Thorkild Jacobsen*. Edited by Tzvi Abusch. Winona Lake, IN: Eisenbrauns, 2002.

Harper, Robert F. *The Code of Hammurabi, King of Babylon, about 2250 B.C.* Chicago: University of Chicago Press, 1904.

Hoffner, Jr., Harry, "Hittite Laws." Pages 213–47 in *Law Collections from Mesopotamia and Asia Minor*. 2nd ed. WAW 6. Atlanta: SBL Press, 1997.

Hölkeskamp, Karl-Joachim. "What's in a Code? Solon's Laws between Complexity, Compilation and Contingency." *Hermes* 133 (2005): 280–93.

Holtz, Shalom. *Neo-Babylonian Trial Records*. WAW 35. Atlanta: SBL Press, 2014.

Horowitz, Wayne, and Takayoshi Oshima. *Cuneiform in Canaan: Cuneiform Sources from the Land of Israel in Ancient Times; Alphabetic Cuneiform Texts*, by Seth Sanders. Jerusalem: Israel Exploration Society and the Hebrew University of Jerusalem, 2006.

Horowitz, Wayne, Takayoshi Oshima, and Filip Vukosavović. "Hazor 18: Fragments of a Cuneiform Law Collection from Hazor." *IEJ* 62.2 (2012): 158–76.

Houtman, Cornelis. *Exodus.* Volume 3: *Chapters 20–40.* HCOT. Leuven: Peeters, 2000.

Izre'el, Shlomo. *Adapa and the South Wind: Language Has the Power of Life and Death.* MC 10. Winona Lake, IN: Eisenbrauns, 2001.

Izre'el, Shlomo. *The Amarna Scholarly Tablets.* CM 9. Groningen: Styx, 1997.

Jackson, Bernard. *Wisdom Laws: A Study of the Mishpatim of Exodus 21:1–22:16.* Oxford: Oxford University Press, 2006.

Jacobsen, Thorkild. "An Ancient Mesopotamian Trial for Homicide." Pages 193–215 in *Toward the Image of Tammuz and Other Essays on Mesopotamian History and Culture.* Edited by William Moran. HSS 21. Cambridge, MA: Harvard University Press, 1970.

Jas, Remko. *Neo-Assyrian Judicial Procedures.* SAAS 5. Helsinki: Neo-Assyrian Text Corpus Project, 1996.

Jasnow, Richard. "Egypt: Middle Kingdom and Second Intermediate Period." Pages 253–88 in vol. 1, *A History of Ancient Near Eastern Law.* Edited by Raymond Westbrook. HdO. Section 1 The Near and Middle East 72. Leiden: Brill, 2003.

Jasnow, Richard. "Egypt: New Kingdom." Pages 289–359 in vol. 1, *A History of Ancient Near Eastern Law.* Edited by Raymond Westbrook. HdO. Section 1 The Near and Middle East 72. Leiden: Brill, 2003.

Jasnow, Richard. "Egypt: Old Kingdom and First Intermediate Period." Pages 93–140 in vol. 1, *A History of Ancient Near Eastern Law.* Edited by Raymond Westbrook. HdO. Section 1 The Near and Middle East 72. Leiden: Brill, 2003.

Jeremias, Johannes. *Moses und Hammurabi.* Leipzig: J.C. Hinrichs, 1903.

Johns, Claude Hermann Walter. *The Oldest Code of Laws in the World: The Code of Laws Promulgated by Hammurabi, King of Babylon, B.C. 2285–2242.* Edinburgh: T&T Clark, 1903.

Justel, Josué. "Women and Family in the Legal Documentation of Emar (with Additional Data from Other Late Bronze Age Syrian Archives)." *KASKAL* 11 (2014): 57–84.

Kawashima, Robert S. "Could a Woman Say 'No' in Biblical Israel?: On the Genealogy of Legal Status in Biblical Law and Literature." *AJSR* 35.1 (2011): 1–22.

Kilhör, Benjamin. "Levirate Marriage in Deuteronomy 25:5–10 and Its Precursors in Leviticus and Numbers: A Test Case for the Relationship between P/H and D." *CBQ* 77.3 (2015): 429–40.

Klein, Jacob, and Tonia Sharlach. "A Collection of Model Court Cases from Old Babylonian Nippur (CBS 11324)." *ZA* 97.1 (2007): 1–25.

Kleinerman, Alexandra. *Education in Early 2nd Millennium BC Babylonia: The Sumerian Epistolary Miscellany.* CM 42. Leiden: Brill, 2011.

Knoppers, Gary N., and Paul B. Harvey, Jr., "The Pentateuch in Ancient Mediterranean Context: The Publication of Local Lawcodes." Pages 105–41 in *The Pentateuch as Torah: New Models for Understanding Its Promulgation and Acceptance.* Edited by Gary N. Knoppers and Bernard M. Levinson. Winona Lake, IN: Eisenbrauns, 2007.

Koch-Westenholz, Ulla. *Mesopotamian Astrology: An Introduction to Babylonian and Assyrian Celestial Divination*. CNIP 19. Copenhagen: Carsten Niebuhr Institute of Near Eastern Studies, Museum Tusculanum Press, University of Copenhagen, 1995.

Koehler, Ludwig, and Walter Baumgartner. "יבם". Page 383 in vol. 1, *The Hebrew and Aramaic Lexicon of the Old Testament*. Translated by M. E. J. Richardson. Revised by Walter Baumgartner and Johann Jakob Stamm. Leiden: Brill, 2001.

Kratz, Reinhard. *The Composition of the Narrative Books of the Old Testament*. Translated by John Bowden. London: T&T Clark, 2005.

Kraus, Fritz R. "Briefschreibübungen im altbabylonischen Schulunterricht." *JEOL* 16 (1964): 16–39.

Kraus, Fritz R. "Ein zentrales Problem des altmesopotamischen Rechtes: Was ist der Codex Hammu-rabi?" *Genava* 8 (1960): 283–96.

Kuyt, Annelies, and Jeremias W. Wesselius. "The Yavne-Yam Ostracon: An Exercise in Classical Hebrew Prose?" *BiOr* 48 (1991): 726–35.

Lafont, Bertrand, and Raymond Westbrook. "Mesopotamia: Neo-Sumerian Period (Ur III)." Pages 183–226 in vol. 1, *A History of Ancient Near Eastern Law*. Edited by Raymond Westbrook. HdO. Section 1 The Near and Middle East 72. Leiden: Brill, 2003.

Landsberger, Benno. "Die Babylonischen Termini für Gesetz und Recht." Pages 219–34 in *Symbolae ad iura Orientis antiqui pertinentes Paulo Koschaker dedicatae*. Edited by Johannes Friedrich, Julius Georg Lautner, Sir John Charles Miles, and Theunis Folkers. Studia et Documenta ad Iura Orientis Antiqui Pertinentia 2. Leiden: Brill, 1939.

Landsberger, Benno. *Die Serie ana ittišu*. MSL 1. Rome: Pontificium Institutum Biblicum, 1937.

Lehman, Jeffrey, and Shirelle Phelps, eds. "Legal Fiction." In *West's Encyclopedia of American Law*. 2nd ed. (2008). The Gale Group. http://legal-dictionary.thefreedictionary.com/legal+fiction.

Levin, Christoph. *Die Verheissung des neuen Bundes in ihrem theologiegeschichtlichen Zusammenhang ausgelegt*. FRLANT 137. Göttingen: Vandenhoeck & Ruprecht, 1985.

Levinson, Bernard M. "The Case for Revision and Interpolation within the Biblical Legal Corpora." Pages 37–59 in *Theory and Method in Biblical and Cuneiform Law: Revision, Interpolation and Development*. Edited by Bernard M. Levinson. Reprint. Sheffield: Sheffield Phoenix Press, 2006.

Levinson, Bernard M. *Deuteronomy and the Hermeneutics of Legal Innovation*. New York: Oxford University Press, 1997.

Levinson, Bernard M. "Is the Covenant Code an Exilic Composition? A Response to John Van Seters." Pages 276–330 in *"The Right Chorale": Studies in Biblical Law and Interpretation*. Winona Lake, IN: Eisenbrauns, 2011.

Levinson, Bernard M. *Legal Revision and Religious Renewal in Ancient Israel*. New York: Cambridge University Press, 2008.

Lieberman, Stephen. "Nippur: City of Decisions." Pages 127–36 in *Nippur at the Centennial: Papers Read at the 35e Rencontre Assyriologique Internationale, Philadelphia 1988*. Edited by Maria deJong Ellis. Occasional Publications of the Samuel Noah Kramer Fund 14. Philadelphia: University Museum, 1992.

Locher, Clemens. "Deuteronomium 22,13–21 vom Prozessprotokoll zum kasuistischen Gesetz." Pages 298–303 in *Das Deuteronomium: Entstehung, Gestalt und Botschaft*. Edited by Norbert Lohfink. BETL 68. Leuven: Leuven University Press, 1985.

Locher, Clemens. *Die Ehre einer Frau in Israel: Exegetische und rechtsvergleichende Studien zu Deuteronomium 22,13–21.* OBO 70. Freiburg, Switzerland: Universitätsverlag; Göttingen: Vandenhoeck & Ruprecht, 1986.

Loewenstamm, Samuel E. "Exodus 21:22–25." *VT* 27 (1977): 352–60.

Lohfink, Norbert. "Distribution of the Functions of Power: The Laws Concerning Public Offices in Deuteronomy 16:18–18:22." Pages 336–52 in *A Song of Power and the Power of Song: Essays on the Book of Deuteronomy*. Edited by Duane L. Christensen. Sources for Biblical and Theological Study 3. Winona Lake, IN: Eisenbrauns, 1993.

Lohfink, Norbert. *Studien zum Deuteronomium und zur deuteronomistischen Literatur II*. Stuttgart: Verlag Katholisches Bibelwerk, 1991.

Magdalene, F. Rachel, Cornelia Wunsch, and Bruce Wells. *Fault, Responsibility, and Administrative Law in Late Babylonian Legal Texts*. MC 23. University Park, PA: Eisenbrauns, 2019.

Malul, Meir. *The Comparative Method in Ancient Near Eastern and Biblical Legal Studies*. AOAT 227. Kevelaer: Butzon und Bercker, 1990.

Malul, Meir. *Studies in Mesopotamian Legal Symbolism*. AOAT 221. Kevelaer: Butzon & Bercker, 1988.

Manning, Sturt W., Carol B. Griggs, Brita Lorentzen, Gojko Barjamovic, Christopher Bronk Ramsey, Bernd Kromer, and Eva Maria Wild. "Integrated Tree-Ring-Radiocarbon High-Resolution Timeframe to Resolve Earlier Second Millennium BCE Mesopotamian Chronology." *PLoS ONE* 11.7 (2016): e0157144 (doi:10.1371/journal.pone.0157144).

Mari, Francesco. *Il Codice di Hammurabi e la Bibbia*. Rome: Desclee, Lefebvre & C. Editori Pontifici, 1903.

Mayer, Walter. *Ausgrabungen in Tall Munbāqa-Ekalte*. Vol. 2, *Die Texte*. Edited by Dittmar Machule. WVDOG 102. Saarbrücken: Saarbrücker Druckerei und Verlag, 2001.

Mendelsohn, Isaac. "The Conditional Sale into Slavery of Free-Born Daughters in Nuzi and the Law of Ex. 21:7–11." *JAOS* 55.2 (1935): 190–95.

Merendino, Rosario P. *Das deuteronomische Gesetz: Eine literarkritische, gattungs- und überlieferungsgeschichtliche Untersuchung zu Dt 12-26*. BBB 31. Bonn: Hanstein, 1969.

Michalowski, Piotr. "The Libraries of Babel: Text, Authority, and Tradition in Ancient Mesopotamia." Pages 105–29 in *Cultural Repertoires: Structure, Function, and Dynamics*. Edited by Gillis J. Dorleijn and Herman L. J. Vanstiphout. GSCC 3. Leuven: Peeters, 2003.

Mieroop, Marc Van De. *King Hammurabi of Babylon: A Biography*. Blackwell Ancient Lives. Malden, MA/Oxford: Blackwell, 2005.

Milstein, Sara. "Insights from Tradition into the Biblical Law of the Slavewoman (Exodus 21,7–11)." *BN* 189 (2021): 29–44.

Milstein, Sara. "Making a Case: The Repurposing of 'Israelite Legal Fictions' as Deuteronomic Law." Pages 161–81 in *Supplementation and the Study of the Hebrew Bible*. Edited by Saul Olyan and Jacob Wright. BJS 361. Providence: Brown Judaic Studies, 2017.

Milstein, Sara. "Separating the Wheat from the Chaff: The Independent Logic of Deuteronomy 22:25–27." *JBL* 137.3 (2018): 625–43.

Milstein, Sara. *Tracking the Master Scribe: Revision through Introduction in Biblical and Mesopotamian Literature*. New York: Oxford University Press, 2016.

Milstein, Sara. "Will and (Old) Testament: Reconsidering the Roots of Deuteronomy 25,5–10." Pages 49–63 in *Writing, Rewriting, and Overwriting in the Books of Deuteronomy and the Former Prophets: Essays in Honour of Cynthia Edenburg*. Edited by Thomas Römer, Ido Koch, and Omer Sergi. BETL 304. Leuven: Peeters, 2019.

Morrow, William. "The Arrangement of the Original Version of Deuteronomy According to Eckart Otto." *ZAR* 25 (2019): 195–206.

Morrow, William. "Have Attempts to Establish the Dependency of Deuteronomy on the Esarhaddon Succession Treaty (EST) Failed?" *HeBAI* 8 (2019): 133–58.

Morrow, William. "Legal Interactions: The *Mišpāṭîm* and the Laws of Hammurabi." *BiOr* 70.3–4 (2013): 309–31.

Muffs, Yochanan. *Studies in the Aramaic Legal Papyri from Elephantine*. Studia et Documenta ad Iura Orientis Antiqui Pertinentia 8. Leiden: Brill, 1969. Reprint with Prolegomenon by Baruch A. Levine. HdO. Section 1 The Near and Middle East 66. Leiden: Brill, 2003.

Neufeld, Ephraim. *Ancient Hebrew Marriage Laws: With Special References to General Semitic Laws and Customs*. London: Longmans, Green, and Co., 1944.

Noth, Martin. *Exodus: A Commentary*. London: SCM Press, 1962.

Oettli, Samuel. *Das Gesetz Hammurabis und die Thora Israels: Eine religions- und rechtsgeschichtliche Parallele*. Leipzig: A. Diechert, 1903.

Ornan, Tallay. "Unfinished Business: The Relief on the Hammurabi Louvre Stele Revisited." *JCS* 71 (2019): 85–109.

Otto, Eckart. "Aspects of Legal Reforms and Reformulations in Ancient Cuneiform and Israelite Law." Pages 160–96 in *Theory and Method in Biblical and Cuneiform Law: Revision, Interpolation and Development*. Edited by Bernard M. Levinson. Reprint. Sheffield: Sheffield Phoenix Press, 2006.

Otto, Eckart. *Das Deuteronomium: Politische Theologie und Rechtsreform in Juda und Assyrien*. BZAW 284. Berlin/New York: De Gruyter, 1999.

Otto, Eckart. *Deuteronomium 1–11: Erster Teilband 1,1–4,43*. HThKAT. Freiburg: Herder, 2012.

Otto, Eckart. *Deuteronomium 12–34: Erster Teilband 12,1–23,15*. HThKAT. Freiburg: Herder, 2016.

Otto, Eckart. "False Weights in the Scales of Biblical Justice? Different Views of Women from Patriarchal Hierarchy to Religious Equality in the Book of Deuteronomy." Pages 128–46 in *Gender and Law in the Hebrew Bible and the Ancient Near East*. Edited by Victor H. Matthews, Tikva Frymer-Kensky, and Bernard Levinson. JSOTSup 262. Sheffield: Sheffield Academic Press, 1998.

Otto, Eckart. "The History of the Legal-Religious Hermeneutics of the Book of Deuteronomy from the Assyrian to the Hellenistic Period." Pages 211–50 in *Law and Religion in the Eastern Mediterranean: From Antiquity to Early Islam*. Edited by Anselm C. Hagedorn and Reinhard Kratz. Oxford: Oxford University Press, 2013.

Otto, Eckart. *Kontinuum und Proprium: Studien zur Sozial- und Rechtsgeschichte des Alten Orients und des Alten Testaments*. OBC 8. Wiesbaden: Harrassowitz, 1996.

Otto, Eckart. "Town and Rural Countryside in Ancient Israelite Law: Reception and Redaction in Cuneiform and Israelite Law." *JSOT* 57 (1993): 3–22.

Otto, Eckart. "Vom Bundesbuch zum Deuteronomium: Die deuteronomische Redaktion in Dtn 12–26." Pages 260–78 in *Biblische Theologie und gesellschaftlicher Wandel: für Norbert Lohfink SJ*. Edited by Georg Braulik, Walter Gross, and Sean McEvenue. Freiburg: Herder, 1993.

Owen, David I. "Widows' Rights in Ur III Sumer." *ZA* 70.2 (1980): 170–84.

Pakkala, Juha. "The Influence of Treaties on Deuteronomy, Exclusive Monolatry, and Covenant Theology." *HeBAI* 8 (2019): 159–83.

Paradise, Jonathan. "Marriage Contracts of Free Persons at Nuzi." *JCS* 39.1 (1987): 1–36.

Paul, Shalom M. *Studies in the Book of the Covenant in the Light of Cuneiform and Biblical Law*. VTSupp 18. Leiden: Brill, 1970.

Perlitt, Lothar. *Bundestheologie im Alten Testament*. WMANT 36. Neukirchen-Vluyn: Neukirchener-Verlag, 1969.

Petschow, Herbert. "Die neubabylonische Zwiegesprächsurkunde und Genesis 23." *JCS* 19.4 (1965): 103–20.

Pfeiffer, Robert H., and E. A. Speiser. *One Hundred New Selected Nuzi Texts*. The Annual of the American Schools of Oriental Research, vol. 16 for 1935–36. New Haven, CT: American Schools of Oriental Research, 1936.

Podany, Amanda. "Hana and the Low Chronology." *JNES* 73.1 (2014): 49–71.

Porten, Bezalel, ed. *The Elephantine Papyri in English: Three Millennia of Cross-Cultural Continuity and Change*. 2nd ed. DMOA, Studies in Near Eastern Archaeology and Civilisation 22. Atlanta: SBL Press, 2011.

Porten, Bezalel. "Structure and Chiasmus in Aramaic Contracts and Letters." Pages 169–82 in *Chiasmus in Antiquity: Structures, Analyses, Exegesis*. Edited by John W. Welch. Hildesheim: Gerstenberg Verlag, 1981.

Pressler, Carolyn. *The View of Women Found in the Deuteronomic Family Laws*. BZAW 216. Berlin: De Gruyter, 1993.

Propp, William H. C. *Exodus 19–40: A New Translation with Introduction and Commentary*. Anchor Bible. New York: Doubleday, 2006.

Rahmouni, Aicha. *Divine Epithets in the Ugaritic Alphabetic Texts*. Translated by J. N. Ford. HdO. Section 1 The Near and Middle East 93. Leiden: Brill, 2008.

Robson, Eleanor. *Mesopotamian Mathematics, 2100–1600 BC: Technical Constants in Bureaucracy and Education*. OECT 14. Oxford: Oxford University Press, 1999.

Robson, Eleanor. "The Tablet House: A Scribal School in Old Babylonian Nippur." *RA* 95.1 (2001): 39–66.

Rofé, Alexander. *Deuteronomy: Issues and Interpretation*. OTS. London: T&T Clark, 2002.

Rofé, Alexander. "Family and Sex Laws in Deuteronomy and the Book of Covenant." *Hen* 9 (1987): 131–59.

Rollston, Christopher. *Writing and Literacy in the World of Ancient Israel: Epigraphic Evidence from the Iron Age*. ABS 11. Atlanta: SBL Press, 2010.

Roth, Martha T. *Babylonian Marriage Agreements, 7th–3rd Centuries B.C.* AOAT 222. Neukirchen-Vluyn: Neukirchener Verlag, 1989.

Roth, Martha T. "Errant Oxen Or: The Goring Ox Redux." Pages 397–404 in *Literature as Politics, Politics as Literature: Essays on the Ancient Near East in Honor of Peter Machinist*. Edited by David S. Vanderhooft and Abraham Winitzer. Winona Lake, IN: Eisenbrauns, 2013.

Roth, Martha T. "Gender and Law: A Case Study from Ancient Mesopotamia." Pages 173–84 in *Gender and Law in the Hebrew Bible and the Ancient Near East*. Edited by Victor H. Matthews, Bernard Levinson, and Tikva Frymer-Kensky. JSOTSup 262. Sheffield: Sheffield Academic Press, 1998.

Roth, Martha T. "Hammurabi's Wronged Man." *JAOS* 122.1 (2002): 38–45.

Roth, Martha T. "The Law Collection of King Hammurabi: Toward an Understanding of Codification and Text." Pages 9–31 in *La codification des lois dans l'Antiquité: Actes du Colloque de Strasbourg, 27–29 novembre 1997*. Edited by Edmond Lévy. Travaux du Centre de Recherche sur le Proche-Orient et la Grèce Antiques 16. Paris: De Boccard, 2000.

Roth, Martha T. *Law Collections from Mesopotamia and Asia Minor*. 2nd ed. WAW 6. Atlanta: SBL Press, 1997.

Roth, Martha T. "Mesopotamian Legal Traditions and the Laws of Hammurabi." *Chicago-Kent Law Review* 71.1 (1995): 13–39.

Roth, Martha T. "Reading Mesopotamian Law Cases PBS 5 100: A Question of Filiation." *JESHO* 44.3 (2001): 243–92.

Roth, Martha T. "Scholastic Tradition and Mesopotamian Law: A Study of FLP 1287, a Prism in the Collection of the Free Library of Philadelphia." PhD diss., University of Pennsylvania, 1979.

Roth, Martha T. "'She Will Die by the Iron Dagger': Adultery and Neo-Babylonian Marriage." *JESHO* 31.2 (1988): 186–206.

Roth, Martha T. "The Slave and the Scoundrel: CBS 10467, A Sumerian Morality Tale?" *JAOS* 103.1 (1983): 275–82.

Rothenbusch, Ralf. *Die kasuistische Rechtssammlung im "Bundesbuch" (Ex 21,2–11.18–22,16) und ihr literarischer Kontext im Licht altorientalischer Parallelen*. AOAT 259. Münster: Ugarit Verlag, 2000.

Rowe, Ignacio Márquez. "Anatolia and the Levant: Ugarit." Pages 719–35 in vol. 1, *A History of Ancient Near Eastern Law*. Edited by Raymond Westbrook. HdO. Section 1 The Near and Middle East 72. Leiden: Brill, 2003.

Rutz, Matthew. *Bodies of Knowledge in Ancient Mesopotamia: The Diviners of Late Bronze Age Emar and Their Tablet Collection*. AMD 9. Leiden: Brill, 2013.

Sallaberger, Walther. *"Wenn Du mein Bruder bist, . . .": Interaktion und Textgestaltung in altbabylonischen Alltagsbriefen*. CM 16. Groningen: Styx, 1999.

Sasson, Jack. *From the Mari Archives: An Anthology of Old Babylonian Letters*. Winona Lake, IN: Eisenbrauns, 2015.

Sayce, A. H. "The Legal Code of Babylonia." *American Journal of Theology* 8.2 (1904): 256–66.

Scheil, Vincent. *Textes élamites-sémitiques, deuxieme Serie*. Mémoires de la Délégation en Perse, Tome IV. Paris: Leroux, 1902.

Schniedewind, William M. *The Finger of the Scribe: How Scribes Learned to Write the Bible*. New York: Oxford University Press, 2019.

Schøyen, Martin. "Statement of Provenance." Pages vii–viii in Andrew R. George and Gabriella Spada, *Old Babylonian Texts in the Schøyen Collection, Part Two: School Letters, Model Contracts, and Related Texts*. CUSAS 43. University Park, PA: Eisenbrauns, 2019.

Schwartz, Glenn M. "Problems of Chronology: Mesopotamia, Anatolia, and the Syro-Levantine Region." Pages 450–52 in *Beyond Babylon: Art, Trade, and Diplomacy in the Second Millennium B.C.* Edited by Joan Aruz, Kim Benzel, and Jean M. Evans. New York: Metropolitan Museum of Art; New Haven, CT: Yale University Press, 2008.

Schwienhorst-Schönberger, Ludger. *Das Bundesbuch (Ex 20,22–23,33): Studien zu seiner Entstehung und Theologie*. BZAW 188. Berlin: De Gruyter, 1990.

Skaist, Aaron J. *The Old Babylonian Loan Contract: Its History and Geography*. Bar-Ilan Studies in Near Eastern Languages and Culture. Ramat Gan: Bar-Ilan University Press, 1994.

Smith, J. C. *The Law of Contract*. Fundamental Principles of Law. London: Sweet & Maxwell, 1989.

Spada, Gabriella. "Addenda et corrigenda to G. Spada, 'A New Fragment of the Laws about Rented Oxen and the Sumerian Verb bu-us2,' RSO 91 (2018): 11–18." *Nouvelles Assyriologiques Brèves et Utilitaires* (2019): 22–23.

Spada, Gabriella. "I modelli di contratto nell'edubba paleo-babilonese: un esempio di contratto di adozione." *AION* 72 (2012): 133–48.

Spada, Gabriella. "I Want to Break Free: Model Contracts Recording Slave Self-Emancipation." Pages 283–99 in ^{d}*Nisaba za3-mi2: Ancient Near Eastern Studies in Honor of Francesco Pomponio*. Edited by Palmiro Notizia, Annunziata Rositani, and Lorenzo Verderame. dubsar 19. Münster: Zaphon, 2021.

Spada, Gabriella. "A New Fragment of the 'Laws about Rented Oxen' and the Sumerian Verb bu-us$_2$." *RSO* 91: 91 (2018): 11–18.

Spada, Gabriella. "Old Babylonian Model Contracts and Related Texts." Pages 73–145 in Andrew R. George and Gabriella Spada, *Old Babylonian Texts in the Schøyen Collection, Part Two: School Letters, Model Contracts, and Related Texts*. CUSAS 43. University Park, PA: Eisenbrauns, 2019.

Spada, Gabriella. Review of Walter Ray Bodine, *How Mesopotamian Scribes Learned to Write Legal Documents: A Study of the Sumerian Model Contracts in the Babylonian Collection at Yale University* (Lewiston, NY: Edwin Mellen Press, 2014). *ZA* 107 (2017): 290–307.

Spada, Gabriella. *Sumerian Model Contracts from the Old Babylonian Period in the Hilprecht Collection Jena*. Texte und Materialien der Frau Professor Hilprecht Collection of Babylonian Antiquities im Eigentum der Friedrich-Schiller-Universität Jena XI. Wiesbaden: Harrassowitz, 2018.

Spada, Gabriella. "Two Old Babylonian Model Contracts." *CDLJ* 2 (2014): 1–13.

Sprinkle, Joe M. *'The Book of the Covenant': A Literary Approach*. JSOTSup 174. Sheffield: Sheffield Academic Press, 1994.

Stackert, Jeffrey. *Rewriting the Torah: Literary Revision in Deuteronomy and the Holiness Legislation*. FAT 52. Tübingen: Mohr Siebeck, 2007.

Steinkeller, Piotr. "Seal Practice in the Ur III Period." Pages 41–53 in *Seals and Sealing in the Ancient Near East*. Edited by McGuire Gibson and Robert D. Biggs. BibMes 6. Malibu: Undena, 1977.

Stol, Marten. *Women in the Ancient Near East*. Translated by Helen and Mervyn Richardson. Boston/Berlin: De Gruyter, 2016.

Szubin, Zvi Henri, and Bezalel Porten. "The Status of a Repudiated Spouse: A New Interpretation of Kraeling 7 (*TAD* B3.8)." *ILR* 35.1 (2001): 46–78.

Talshir, Zipora. "The Detailing Formula 'וזה (ה)דבר'." *Tarbiz* 41 (1981–82): 23–36 (Heb.).

Tinney, Steve. "On the Curricular Setting of Sumerian Literature." *Iraq* 61 (1999): 159–72.

Tombazzi, Nicole. "'If There Was an Attack': A Reinterpretation of *'ason* as Intentional Assault." BA Honours Thesis, The University of British Columbia, 2021.

Toorn, Karel van der. "Cuneiform in Syria-Palestine: Texts, Scribes, and Schools." Pages 139–56 in *God in Context: Selected Essays on Society and Religion in the Early Middle East*. FAT 123. Tübingen: Mohr Siebeck, 2018.

Toorn, Karel van der. *Scribal Culture and the Making of the Hebrew Bible*. Cambridge, MA: Harvard University Press, 2009.

Van Seters, John. *A Law Book for the Diaspora: Revision in the Study of the Covenant Code*. New York: Oxford University Press, 2003.

Van Wolde, Ellen. "Does *'innâ* Denote Rape? A Semantic Analysis of a Controversial Word." *VT* 52.4 (2002): 528–44.

Veijola, Timo. *Das fünfte Buch Mose (Deuteronomium) Kapitel 1,1–16,17*. ATD 8/1. Göttingen: Vandenhoeck & Ruprecht, 2004.

Veldhuis, Niek. *History of the Cuneiform Lexical Tradition*. GMTR 6. Münster: Ugarit-Verlag, 2014.

Veldhuis, Niek. *Religion, Literature, and Scholarship: The Sumerian Composition "Nanše and the Birds," With a Catalogue of Sumerian Bird Names*. CM 22. Leiden: Brill, 2004.

Wells, Bruce. "The Covenant Code and Near Eastern Legal Traditions: A Response to David P. Wright." *Maarav* 13.1 (2006): 85–118.

Wells, Bruce. "The Hated Wife in Deuteronomic Law." *VT* 60.1 (2010): 131–46.

Wells, Bruce. "Is It Law or Religion? Legal Motivations in Deuteronomic and Neo-Babylonian Texts." Pages 287–309 in *Law and Religion in the Eastern Mediterranean: From Antiquity to Early Islam*. Edited by Anselm C. Hagedorn and Reinhard G. Kratz. Oxford: Oxford University Press, 2013.

Wells, Bruce. "Sex, Lies, and Virginal Rape: The Slandered Bride and False Accusation in Deuteronomy." *JBL* 124.1 (2005): 41–72.

Wenham, Gordon J. "*Betûlāh*: 'A Girl of Marriageable Age.'" *VT* 22.3 (1972): 326–48.

Wenham, Gordon J., and J. G. McConville. "Drafting Techniques in Some Deuteronomic Laws." *VT* 30.2 (1980): 248–52.

Westbrook, Raymond. "Anatolia and the Levant: Emar and Vicinity." Pages 657–91 in vol. 1, *A History of Ancient Near Eastern Law*. Edited by Raymond Westbrook. HdO. Section 1 The Near and Middle East 72. Leiden: Brill, 2003.

Westbrook, Raymond. "Biblical and Cuneiform Law Codes." Pages 3–20 in *Law from the Tigris to the Tiber: The Writings of Raymond Westbrook*, vol. 1, *The Shared Tradition*. Edited by Bruce Wells and F. Rachel Magdalene. Winona Lake, IN: Eisenbrauns, 2009.

Westbrook, Raymond. "The Character of Ancient Near Eastern Law." Pages 1–90 in vol. 1, *A History of Ancient Near Eastern Law*. Edited by Raymond Westbrook. HdO. Section 1 The Near and Middle East 72. Leiden: Brill, 2003.

Westbrook, Raymond. "The Female Slave." Pages 149–74 in *Law from the Tigris to the Tiber*, vol. 2, *Cuneiform and Biblical Sources*. Edited by Bruce Wells and F. Rachel Magdalene. Winona Lake, IN: Eisenbrauns, 2009.

Westbrook, Raymond. "The Laws of Biblical Israel." Pages 317–40 in *Law from the Tigris to the Tiber*, vol. 2, *Cuneiform and Biblical Sources*. Edited by Bruce Wells and F. Rachel Magdalene. Winona Lake, IN: Eisenbrauns, 2009.

Westbrook, Raymond. "Lex Talionis and Exodus 21:22–25." Pages 341–60 in *Law from the Tigris to the Tiber*, vol. 2, *Cuneiform and Biblical Sources*. Edited by Bruce Wells and F. Rachel Magdalene. Winona Lake, IN: Eisenbrauns, 2009.

Westbrook, Raymond. "The Nature and Origins of the Twelve Tables." Pages 21–71 in *Law from the Tigris to the Tiber: The Writings of Raymond Westbrook*, vol. 1, *The Shared Tradition*. Edited by Bruce Wells and F. Rachel Magdalene. Winona Lake, IN: Eisenbrauns, 2009.

Westbrook, Raymond. *Old Babylonian Marriage Law*. AfOB 23. Horn: Verlag Ferdinand Berger & Söhne, 1988.

Westbrook, Raymond. "The Prohibition on Restoration of Marriage in Deuteronomy 24:1–4." Pages 387–404 in *Law from the Tigris to the Tiber*, vol. 2, *Cuneiform and Biblical Sources*. Edited by Bruce Wells and F. Rachel Magdalene. Winona Lake, IN: Eisenbrauns, 2009.

Westbrook, Raymond. *Property and the Family in Biblical Law*. JSOTSup 113. Sheffield: Sheffield Academic Press, 1991.

Westbrook, Raymond. "Social Justice and Creative Jurisprudence in Late Bronze Age Syria." Pages 101–26 of *Law from the Tigris to the Tiber*, vol. 2, *Cuneiform and Biblical Sources*. Edited by Bruce Wells and F. Rachel Magdalene. Winona Lake, IN: Eisenbrauns, 2009.

Westbrook, Raymond. *Studies in Biblical and Cuneiform Law*. Cahiers de la Revue Biblique 26. Paris: J. Gabalda et Cie, 1988.

Wilcke, Claus. "AḪ, die 'Brüder' von Emar: Untersuchungen zur Schreibtradition am Euphratknie." *AuOr* 10 (1992): 115–50.

Wilcke, Claus. "Mesopotamia: Early Dynastic and Sargonic Periods." Pages 141–81 in vol. 1, *A History of Ancient Near Eastern Law*. Edited by Raymond Westbrook. HdO. Section 1 The Near and Middle East 72. Leiden: Brill, 2003.

Willetts, Ronald. *The Law Code of Gortyn*. Kadmos/Supplemente 1. Berlin: De Gruyter, 1967.

Winckler, Hugo. *Die Gesetze Hammurabis, Königs von Babylon um 2250 v. Chr. Das älteste Gesetzbuch der Welt*. Leipzig: J.C. Hinrichs, 1902.

Winitzer, Abraham. *Early Mesopotamian Divination Literature: Its Organizational Framework and Generative and Paradigmatic Characteristics*. AMD 12. Boston: Brill, 2017.

Wright, David P. *Inventing God's Law: How the Covenant Code of the Bible Used and Revised the Laws of Hammurabi*. New York: Oxford University Press, 2009.

Zaccagnini, Carlos. "Mesopotamia: Nuzi." Pages 565–617 in vol. 1, *A History of Ancient Near Eastern Law*. Edited by Raymond Westbrook. HdO. Section 1 The Near and Middle East 72. Leiden: Brill, 2003.

INDEX OF AUTHORS

INDEX OF SUBJECTS